THE RIDE OF A LIFETIME

THE RIDE OF
A LIFETIME

LESSONS LEARNED
FROM 15 YEARS AS CEO OF THE
WALT DISNEY COMPANY

ROBERT IGER

RANDOM HOUSE
NEW YORK

Published in the United States by Random House, an imprint and division of Penguin Random House LLC, New York.

RANDOM HOUSE and the HOUSE colophon are registered trademarks of Penguin Random House LLC.

Hardback ISBN 978-0-399-59209-6
International edition ISBN 978-1-9848-0146-3
Ebook ISBN 978-0-399-59210-2

Printed in India

randomhousebooks.com

19

First Edition

To Willow: This ride would not have been possible without you.

Kate, Amanda, Max, and Will: Thank you for your love and understanding and for all the joy you have given me.

To the thousands of Disney cast members and employees past and present: My pride in you and appreciation of you is boundless.

CONTENTS

PART TWO

LEADING

I N JUNE 2016 I made my fortieth trip to China in eighteen years, my eleventh in the past six months. I was there to oversee the final preparations before the opening of Shanghai Disneyland. I'd been CEO of the Walt Disney Company for eleven years at that point, and my plan was to open Shanghai and then retire. It had been a thrilling run, and the creation of this park was the biggest accomplishment of my career. It felt like the right time to move on, but life doesn't always go the way you expect it will. Things happen that you can't possibly anticipate. The fact that I'm still running the company as I write this is a testament to that. Much more profoundly, so are the events of that week in Shanghai.

We were opening the park on Thursday, June 16. That Monday, the first wave of VIPs was scheduled to arrive: Disney board members and key executives and their families, creative partners, investors and Wall Street analysts. There was a huge international media contingent already there and more coming in. I'd been in Shanghai for two weeks and was running on adrenaline. Since my first location-scouting trip to China in 1998, I was the only person who had been involved in the project from day one, and I couldn't wait to show it to the world.

In the sixty-one years since Walt Disney built Disneyland in Anaheim, California, we'd opened parks in Orlando and Paris and Tokyo and Hong Kong. Disney World in Orlando remains our largest, but Shanghai was of a different order than all the others. It was one of the biggest investments in the history of the company. Numbers don't really do the park justice, but here are a few to give some sense of its scope. Shanghai Disneyland cost about $6 billion to build. It is 963 acres, about eleven times the size of Disneyland. At various stages of its construction, as many as fourteen thousand workers lived on the property. We held casting calls in six cities in China to discover the thousand singers, dancers, and actors who perform in our stage and street shows. Over the eighteen years it took to complete the park, I met with three presidents of China, five mayors of Shanghai, and more party secretaries than I can remember (one of whom was arrested for corruption and banished to northern China in the middle of our negotiations, setting the project back nearly two years).

We had endless negotiations over land deals and partnership splits and management roles, and considered things as significant as the safety and comfort of Chinese workers and as tiny as whether we could cut a ribbon on opening day. The creation of the park was an education in geopolitics, and a constant balancing act between the possibilities of global expansion and the perils of cultural imperialism. The overwhelming challenge, which I repeated to our team so often it became a mantra for everyone working on the project, was to create an experience that was "authentically Disney and distinctly Chinese."

In the early evening on Sunday, June 12, I and the rest of my team in Shanghai received news of a mass shooting at the Pulse nightclub in Orlando, fifteen miles from Disney World. We have more than seventy thousand employees in Orlando, and we waited in horror for confirmation that some of them were at the club that night. Our head of security, Ron Iden, was with us in Shanghai, and he immediately began calling his network of security contacts in the States. It was twelve hours earlier—just before dawn—in Orlando when we first heard the news. Ron told me he'd have more information when I got up in the morning.

My first event the next day was a presentation to investors over breakfast. Then I had to shoot a long interview with Robin Roberts of *Good Morning America,* which included touring the park and riding attractions with Robin and her crew. Then there was a meeting with Chinese officials about protocol for the opening ceremonies, a dinner with members of our board and senior executives, and finally a rehearsal for the opening-night concert that I was hosting. Ron periodically gave me updates as I moved through the day.

We knew that more than fifty people had been killed and nearly as many injured, and that the shooter was a man named Omar Mateen. Ron's security team ran Mateen's name through our database and found that he'd visited the Magic Kingdom a couple of months before the shooting, then again the weekend before. There was closed-circuit television footage of him on that last visit, pacing outside a park entrance near the House of Blues, in Downtown Disney.

What we learned next shook me in a way few things have over the course of my career. It wouldn't be made public until nearly two years later, during the trial of Mateen's wife as an accomplice to the murders (she was later acquitted), but federal investigators informed Ron that they believed Disney World had been Mateen's primary target. They'd found his phone at the scene of the shooting, and determined that it had been pinging off one of our cell towers earlier that night. They studied the CCTV footage and saw him, again, walking back and forth in front of the entrance near the House of Blues. There was a heavy metal concert there that night, which meant extra security—five armed police officers—and after a few minutes of casing the area, Mateen could be seen walking back to his car.

Security cameras picked up two weapons in Mateen's possession, a semiautomatic rifle and a semiautomatic pistol, hidden inside a child's stroller, along with a baby blanket that hadn't yet been taken out of its packaging. Investigators suspected that his plan was to cover his weapons with the blanket and wheel them up to the entrance before pulling them out.

Our head of Parks and Resorts, Bob Chapek, was also in Shanghai, and he and I consulted throughout the day as Ron passed on more news. We were still anxiously waiting to hear if any of our people had been at the nightclub, and now we were concerned that the news of our being a target would soon be leaked. It would be a big story and would take a difficult emotional toll on the community there. The bond you form in high-stress moments like this, when you're sharing information that you can't discuss with anyone else, is a powerful one. In every emergency I've encountered as CEO, I've been grateful for the competence and cool heads and humanity of the team around me. Bob's first move was to send the head of Walt Disney World, George Kalogridis, back to Orlando from Shanghai, to give his people on the ground more executive support.

The data on Mateen's phone showed that once he got back to his car, he typed in a search for nightclubs in Orlando. He drove to the first club that came up, but there was construction going on in front of the entrance, and traffic was backed up. The second result was Pulse, where he ultimately committed his massacre. As the details of the investigation trickled in, I felt horror and grief for the victims of the shooting, and at the same time a sickening "there but for the grace of God" relief that he'd been deterred by the security we had in place.

I'm often asked what aspect of the job most keeps me up at night. The honest answer is that I don't agonize over the work very much. I don't know if it's a quirk of brain chemistry, or a defense mechanism I developed in reaction to some family chaos in my youth, or the result of years of discipline—some combination of all of those things, I suppose—but I tend not to feel much anxiety when things go awry. And I tend to approach bad news as a problem that can be worked through and solved, something I have control over rather than something happening to me. But I'm also all too aware of the symbolic power of Disney as a target, and the one thing that weighs heavily on me is the knowledge that no matter how vigilant we are, we can't prepare for everything.

When the unexpected does happen, a kind of instinctive triage kicks in. You have to rely on your own internal "threat scale." There are drop-everything events, and there are others when you say to yourself, *This is serious, I need to be engaged right now, but I also need to extricate myself and focus on other things and return to this later.* Sometimes, even though you're "in charge," you need to be aware that in the moment you might have nothing to add, and so you don't wade in. You trust your people to do their jobs and focus your energies on some other pressing issue.

That's what I was telling myself in Shanghai, half a world away from Orlando. This was the most momentous thing the company had embarked on since Disney World opened in 1971. We had never invested so much in something, with so much potential—for success or failure—in our nearly hundred-year history. I had no choice but to compartmentalize, to focus on the last-minute details of the opening ceremonies, and trust in my team in Orlando and in the protocols we had in place.

We have a system that tracks employees whenever a disaster occurs. If there's a plane crash or a hurricane or a wildfire, I get reports on who's unaccounted for, who's had to evacuate their homes, who lost a friend or relative or pet, whose property was damaged. We have well over two hundred thousand employees around the world, so if something catastrophic happens, the odds aren't insignificant that one of our people has been touched by it. After the 2015 terror attacks in Paris, I learned within hours that vendors from an ad agency we work with were killed. In the aftermath of the Las Vegas shooting in the fall of 2017, I got reports right away that more than sixty of our employees were at the outdoor concert that night. Fifty of them knew someone who was either killed or injured. Three had been shot themselves. And one, an employee at Disneyland, had been killed.

By Tuesday morning in Shanghai, we'd learned that two of our part-time employees were among those killed in the nightclub shooting. Several other employees were friends or relatives of victims. Our trauma and grief counselors went to work, contacting those affected and arranging mental health services.

MY ITINERARY FOR those days leading up to the park's opening was scheduled down to the minute: leading park tours and giving interviews and attending rehearsals to give final notes on the opening-ceremony performances; hosting lunches and dinners and meetings with shareholders and vendors and members of our board; meeting with Chinese dignitaries to pay proper respects; dedicating a wing of the Shanghai Children's Hospital; practicing a brief speech, part of which was in Mandarin, that I'd be giving at the opening ceremony. There were even small intervals during which I was scheduled to get makeup, change my clothes, or sneak a quick snack. On Wednesday morning, I was leading a VIP tour of about a hundred guests. Jerry Bruckheimer was there, and George Lucas. Some of my direct reports were there with their families. My wife, Willow, and our kids were there. Everyone wore headsets, and I spoke into a microphone as I led them through the park.

I remember exactly where we were—between Adventure Island and Pirate Cove—when Bob Chapek approached me and pulled me aside. I assumed he had more news from the shooting investigation, and I leaned in so that he could privately give me an update. "There was an alligator attack in Orlando," Bob whispered. "An alligator attacked a young child. A little boy."

We were surrounded by people, and I hid my rising sense of horror as Bob told me what he knew so far. The attack had occurred at our Grand Floridian Hotel resort at about 8:30 in the evening. It was now around 10:30 A.M. in Shanghai, so, two hours ago. "We don't know the status of the child," Bob said.

I instinctively started praying that somehow the boy was not killed. And then I started scrolling through the history in my mind. Had this ever happened before? In the forty-five years the park had been open, as far as I knew, a guest had never been attacked. I started to visualize the property. Bob told me it happened on the beach at the resort. I've stayed in the Grand Floridian many times and know that beach well. There's a lagoon there, but I've never seen anyone swimming in it. Wait, that wasn't true. The image of a man swimming out to retrieve a balloon that his child had lost came to mind. It was about five years earlier. I remembered taking a picture of him as he swam back to shore, balloon in hand, laughing to myself at the things parents are willing to do for their kids.

I finished the tour and waited for more news. There's a protocol for what rises to me and what gets handled by someone else, and my team will regularly wait to tell me something until they're sure it's accurate. (To their frustration, I sometimes chide them that they don't report bad news to me fast enough.) This time the news came to me immediately, but I felt desperate for more.

George Kalogridis, whom we'd sent back in the aftermath of the nightclub shooting, landed right around the time of the attack and began to deal with it instantly, passing information on to us as it became available. I soon learned the boy was missing. Rescue teams hadn't found the body. His name was Lane Graves. He was two years old. The Graves family was staying at the Grand Floridian and had gone down to the beach for a scheduled movie night. The movie was canceled because of lightning, but they and some other families decided to stay and let their kids play. Lane took a bucket to fill at the water's edge. It was dusk, and an alligator that had come up to the surface to feed was right there in the shallow water. It grabbed the boy and took him under. The Graves family had come to Disney World from Nebraska, George told me. A crisis team was with them. I knew a couple of members of that team. They were exceptional at their jobs, and I was grateful they were there, but this would test them in the extreme.

That night was our opening concert in Shanghai, to be performed by a five-hundred-piece orchestra and featuring the world-famous pianist Lang Lang, along with a lineup of the most revered composers and singers and musicians in China. Prior to the concert, I was hosting a dinner for a group of Chinese officials and visiting dignitaries. I did everything I could to focus on my responsibilities, but my mind returned constantly to the Graves family in Orlando. The thought that they had come to Disney World, of all places, and suffered such an unimaginable loss, loomed over everything.

Thursday morning, June 16, was opening day. I woke at 4:00 A.M. and worked out, to try to clear my head, then wandered to a lounge on our floor and met with Zenia Mucha, our chief communications officer. Zenia and I have worked together for more than a dozen years. She's been with me through it all, good and bad. She's tough, she'll tell me straight to my face when she thinks I'm making a mistake, and she always has the best interests of the company at heart.

The story was being reported widely now, and I wanted our response to come from me. I've seen other companies deal with crises by letting a "company spokesperson" be their official voice, and that strategy has always struck me as cold and a bit cowardly. Corporate systems often work to insulate and protect CEOs, sometimes to a fault, and I was determined not to do that now. I told Zenia I had to issue a statement, and she immediately agreed that it was the right thing to do.

There is so little you can say to make sense of something like this, but we sat there in the lounge and I dictated my feelings to Zenia as honestly as I could. I talked about being a father and a grandfather, and how that gave me the slightest window into the parents' unimaginable pain. Fifteen minutes after our conversation, the statement went out. I returned to my room to start to get ready for the opening. Willow was up and out, and my boys were asleep. I couldn't seem to do what I needed to do next, though, and after several minutes I called Zenia again. When she answered her phone, I said, "I have to speak with the family."

This time I expected pushback from her and from our general counsel, Alan Braverman. This could become a complicated legal situation, and lawyers want to restrict the possibility of saying anything that might exacerbate liability. In this case, though, they both knew this was something I needed to do, and neither of them offered resistance. "I'll get you a number," Zenia said, and within minutes I had the phone number of Jay Ferguson, a friend of Matt and Melissa Graves, the boy's parents, who'd flown to Orlando immediately to be with them.

I sat on the edge of the bed and dialed. I didn't know what I was going to say, but when Jay answered, I explained who I was and that I was in Shanghai. "I don't know if they'll want to talk with me," I said, "but if they do, I would like to express my sympathies. If they don't, I'll express them to you and ask you to pass them on."

"Give me a minute," Jay said. I could hear talking in the background, and then suddenly Matt was there on speaker. I just started talking. I reiterated what I'd said in the statement, that I was a parent and a grandparent, that I couldn't fathom what they must be going through. I told him that I wanted him to know from me, the person at the top of this company, that we would do anything we could possibly do to get them through this. I gave him my direct number and told him to call it if he needed anything, and then asked if there was anything I could do for them now.

"Promise me that my son's life won't be in vain," he said. He was speaking through heaving sobs, and I could hear Melissa also sobbing in the background. "Promise me you'll do whatever you can to prevent this from ever happening to another child."

I gave him my promise. I knew from a lawyer's perspective that I should be careful about what I was saying, that I should consider whether that was somehow an admission of negligence. When you work in a corporate structure for so long, you become trained to give legalistic, corporate responses, but I didn't care about any of that in this moment. I reiterated to Jay that he should call me if there was anything they needed, and then we hung up, and I sat there shaking on the edge of my bed. I'd been crying so hard that both of my contact lenses had come out, and I was vaguely searching for them when Willow walked into the room.

"I just talked with the parents," I said. I was at a loss for how to explain what I felt. She came to me and wrapped her arms around me. She asked what she could do. "I just have to keep going," I said. But I didn't have anything left. The adrenaline that had been powering me for the last two weeks, all that this project meant to me and the thrill I'd felt at sharing it, had drained away. In thirty minutes, I was scheduled to meet the vice premier of China, the U.S. ambassador to China, the Chinese ambassador to the United States, the party secretary of Shanghai, and the mayor of Shanghai, and lead them on a tour of the park. I felt like I couldn't move.

Eventually I called my team and said to meet me in the hotel lounge. I knew if I described the conversation to them, I would start crying again, so I kept it short and told Bob Chapek what I'd promised Matt Graves. "We're on it," Bob said, and sent word back to his team in Orlando right away. (What they did there was remarkable. There are hundreds of lagoons and canals on the property, and thousands of alligators. Within twenty-four hours, they had ropes and fences and signs up throughout the park, which is twice the size of Manhattan.)

I went off to meet the dignitaries. We rode rides and posed for pictures. I struggled to smile and go on with the show. It was a stark example of the truth that what people see on the outside so often doesn't reflect what's happening on the inside. When the tour was over, I was scheduled to give a speech to the thousands of people gathered there in the park, and millions more in China watching on TV, then cut a ribbon and officially open Shanghai

Disneyland to the world. Disney coming to mainland China was a major event. There were members of the press there from all over the globe. Both President Xi and President Obama had written letters that we were planning to read at the opening. I was well aware of the weight of it all, but I also couldn't stop thinking of the anguish of Matt Graves's voice on the phone.

As I walked away from the vice premier, the president of Shanghai Shendi Group, the Chinese company we'd partnered with, caught up to me and took me by the arm. "You're not going to talk about Orlando, are you?" he said. "It's a happy day. This is a happy day." I assured him I wouldn't say anything to dampen the mood.

Less than half an hour later, I found myself sitting alone on a banquette in the Disney castle, waiting for a stage manager to give me the cue that it was time for my speech. I'd memorized the lines in Mandarin that I was planning to deliver, and now I was struggling to recall them. It was true, it was a happy day, and I needed to try to focus on that and recognize what it meant for all the people who had worked so hard, for so long, to make this day happen; and for the people of China, who would have this place to dream about in the same way that I and so many American kids dreamed of going to Disneyland. It was a happy day. It was also the saddest of my career.

I'VE WORKED FOR the same company for forty-five years: twenty-two of them at ABC, another twenty-three at Disney, after Disney acquired ABC in 1995. For the past fourteen years, I've had the enviable task of being the sixth CEO to run the company since Walt founded it in 1923.

There have been difficult, even tragic, days. But for me this has also been, to steal from a phrase, the happiest job on earth. We make movies and television shows and Broadway musicals, games and costumes and toys and books. We build theme parks and rides, hotels and cruise ships. We stage parades and street shows and concerts every day in our fourteen parks across the world. We manufacture fun. Even after all of these years, I still sometimes find myself thinking, *How did this happen? How did I get so lucky?* We used to call our biggest, most exciting theme-park attractions "E-Tickets." That's what comes to mind when I think about the job, that it's been a fourteen-year ride on a giant E-Ticket attraction known as the Walt Disney Company.

But Disney also exists in the world of quarterly earnings reports and shareholder expectations and countless other obligations that come with running a company that operates in nearly every country in the world. On the least eventful days, this job requires an ability to constantly adapt and re-adapt. You go from plotting growth strategy with investors, to looking at the design of a giant new theme-park attraction with Imagineers, to giving notes on the rough cut of a film, to discussing security measures and board governance and ticket pricing and pay scale. The days are challenging and dynamic, but they're also a never-ending exercise in compartmentalization. You address one thing—What are the attributes of a Disney princess in today's world and how should they manifest in our products?—then you put it away and shift your focus to the next: What will our slate of Marvel films be for the next eight years? And those are the rare days when things actually unfold according to schedule. As the week described above makes all too clear, there are also, always, crises and failures for which you can never be fully prepared. Few will be as tragic as the events of that week, but something will always come up.

This is true not just of the Walt Disney Company but of any company or institution. Something will always come up. At its simplest, this book is about being guided by a set of principles that help nurture the good and manage the bad. I was reluctant to write it for a long time. Until fairly recently, I even avoided talking publicly about my "rules for leadership" or any such ideas, because I felt I hadn't fully "walked the walk." After forty-five years, though—

and especially after the past fourteen—I've come to believe that I have insights that could be useful beyond my own experience.

If you run a business or manage a team or collaborate with others in pursuit of a common goal, this book might be helpful to you. My experiences from day one have all been in the media and entertainment world, but these strike me as universal ideas: about fostering risk taking and creativity; about building a culture of trust; about fueling a deep and abiding curiosity in oneself and inspiring that in the people around you; about embracing change rather than living in denial of it; and about operating, always, with integrity and honesty in the world, even when that means facing things that are difficult to face. These are abstractions, but my hope is that the stories and examples that are significant to me as I look back at the long arc of my career will help them feel more concrete and relatable, not just to the aspiring CEOs of the world but to anyone wanting to be less fearful, more confidently themselves, as they navigate their professional and even personal lives.

For the most part, the book is organized chronologically. Since my first day at ABC, I've had twenty jobs and fourteen bosses. I've been the lowliest crew member working on a daytime soap opera and run a network that produced some of the most innovative television (and one of the most infamous flops) of all time. I've twice been on the side of the company being taken over, and I've acquired and assimilated several others, among them Pixar, Marvel, Lucasfilm, and, most recently, 21st Century Fox. I've schemed about the future of entertainment with Steve Jobs and become the keeper of George Lucas's Star Wars mythology. I've thought every day about how technology is redefining the way we create, deliver, and experience media, and what it means to be both relevant to a modern audience and faithful to a nearly hundred-year-old brand. And I've worked hard and thoughtfully to make a connection between that brand and billions of people around the globe.

As I near the end of all of that and think back on what I've learned, these are the ten principles that strike me as necessary to true leadership. I hope they'll serve you as well as they've served me.

Optimism. One of the most important qualities of a good leader is optimism, a pragmatic enthusiasm for what can be achieved. Even in the face of difficult choices and less than ideal outcomes, an optimistic leader does not yield to pessimism. Simply put, people are not motivated or energized by pessimists.

Courage. The foundation of risk-taking is courage, and in ever-changing, disrupted businesses, risk-taking is essential, innovation is vital, and true innovation occurs only when people have courage. This is true of acquisitions, investments, and capital allocations, and it particularly applies to creative decisions. Fear of failure destroys creativity.

Focus. Allocating time, energy, and resources to the strategies, problems, and projects that are of highest importance and value is extremely important, and it's imperative to communicate your priorities clearly and often.

Decisiveness. All decisions, no matter how difficult, can and should be made in a timely way. Leaders must encourage a diversity of opinion balanced with the need to make and implement decisions. Chronic indecision is not only inefficient and counterproductive, but it is deeply corrosive to morale.

Curiosity. A deep and abiding curiosity enables the discovery of new people, places, and ideas, as well as an awareness and an understanding of the marketplace and its changing dynamics. The path to innovation begins with curiosity.

Fairness. Strong leadership embodies the fair and decent treatment of people. Empathy is essential, as is accessibility. People committing honest mistakes deserve second chances, and judging people too harshly generates fear and anxiety, which discourage communication and innovation. Nothing is worse to an organization than a culture of fear.

Thoughtfulness. Thoughtfulness is one of the most underrated elements of good leadership. It is the process of gaining knowledge, so an opinion rendered or decision made is more credible and more likely to be correct. It's simply about taking the time to develop informed opinions.

Authenticity. Be genuine. Be honest. Don't fake anything. Truth and authenticity breed respect and trust.

The Relentless Pursuit of Perfection. This doesn't mean perfectionism at all costs, but it does mean a refusal to accept mediocrity or make excuses for something being "good enough." If you believe that something can be made better, put in the effort to do it. If you're in the business of making things, be in the business of making things great.

Integrity. Nothing is more important than the quality and integrity of an organization's people and its product. A company's success depends on setting high ethical standards for all things, big and small. Another way of saying this is: The way you do anything is the way you do everything.

PART ONE

LEARNING

CHAPTER 1

STARTING AT THE BOTTOM

THIS BOOK IS not a memoir, but it's impossible to talk about the traits that have served me well over the course of my professional life and not look back at my childhood. There are certain ways I've always been, things I've always done, that are the result of some inscrutable mix of nature and nurture. (I've always woken early, for example, as far back as I can remember, and cherished those hours to myself before the rest of the world wakes up.) There are other qualities and habits that are the result of purposeful decisions I made along the path. As is the case with many of us, those decisions were partially made in response to my parents, in particular my father, a brilliant and complicated man who shaped me more than anyone.

He certainly made me curious about the world. We had a den lined with shelves full of books, and my dad had read every one of them. I didn't become a serious reader until I was in high school, but when I did finally fall in love with books, it was because of him. He had complete sets that he ordered from the Book of the Month

Club of the works of all the American literary giants—Fitzgerald and Hemingway and Faulkner and Steinbeck and so on. I'd pull down from the shelves his copy of *Tender Is the Night* or *For Whom the Bell Tolls* or dozens of others and devour them, and he'd urge me to read even more. We also spent our dinners discussing world events, and as young as ten years old, I'd grab the *New York Times* on our front lawn and read it at the kitchen table before anyone else woke up.

We lived in a split-level house in a small, mostly working-class town on Long Island called Oceanside. I was the older of two kids; my sister is three years younger. My mother was warm and loving, a stay-at-home mom until I went to high school, at which point she got a job in the local junior high school library. My dad was a Navy veteran who came back from the war and played the trumpet with some "lesser" big bands, but he figured he could never make much of a living as a musician, so never tried to do it full-time. He majored in marketing at the University of Pennsylvania's Wharton School, and his first job was working in marketing for a food manufacturing company, and that led him into advertising. He became an account executive at an advertising agency on Madison Avenue—he handled the Old Milwaukee and Brunswick bowling accounts—but eventually lost that job. He changed agencies several times, almost always lateral moves. By the time I was ten or eleven, he'd changed jobs so many times that I began to wonder why.

He was always deeply politically engaged and had a very strong liberal bias. He once lost a job because he was determined to go to the March on Washington and see Martin Luther King, Jr., speak. His boss wouldn't give him the day off, but he went anyway. I don't know if he quit and went to the speech or if he was fired for going after he'd been told he couldn't, but it was just one of several such endings.

I was proud of his strong character and his politics. He had a fierce sense of what was right and fair, and he was always on the side of the underdog. But he also had trouble regulating his moods and would often say things that got him into trouble. I later learned that he'd been diagnosed with manic depression, and that he'd tried several therapies, including electroshock therapy, to treat his illness. As the older child, I bore the brunt of his emotional unpredictability. I never felt threatened by his moods, but I was acutely aware of his dark side and felt sad for him. We never knew which Dad was coming home at night, and I can distinctly recall sitting in my room on the second floor of our house, knowing by the sound of the way he opened and shut the door and walked up the steps whether it was happy or sad Dad.

He would sometimes check in on his way past my room to make sure I was "spending time productively," as he put it. That meant reading or doing homework or being engaged in something that would "better" me in some way. He wanted my sister and me to have fun, but it also was very important to him that we use our time wisely and work in a focused way toward our goals. I'm certain that my vigilance (some might say obsessiveness) about time-management comes from him.

I felt early on that it was my job to be the steady center of our family, which extended even to practical matters around the house. If something broke, my mother would ask me to fix it, and I learned as a young kid how to repair whatever needed repairing. That's part of where my curiosity about technology comes from, too, I think. I liked using tools and taking things apart and understanding how they worked.

My parents were worriers. There was a sense with both of them that something bad would soon be coming down the pike. I don't know how much of it is a fluke of genetics and how much is a learned reaction to their anxiety, but I've always been the opposite of that. With few exceptions in my life, I've never worried too much about the future, and I've never had too much fear about trying something and failing.

As I grew older, I became more aware of my father's disappointment in himself. He'd led a life that was unsatisfying to him and was a failure in his own eyes. It's part of why he pushed us to work so hard and be productive, so that we might be successful in a way that he never was. His employment troubles meant that if I wanted to have any spending money, I needed to find my own jobs. I started working in eighth grade, shoveling snow and babysitting and working as a stock boy in a hardware store. At fifteen, I got a job as the summer janitor in my school district. It involved cleaning every heater in every classroom, then moving on to the bottom of every desk, making sure they were gum-free when the school year started. Cleaning gum from the bottoms of a thousand desks can build character, or at least a tolerance for monotony, or something . . . .

I attended Ithaca College and spent nearly every weekend night my freshman and sophomore year making pizza at the local Pizza Hut. I got mostly B's and a few A's in high school, but academics was never my passion. Something clicked for me when I went to college, though. I was determined to work hard and learn as much as I could learn, and I think that, too, was related to my father— a function of never wanting to experience the same sense of failure that he felt about himself. I didn't have a clear idea of what "success" meant, no specific vision of being wealthy or powerful, but I was determined not to live a life of disappointment. Whatever shape my life took, I told myself, there wasn't a chance in the world that I was going to toil in frustration and lack fulfillment.

I don't carry much pain with me from those early years, other than the pain that my dad didn't live a happier life, and that my mother suffered, too, as a result. I wish he could have felt prouder of himself. My sister and I were never deprived of love as kids. We always had a roof over our heads and food on the table, but there was little or no money for much else. Vacations were usually spent driving to mundane places in our car or going to the beach a few minutes away from our house. We had enough clothes to look presentable, but nothing extra, and when I tore a pair of pants in the fall, I was typically told to wear them with a patch until we had the money to replace them, which could be months. I never felt poor, and no one viewed me as such. Things were a lot thinner than they looked, though, and as I grew older I became aware of that.

Late in life, after I'd become CEO of Disney, I took my father to lunch in New York. We talked about his mental health and his perspective on his life. I told him how much I appreciated everything that he and my mom had done for us, the ethics they instilled, and the love they gave us. I told him that was enough, more than enough, and wished that my gratitude might liberate him in some small way from disappointment. I do know that so many of the traits that served me well in my career started with him. I hope that he understood that, too.

I STARTED MY career at ABC on July 1, 1974, as a studio supervisor for ABC Television. Before that, I'd spent a year as a weatherman and feature news reporter at a tiny cable TV station in Ithaca, New York. That year of toiling in obscurity (and performing with mediocrity) convinced me to abandon the dream I'd had since I was fifteen years old: to be a network news anchorman. I'm only half-joking when I say that the experience of giving the people of Ithaca their daily weather report taught me a necessary skill, which is the ability to deliver bad news. For roughly six months of the year, the long bleak stretch from October through April, I was far from the most popular guy in town.

I came to ABC thanks to my uncle Bob's bad eyesight. My mother's brother, whom I adored, spent a few days in a Manhattan hospital after eye surgery, and his roommate was a lower-level ABC executive, who for whatever reasons wanted my uncle to believe he was a big network mogul. He would fake taking phone calls in his hospital bed, as if there were important network decisions that only he could make, and my uncle fell for it. Before he was discharged, my uncle mentioned to his roommate that his nephew was looking for a job in television production in New York. The guy gave him his number and said, "Tell your nephew to give me a call."

He was surprised and a little confused about who I was when I actually followed through. Based on what my uncle had described, I was expecting a powerful network executive whose influence was felt at the highest reaches of the company. He was far from that, but to his credit, he did manage to get me an interview in the small department he ran at the network, Production Services, and not long after that I was hired on as a studio supervisor.

The position paid $150 per week and was about as low as you could go on the ABC ladder. There were a half dozen of us who did all manner of menial labor, on game shows and soap operas and talk shows and news shows and made-for-TV specials—basically anything produced at ABC's sprawling Manhattan studios. I was assigned to a whole gamut of programming: *All My Children* and *One Life to Live* and *Ryan's Hope*, *The $10,000 Pyramid* and *The Money Maze* and *Showdown*. *The Dick Cavett Show.* Geraldo Rivera's *Good Night America*. *The ABC Evening News with Harry Reasoner.*

The job description was pretty simple: Show up whenever they needed me, for whatever task. Often that meant being at a studio at 4:30 A.M. for "lighting calls." Soap opera sets were set up the night before a shoot, and my job was to let in the lighting director and stagehands long before the sun came up, so the lights would be in place when the director and actors arrived for their first run-throughs. I coordinated all the carpenters and prop masters and electricians, makeup artists and costume people and hairstylists, checking everybody in and making sure they had their marching orders for the day. I kept track of their hours and their grievances and their violations of union rules. I made sure catering was in place and the air-conditioning had cooled the studios enough to begin shooting under the hot lights. It was the opposite of glamorous, but I learned the ins and outs of all of those shows. I spoke the lingo. I got to know all of the people who made a TV show work. Maybe most important, I learned to tolerate the demanding hours and the extreme workload of television production, and that work ethic has stayed with me ever since.

To this day, I wake nearly every morning at four-fifteen, though now I do it for selfish reasons: to have time to think and read and exercise before the demands of the day take over. Those hours aren't for everyone, but however you find the time, it's vital to create space in each day to let your thoughts wander beyond your immediate job responsibilities, to turn things over in your mind in a less pressured, more creative way than is possible once the daily triage kicks in. I've come to cherish that time alone each morning, and am certain I'd be less productive and less creative in my work if I didn't also spend those first hours away from the emails and text messages and phone calls that require so much attention as the day goes on.

IT WAS A very different industry back then. In some ways it was better. The competition was simpler, the world less atomized. Certainly there was a mostly shared American narrative, organized around a general societal belief in basic facts. In many other ways, though, it was worse. For one, there was a shrugging tolerance of a level of disrespect that would be unacceptable today. It was without a doubt much more difficult on a day-to-day basis for women and members of underrepresented groups than it ever was for me. But even in my case, being low on the food chain meant exposure to the occasional, casual abuse that people would be fired for now.

One example that captures so much of that time: *The Evening News* was broadcast at 6:00 P.M. Eastern Standard Time. The moment we wrapped, the anchorman Harry Reasoner and his stage manager, a man called Whitey, would walk off the set and park themselves at the bar of the Hotel des Artistes on West Sixty-seventh Street. (*The Evening News* was broadcast from a converted ballroom in the old hotel.) Every evening, Harry would down a double extra-dry Beefeater martini on the rocks with a twist.

One of my responsibilities was to wait while the producer reviewed the show, then pass on word to Harry and the studio crew if any updates or fixes needed to be made before it aired in later time zones. One night Harry was ready to move on to martini number two, and he asked me to run back to the studio and find out from the producer where things stood. I ventured into the control room and said, "Harry sent me to find out how it looks." The producer looked at me with complete disdain. Then he unzipped his pants, pulled out his penis, and replied, "I don't know. You tell me how it looks." Forty-five years later, I still get angry when I recall that scene. We've become much more aware of the need for fair, equal, non-abusive treatment in the workplace, but it has taken too long.

In the fall of 1974, I got assigned to work *The Main Event,* a Frank Sinatra concert at Madison Square Garden that ABC was televising live in prime time. I was the studio supervisor onsite, which meant that I had to be on hand to run errands for the enormous Madison Square Garden stage crew. This was a plum assignment, and it was a big deal for me, personally. My father played Sinatra records endlessly on the turntable in our house. To this day, I can remember perfectly the image of my dad standing in the living room, blowing on his trumpet in accompaniment as Frank crooned.

To be in the same building as Sinatra, attending rehearsals and doing my small part to make sure the production went smoothly—I couldn't believe my good fortune. The high point came a few hours before the concert was scheduled to begin, when I was told by an associate producer to run out and get a bottle of mouthwash and deliver it as fast as I could to Mr. Sinatra's dressing room. I ran a few blocks to a pharmacy uptown and bought the largest bottle of Listerine I could find, thinking the whole time that Frank was having throat issues and the entire broadcast rested on my shoulders!

Nervous and out of breath, I knocked on the dressing room door, mouthwash in hand. The door swung open, and I was greeted by an imposing bodyguard, who wanted to know what the hell I was doing there. "I'm delivering Mr. Sinatra's Listerine," I said.

Before he could respond, I heard that familiar voice, from somewhere deep in the room: "Let him in." Moments later I was standing in front of the Chairman of the Board.

"What's your name, kid?"

"Bob."

"Where're you from?"

For some reason I said, "Brooklyn," which is where I was born and lived until my family moved to Long Island when I was five years old. I think I must have wanted to seem more real to him in some way, and "Oceanside" didn't quite have the same romance.

"Brooklyn!" Frank said, like it was the next best thing to Hoboken, and then he handed me a crisp hundred-dollar bill. When the show ended, he gave every member of the crew a sleek gold cigarette lighter, inscribed LOVE, SINATRA. I spent the hundred dollars almost immediately, but the lighter sits in a drawer in my desk to this day.

The Main Event was produced by Jerry Weintraub and Roone Arledge, then the brash forty-three-year-old head of ABC Sports. By 1974, Roone was already a legendary television executive. He'd stacked the crew with various producers who worked for him at Sports. The night before the concert, they rehearsed the entire show. Howard Cosell kicked it off, introducing Frank onto the stage like a prizefighter (the stage itself was made to look like a boxing ring in the center of the arena), and then Frank came on and performed for nearly two hours.

It was the first time I'd ever seen Roone in action. He watched it all, and when the rehearsal was over he decided that more or less everything needed to be scrapped and redone. The set needed to be redesigned, Howard's intro needed to be reworked, the lighting needed to be radically changed. The entire way in which Frank interacted with the audience, Roone said, needed to be reconceived.

I did my small tasks and watched as it all came down and went back up, to no small amount of swearing and moaning from the crew. There was no denying that the show that aired less than twenty-four hours later was of a different order than the one that had been rehearsed. I didn't understand how he did it, but I'd later learn that this was classic Roone, absolutely unwilling to accept "good enough," and completely comfortable pushing right up against an unmovable deadline (and exhausting a lot of people along the way) to make it great.

The thrill of working on *The Main Event* wore off as soon as I returned to my mundane world of soap operas and game shows. Before long I had my own drama to contend with, however. The head of the small department I worked for was a corrupt bully who was paying vendors and suppliers out of our department's budget to do work ("government jobs," he called them) for himself and other executives at ABC, then filling his own pockets with the kickbacks. He was also buying furniture that he claimed was for soap opera sets, then using stagehands to move it all into an apartment in Midtown that he'd set up for a mistress. I'd been asked to go along with all of this, either by helping out or by looking the other way, and it irritated me to no end. I started asking some people in the department if there was anything I could do about it, and word got back to him.

One day he summoned me to his office. When I walked in, he immediately accused me of violating company rules. "What are you up to?" he said. "I hear you used our truck to move in to a new apartment."

In fact, I'd briefly had access to a company pickup, and I'd joked to some colleagues that maybe I should use the truck to move in to an apartment I'd just rented. I never did it, and I told him so, but it dawned on me in that moment that someone must have told him I was a troublemaker.

"You're spreading rumors about me," he said. When I didn't deny that I'd been talking about him, he stared me down for a while before telling me, "You know what, Iger? You're no longer promotable."

He gave me two weeks to find a job in another department or I was done at the company. I was twenty-three and certain my career in television was already over. But I went to the ABC job-posting site—in those days it was a clipboard hanging on a wall—and there, in a list of about twenty-five other jobs I wasn't qualified for, was the description of an opening at ABC Sports. I immediately called one of the guys I knew from the Sinatra concert and explained that I was in a tough spot. He told me to come down to 1330 (ABC's corporate headquarters, 1330 Avenue of the Americas), and a month later I was hired as a studio operations supervisor at ABC Sports. If you squinted, this new position was slightly more illustrious than the job I'd just lost. But it was the break that made all the difference, part of which I like to think I owe to Frank Sinatra, and part to a guy who later got fired from the company for embezzlement.

DURING ITS HEYDAY in the '70s and early '80s, ABC Sports was one of the network's most profitable divisions, largely because *Monday Night Football* and *Wide World of Sports* were so wildly popular. It also had a great lineup of college football and Major League Baseball and many of the major golf tournaments and boxing championships, and programs like *The American Sportsman* and *The Superstars*. Plus every four years, ABC was the "network of the Olympics," having covered most of the Olympic Games from 1964 to 1988.

The guys who worked in Sports were the "cool kids" at the company, a status reflected in pretty much everything about them, the way they dressed (tailored suits and Gucci loafers with no socks), what they ate and drank (expensive wine and scotch, often at lunch), and the Hollywood stars and famous athletes and politicians they fraternized with. They were always off to somewhere exotic, often flying the Concorde to our European office in Paris, and then going from there to cover events in places like Monte Carlo and Saint Moritz.

Eventually I rose high enough in the ranks that I had a seat on the Concorde, too. The traveling I did, especially for *ABC's Wide World of Sports,* changed my life. I hadn't been out of the country before then, and suddenly I was flying all over the world. (As Jim McKay's opening voiceover intoned week after week, we were "spanning the globe to bring you the constant variety of sports.") On any given weekend, I might be at a surfing championship in Hawaii or a figure-skating event in Prague, a weight-lifting competition in Budapest or the Frontier Days rodeo in Cheyenne. There was cliff diving in Acapulco and downhill skiing in Kitzbuhel, gymnastics in China or Romania or the U.S.S.R. . . .

ABC Sports showed me the world and made me more sophisticated. I got exposed to things I'd never contemplated before. I remember exactly where and when I ate my first fine French meal in Paris, the first time I ever uttered the word *Montrachet,* and my first experience driving through Monaco in a luxury sports car. For a kid who'd grown up in a split-level house in Oceanside, New York, it all felt a little head-spinning. It was much more than the high life, though. I traveled regularly to the developing world and arranged for coverage of events in the Communist bloc, negotiating with intransigent governing bodies and navigating often corrupt and byzantine systems. I witnessed firsthand how people lived behind the Iron Curtain, and got a sense of the daily challenges of their lives. (I can still remember looking out over darkened Bucharest during the nightly brownouts when the government shut down the electrical grid in winter.) I also saw the ways in which their dreams were no different from the dreams of the average person in America. If politicians had an urge to divide the world or generate an us-versus-them, good-versus-bad mentality, I was exposed to a reality much more nuanced than that.

As for all the glamour, there is (and eventually there was) a convincing argument to be made that living that high off the hog was irresponsible. However, at that time ABC Sports existed in its own orbit, often immune from the laws that governed the rest of ABC.

Roone Arledge was at the center of that orbit. Roone had been tapped to run ABC Sports in the early 1960s, and by the time I arrived he was already television royalty. More than anyone in the history of broadcasting, he changed the way we experience televised sports.

He knew, first and foremost, that we were telling stories and not just broadcasting events, and to tell great stories, you need great talent. He was the most competitive person I've ever worked for, and a relentless innovator, but he also knew that he was only as good as the people he surrounded himself with. Jim McKay, Howard Cosell, Keith Jackson. Frank Gifford, Don Meredith, Chris Schenkel, Bob Beattie in skiing, Jackie Stewart in auto racing. They all had magnetic broadcast personalities, and Roone turned them into household names.

"The human drama of athletic competition"—to cite another line from that *Wide World of Sports* opening—that's really how Roone saw the events that we covered. Athletes were characters in unfolding narratives. Where did they come from? What did they have to overcome to get here? How was this competition analogous to geopolitical dramas? How was it a window into different cultures? He reveled in the idea that we were bringing not just sports but the world into the living rooms of millions of Americans.

He was also the first person I ever worked for who embraced technological advancements to revolutionize what we did and how we did it. Reverse-angle cameras, slow-motion replays, airing events live via satellite—that's all Roone. He wanted to try every new gadget and break every stale format. He was looking, always, for new ways to connect to viewers and grab their attention. Roone taught me the dictum that has guided me in every job I've held since: Innovate or die, and there's no innovation if you operate out of fear of the new or untested.

He was also a relentless perfectionist. In my early years in Sports, I spent most of my weekends in a basement control room on Sixty-sixth Street. My job entailed taking in feeds from all over the world and delivering them to producers and editors, who would cut them and lay in voiceovers before they went to air. Roone would often show up in the control room, or if he didn't appear in person, he'd call in from wherever he was. (There was a red "Roone phone" in each of our control rooms, as well as in the mobile units at every event we covered.) If he was at home watching a broadcast—he was always watching from somewhere—and saw something he didn't like, he'd call in and tell us. This camera angle is wrong. That story line needs more emphasis. We're not telling people what's coming up!

No detail was too small for Roone. Perfection was the result of getting all the little things right. On countless occasions, just as I'd witnessed at the Sinatra concert, he would rip up an entire program before it aired and demand the team rework the whole thing, even if it meant working till dawn in an editing room. He wasn't a yeller, but he was tough and exacting and he communicated in very clear terms what was wrong and that he expected it to get fixed, and he didn't much care what sacrifice it required to fix it. The show was the thing. It was everything to him. The show was more important to Roone than to the people who made it, and you had to make peace with that if you worked for him. His commitment to making things great was galvanizing. It was often exhausting, often frustrating (largely because he would wait until very late in the production process to give notes or demand changes), but it was inspiring, too, and the inspiration far outweighed the frustration. You knew how much he cared about making things great, and you simply wanted to live up to his expectations.

His mantra was simple: "Do what you need to do to make it better." Of all the things I learned from Roone, this is what shaped me the most. When I talk about this particular quality of leadership, I refer to it as "the relentless pursuit of perfection." In practice that means a lot of things, and it's hard to define. It's a mindset, really, more than a specific set of rules. It's not, at least as I have internalized it, about perfectionism at all costs (something Roone wasn't especially concerned about). Instead, it's about creating an environment in which you refuse to accept mediocrity. You instinctively push back against the urge to say *There's not enough time,* or *I don't have the energy,* or *This requires a difficult conversation I don't want to have,* or any of the many other ways we can convince ourselves that "good enough" is good enough.

Decades after I stopped working for Roone, I watched a documentary, *Jiro Dreams of Sushi,* about a master sushi chef from Tokyo named Jiro Ono, whose restaurant has three Michelin stars and is one of the most sought-after reservations in the world. In the film, he's in his late eighties and still trying to perfect his art. He is described by some as being the living embodiment of the Japanese word *shokunin,* which is "the endless pursuit of perfection for some greater good." I fell in love with Jiro when I watched it and became fascinated by the concept of *shokunin.* In 2013, I traveled to Tokyo for work and went to the restaurant with some colleagues. We met Jiro, who made us our dinner, and I watched in awe as he deftly laid out nineteen gorgeous pieces of sushi, one after the other, over the course of thirty-five minutes. (The speed of the meal was due to his commitment to serve the sushi on rice that was at body temperature. If the meal took too long, the rice would drop a couple of degrees below 98.6 degrees Fahrenheit, which to Jiro was unacceptable.)

I loved the documentary so much that I showed excerpts of it to 250 executives at a Disney retreat. I wanted them to understand better, through the example of Jiro, what I meant when I talked about "the relentless pursuit of perfection." This is what it looks like to take immense personal pride in the work you create, and to have both the instinct toward perfection and the work ethic to follow through on that instinct.

ONE OF MY favorite interactions with Roone came at the beginning of my tenure at ABC Sports. Even though we worked on the same floor and Sports was a relatively small division, Roone never came across as accessible to me in those days. Other than perfunctory hellos, he barely acknowledged me. One day I found myself standing next to him at a urinal. To my surprise, Roone began to talk with me. "How's it going?"

After a moment of stunned silence, I said, "Well, some days I feel like it's tough just keeping my head above water."

Roone looked straight ahead. Without missing a beat, he said, "Get a longer snorkel." Then he finished his business and walked out.

He wasn't much for excuses. Only later, when I worked more closely with him, would I discover what people meant when they said that he refused to accept no for an answer. If he asked you to do something, you were expected to exhaust every possible method to accomplish it. If you came back and said you tried and it couldn't be done, he'd just tell you, "Find another way."

In 1979, the World Table Tennis Championships were being held in Pyongyang, North Korea. Roone called me into his office one day and said, "This is going to be interesting. Let's cover it on *Wide World of Sports*." I thought he was joking. He surely knew it would be impossible to secure the rights to an event in North Korea.

He wasn't joking.

I then embarked on a worldwide pursuit to secure the rights. The first stop was Cardiff, Wales, to meet with the head of the World Table Tennis Federation, and then from there, since I wasn't allowed to travel to North Korea, to Beijing to meet with the North Korean contingent. After a few months of intense negotiations, we were on the eve of closing the deal when I received a call from someone on the Asian desk in the U.S. State Department. "Everything you're doing with them is illegal," he said. "You're in violation of strict U.S. sanctions against doing any business with North Korea."

That certainly seemed like the end of the road, but I also had Roone in my mind, telling me to find another way. It turned out that the State Department wasn't opposed to our entering North Korea; they actually liked the idea of our going in with cameras and capturing what images we could there. They just wouldn't allow us to pay the North Koreans for the rights or enter into any contract with them. When I explained this to the North Korean contingent, they were livid, and it appeared that the whole thing would collapse. I eventually arrived at a workaround that involved securing the rights not through the host country but through the World Table Tennis Federation. The North Korean government, though we were no longer paying them, still agreed to let us in, and we became the first U.S. media team to enter North Korea in decades—a historic moment in sports broadcasting. Roone never knew the lengths I'd gone to to get it done, but I know I wouldn't have done it had I not been driven in part by his expectations and my desire to please him.

It's a delicate thing, finding the balance between demanding that your people perform and not instilling a fear of failure in them. Most of us who worked for Roone wanted to live up to his standards, but we also knew that he had no patience for excuses and that he could easily turn on anyone, in his singularly cutting, somewhat cruel, way, if he felt we weren't performing to his satisfaction.

Every Monday morning, the top executives in Sports would gather around a conference table to review the past weekend's coverage and plan for what was coming up. The rest of us sat in a ring of chairs around the outer edge of the room, true backbenchers, waiting for critiques of the work we'd just completed and orders for the week ahead.

One morning—this was early in my time at *Wide World of Sports*, right around the time of the snorkel exchange—Roone walked in and began excoriating the entire team for missing a world record for the mile set by the great British middle-distance runner, Sebastian Coe, at a track-and-field event in Oslo, Norway. We were normally on top of such things, but there were unexpected complications in this case, and I hadn't been able to procure the rights to the race in time to air it. I suspected it was going to be a problem come Monday, but I held on to an unrealistic hope that it might slip by without mention.

No such luck. Roone looked around the table at his senior team, wanting to know who was at fault. From the outer edges of the room, I raised my hand and said that it was my mistake. The room went silent; two dozen heads turned toward me. Nobody said anything, and we moved on, but after the meeting, various people came up to me and murmured, "I can't believe you did that."

"Did what?"

"Admitted it was your fault."

"What do you mean?"

"No one ever does that."

Roone never said anything to me about it, but he treated me differently, with higher regard, it seemed, from that moment on. In my early days, I thought there was only one lesson in this story, the obvious one about the importance of taking responsibility when you screw up. That's true, and it's significant. In your work, in your life, you'll be more respected and trusted by the people around you if you honestly own up to your mistakes. It's impossible not to make them; but it is possible to acknowledge them, learn from them, and set an example that it's okay to get things wrong sometimes. What's not okay is to undermine others by lying about something or covering your own ass first.

There's a related lesson, though, that I only came to fully appreciate years later, when I was in a position of real leadership. It's so simple that you might think it doesn't warrant mentioning, but it's surprisingly rare: Be decent to people. Treat everyone with fairness and empathy. This doesn't mean that you lower your expectations or convey the message that mistakes don't matter. It means that you create an environment where people know you'll hear them out, that you're emotionally consistent and fair-minded, and that they'll be given second chances for honest mistakes. (If they don't own up to their mistakes, or if they blame someone else, or if the mistake is the result of some unethical behavior, that's a different story, and something that shouldn't be tolerated.)

There were people at ABC Sports who lived in fear of Roone turning on them, and as a result, they avoided taking risks or sticking their necks out too far. I never felt that way, but I could see it in others, and I understood where it came from. He was a capricious boss, and over time capriciousness takes a huge toll on a staff's morale. One day he would make you feel like you were the most important person in the division; the next he would deliver withering criticism or would put a knife in your back for reasons that were never quite clear. He had a way of playing people off each other, and I could never tell if it was a purposeful strategy or a function of his personality. For all of his immense talent and success, Roone was insecure at heart, and the way he defended against his own insecurity was to foster it in the people around him. Oftentimes it worked, in its way, and made you work that much harder to please him, but there were times when he drove me so crazy I was sure I was going to quit. I wasn't alone in thinking this.

I didn't quit, though. I was able to make peace with the way Roone exercised his authority, to be motivated by the good and not be too personally wounded by the bad. I was naturally resilient, I think, and working for Roone made me more so. And I prided myself on working hard, especially in a place where so many of the people around me were better educated and from more sophisticated backgrounds. It was important to me to know that when it came down to it, I could outwork anyone else, and so I was focused much more on that than I was on the vicissitudes of Roone's moods.

It was only later, looking back, that I realized that so much of what we accomplished didn't have to come at such a cost. I was motivated by Roone's drive for perfection and have carried it with me ever since. But I learned something else along the way, too: Excellence and fairness don't have to be mutually exclusive. I wouldn't have articulated it that way at the time. Mostly I was just focused on doing my job well and certainly wasn't thinking about what I'd do differently if I were in Roone's shoes. But years later, when I was given the chance to lead, I was instinctively aware of both the need to strive for perfection and the pitfalls of caring only about the product and never the people.

CHAPTER 2

BETTING ON TALENT

I N MARCH 1985, I was thirty-four years old and had just been made vice president at ABC Sports, when Leonard Goldenson, ABC's founder, chairman, and CEO, agreed to sell the corporation to a much smaller company, Capital Cities Communications. Cap Cities, as they were called, was a quarter the size of ABC, and they bought us for $3.5 billion. Everyone at ABC was blindsided by the announcement. How could a company like Cap Cities suddenly own a major television network? Who were these guys? How did this happen?

These guys were Tom Murphy and Dan Burke. Over the years, they'd built Cap Cities, starting a small television station in Albany, New York, acquisition by acquisition. With help from Tom's close friend Warren Buffett, who backed the $3.5 billion deal, they were able to swallow our much larger company. (As Tom Murphy put it, they were "the minnow that ate the whale.")

Tom and Dan weren't from our world. In our eyes, they were small-time. They owned local TV and radio stations, a sprawling publishing business, including some midsize newspapers. They were church-going Catholics (their New York office was in a building on Madison Avenue owned by the Catholic Archdiocese of New York) with no network experience, no connection to Hollywood, and a reputation for drastic penny-pinching. We had no idea what was going to happen when they took over, but we knew that nothing we were used to would remain the same.

The deal closed in January 1986. Shortly afterward, Tom and Dan held a corporate retreat in Phoenix. I didn't rank high enough to get invited, but I heard plenty of complaints and snickering from other ABC execs in the aftermath, about corny team-building exercises and Tom and Dan's homespun values. I'd later realize we were all being cynics and snobs. Over the next few years, those corny traditions would help form a genuine camaraderie within the company. And Tom and Dan's allergies to Hollywood didn't mean they were unsophisticated, as a lot of executives at ABC assumed early on. It was just who they were: no-nonsense businesspeople who focused on the work and had zero interest in the glitz.

It was true, though, that running a huge entertainment company was like nothing they'd done before. For one thing, they had never managed world-class executive talent. Nowhere was this more evident than in their relationship with Roone. By the time Cap Cities acquired us, Roone was running both Sports and ABC News, which he'd taken over in 1977, when it was in the ratings tank. He'd transformed it as he had Sports, by putting his most high-profile anchors—Peter Jennings, Barbara Walters, Ted Koppel, and Diane Sawyer—on a pedestal and using them across a range of shows. He created 20/20 and World News Tonight, then Nightline, which grew out of ABC's coverage of the Iranian hostage crisis. He brought the same relentless competitive spirit and striking visual sensibility to news coverage as he had to sports broadcasting, and the division thrived under him.

Tom and Dan respected Roone, and they were well aware of his talent and reputation, but they were also a little intimidated by him. He spoke a language and moved in a world they weren't familiar with, and Roone leveraged that to his advantage. He was aloof and sometimes openly critical of them. He'd show up late for meetings or would at times blatantly disregard some policy issued by the "bean counters," as he saw them. I was one of the last of the old guard from Sports still around in those days, and Roone often commiserated with me. I'd get a call from his assistant at the end of the day, asking me to come over to News, and when I arrived, Roone would pull out a bottle of a white Italian wine that he loved. We'd sit in his office, surrounded by Emmy awards, while he griped about how Tom and Dan were crimping his style. "They don't get it," he'd say. "You can't save your way to success."

Roone believed in sparing no expense in the pursuit of greatness, and he didn't want anyone telling him he had to change the way he did things to meet some arbitrary budgetary goals. He didn't care about the business side of things, but if pressed, he could always point to the revenue we'd brought in over the years and say that the profligate spending allowed us not just to make amazing television but to create an aura of sophistication and glamour that advertisers wanted to be a part of.

That wasn't how Tom and Dan worked. They came in and immediately stripped away all the perks we'd grown used to. No more limos lined up in front of ABC headquarters waiting for executives. No more trips on the Concorde or first-class travel. No more bottomless expense accounts. They saw how our business was changing in a way a lot of people at ABC didn't want to accept. Margins were getting tighter; competition was tougher. Within our own company, even, ESPN was beginning to find its footing, which eventually would have a direct impact on ABC Sports.

Tom and Dan weren't just meat-and-potatoes guys who didn't "get it." They were shrewd businesspeople who sensed which way the winds were blowing. (It also should be said that when they felt it was important to spend money, they did. Roone benefited from that more than anyone when they gave him the go-ahead to woo

Diane Sawyer from CBS and David Brinkley from NBC to round out the all-star team at ABC News.)

One of the first things they did after taking over was to tell Roone they didn't want him running both Sports and News. They gave him a choice, and Roone chose News—with the one stipulation, that he would be the executive producer of our '88 Winter Olympics coverage in Calgary. I assumed they'd replace him with someone from within the division (I thought there was a chance it might even be me), but instead they brought in Dennis Swanson, who, prior to becoming the head of the vaunted ABC Sports division, had managed a half dozen or so local TV stations for ABC. (Dennis's great—and legitimate—claim to fame was that he was the guy who put Oprah Winfrey on TV in Chicago in 1983.)

Overnight, I went from working for the most successful sports television executive of all time to working for someone who'd never spent a minute at a network or in sports broadcasting. My former boss, Jim Spence, was one of the people who also got passed over for Roone's job. When Tom and Dan announced they were bringing in Dennis, Jim quit, and other senior executives followed him out the door. Jim went to the talent agency ICM to start a sports division. I hung around, hoping something might open up for me. After a short time working for Dennis, though, I called Jim to say it seemed like there was nothing for me there anymore and I needed to get out. Jim asked me to come join him at ICM, and we quickly crafted a deal. I was under contract at ABC, but I figured they'd let me out of it, and the next day I went into work planning to give Dennis my notice.

Before I could set up a time to talk with him, I spoke with Steve Solomon, the head of Human Resources for ABC, whom Dennis had brought in to help him run Sports. I told Steve I was planning to leave. "We need to talk with Dennis," he said. "He has another idea for you." When I stepped into Dennis's office, he said, "I've got news for you. I'm going to make you senior vice president for programming. I want you to create a blueprint for all of ABC's sports programming."

I was completely thrown. "I was about to tell you I was leaving," I finally said.

"Leaving?"

"I didn't really think there was a path for me here anymore." I explained that Jim Spence was starting a sports business at ICM and that I'd made a decision to join him.

"I think that's a mistake," Dennis said. He wasn't so sure the company would let me out of my contract, for one. "This is a big opportunity for you, Bob. I don't think you should just let it go." He gave me twenty-four hours to give him an answer.

I went home that night and had a long conversation with my then wife, Susan. We weighed my misgivings about working for Dennis against the potential of this new job. We talked about our two daughters, and the security of being in a place I knew well, versus taking a risk on a new venture. Ultimately I decided to stay where I was because ABC Sports had been such a good place for me over the years, and I still wasn't ready to give up on it.

There are moments in our careers, in our lives, that are inflection points, but they're often not the most obvious or dramatic ones. I wasn't sure I was making the right decision. It was probably the safer one, really, to stay at the place I knew. But I also didn't want to leave too impulsively, because my ego had been bruised or because I had some feeling of superiority when it came to Dennis. If I was ultimately going to leave, it had to be because there was an opportunity that was too great to say no, and the ICM job wasn't that.

Taking Dennis up on his offer proved to be one of the best career decisions I ever made. I'd soon learn that I had been totally wrong in my assessment of him. He was an amiable, funny guy; his energy and optimism were infectious; and, crucially, he knew what he didn't know. This is a rare trait in a boss. It's easy to imagine another person in Dennis's shoes overcompensating for the fact that he'd never worked at a network by exuding a kind of fake authority or knowledge, but that wasn't how Dennis was wired. We would sit in meetings and something would come up and rather than bluffing his way through it, Dennis would say he didn't know, and then he'd turn to me and others for help. He regularly asked me to take the lead in conversations with higher-ups while he sat back, and he took every opportunity to extol my virtues to Tom and Dan. In the lead-up to the Winter Olympics, Dennis asked me to present our plans to them and the highest-ranking executives in the company. It was an enormous opportunity for me, and a perfect example of how Dennis never put himself ahead of anyone else.

It was who he was, a naturally generous man, but it was also a function of the culture that Tom and Dan created. They were two of the most authentic people I've ever met, genuinely themselves at all times. No airs, no big egos that needed to be managed, no false sincerity. They comported themselves with the same honesty and forthrightness no matter who they were talking to. They were shrewd businesspeople (Warren Buffett later called them "probably the greatest two-person combination in management that the world has ever seen or maybe ever will see"), but it was more than that. I learned from them that genuine decency and professional competitiveness weren't mutually exclusive. In fact, true integrity—a sense of knowing who you are and being guided by your own clear sense of right and wrong—is a kind of secret weapon. They trusted in their own instincts, they treated people with respect, and over time the company came to represent the values they lived by. A lot of us were getting paid less than we would have been paid if we went to a competitor. We knew they were cheap. But we stayed because we felt so loyal to these two men.

Their business strategy was fairly simple. They were hypervigilant about controlling costs, and they believed in a decentralized corporate structure. Meaning: They didn't think every key decision should be made by the two of them or by a small group of strategists in corporate headquarters. They hired people who were smart and decent and hardworking, they put those people in positions of big responsibility, and they gave them the support and autonomy needed to do the job. They were also tremendously generous with their time and always accessible. Because of this, executives working for them always had a clear sense of what their priorities were, and their focus enabled us all to be focused, too.

IN FEBRUARY 1988, we went to Calgary to cover the Winter Games. As agreed, Roone was executive producer, and I was the senior program executive. Which meant that in the long run-up to the Olympics I was in charge of the intricate scheduling of all televised events, communicating and negotiating with the Olympic Organizing Committee and the various governing bodies around the world, and helping to plan our coverage in advance of the games. A couple of days before the games began, Roone showed up in Calgary and called me to his suite. "Okay," he said. "What are we doing?"

It had been two years since we'd worked together, but right away it was like nothing had changed—in good ways and bad. We were scheduled to air a three-hour Olympics preview the night before the opening ceremonies, and for weeks I'd been trying to get Roone to focus on it. He finally watched it after arriving in Calgary, the night before it was scheduled to air. "It's all wrong," he said. "There's no excitement. No tension." A team of people worked through the night to execute all of his changes in time to get it on the air. He was right, of course. His storytelling instincts were as sharp as ever. But it was such a stressful way to kick things off, and a reminder of how one person's unwillingness to give a timely response can cause so much unnecessary strain and inefficiency.

We set up our operations in a cavernous warehouse on the outskirts of Calgary. There were several trailers and smaller buildings inside the warehouse that housed various production and tech crews. Our control room was in there, too, with Roone in the captain's chair and me in the back row dealing with logistics. Behind the control room was a glass-enclosed observation booth for VIPs. Throughout the games, Tom and Dan and several board members and guests would spend time in the booth, watching us work.

The first few days went off without a hitch, and then everything changed overnight. Strong chinook winds rolled in and the temperature shot up into the sixties. The snow on the alpine course and the ice on the bobsled runs melted. Event after event got canceled, and even those that took place proved to be a challenge because our cameras couldn't see anything through the fog.

Every morning for the next several days, I'd arrive at the control room having almost no idea what we were going to put on the air that night. It was a perfect example of the need for optimism. Things were dire, for sure, but I needed to look at the situation not as a catastrophe but as a puzzle we needed to solve, and to communicate to our team that we were talented and nimble enough to solve these problems and make something wonderful on the fly.

The big challenge was finding programming to fill our prime-time hours, which were now filled with gaping holes where big-ticket Olympic events used to be. This meant dealing with an Olympic committee that was struggling to solve its own scheduling crises. Even before the games began, I'd pushed my luck with them. The original draw for the hockey tournament had the United States playing two of the toughest teams in the world in the first two games. I assumed they would lose both contests, and viewer interest would drop off a cliff after they were eliminated. So I'd traveled all over the world meeting with national hockey federations and Olympic committees to convince them to redraw the bracket. Now I was on the phone with the Calgary Olympic committee several times a day, begging them to change the schedule of events so that we'd have something to show in prime time.

The meetings with Roone before each night's telecast were almost comical. He'd come into the booth every afternoon and say,

"What are we gonna do tonight?" And I'd reply, "Well, we've got Romania versus Sweden in hockey" or some such thing, and then I'd walk him through the rescheduled events, which were often lacking. Since we didn't have the competitions we needed, each day a team of producers was sent out to uncover compelling human-interest stories. Then they'd pull the features together and slot them into that night's telecast. The Jamaican bobsled team was a godsend. As was Eddie "The Eagle" Edwards, the quixotic British ski jumper who finished last in both 70- and 90-meter events. It was a high-wire act, but it was fun, too. And it was satisfying to face the challenge of each day knowing that the only way through was to stay laser-focused and to exude as much calmness as possible to the people around me.

Somehow it all worked. The ratings were historically high. Tom and Dan were pleased. The added drama of having to improvise so much of it was a fitting end to Roone's reign over sports television. It was also the last Olympics ABC would televise, after a forty-two-year run. We no longer held the rights after those games. On the final night of coverage, after we signed off, several of us hung around in the control room and drank champagne, toasting our efforts and laughing about how closely we'd averted disaster. One by one people filed out and headed back to the hotel. I was the last one left in the control room and stayed there for a while taking in the silence and stillness after so much action. Then I turned out the lights and headed home.

A FEW WEEKS LATER, I got called into a meeting with Tom and Dan. "We want to get to know you better," Tom said. He told me they'd watched me closely in Calgary, and they were impressed with how I'd handled myself under pressure. "Some things might be opening up," Dan said, and they wanted me to know they had their eyes on me. My first thought was that maybe I had a chance at the top job at ESPN, but shortly after that meeting they gave it to the guy who was executive vice president of ABC Television at the time. There I was, frustrated at being passed over again, when they called me back in and gave me his job. "We want to park you there for a little while," Dan said. "But we have bigger plans."

I didn't know what those plans were, but the job they'd just given me—number two at ABC TV—felt like a pretty far reach. I was thirty-seven years old, I'd primarily worked in sports, and now I would be running daytime and late-night and Saturday morning television, as well as managing business affairs for the entire network. I knew precisely nothing about how any of that was done, but Tom and Dan seemed confident I could learn on the job.

My instinct throughout my career has always been to say yes to every opportunity. In part this is just garden-variety ambition. I wanted to move up and learn and do more, and I wasn't going to forgo any chance to do that, but I also wanted to prove to myself that I was capable of doing things that I was unfamiliar with.

Tom and Dan were the perfect bosses in this regard. They would talk about valuing ability more than experience, and they believed in putting people in roles that required more of them than they knew they had in them. It wasn't that experience wasn't important, but they "bet on brains," as they put it, and trusted that things would work out if they put talented people in positions where they could grow, even if they were in unfamiliar territory.

Tom and Dan brought me into their inner circle. They let me in on their decision-making and confided in me about people, including Brandon Stoddard, who ran prime time as president of ABC Entertainment. Brandon was a talented executive who had great taste in television, but like a lot of others who'd come up in entertainment, he didn't have the temperament for working in a corporate structure. Brandon had Hollywood figured out, and to him Tom and Dan were "station guys" who had no clue about his business. He was unable to hide his disdain for them and unwilling to adapt to their way of doing things, or even make an effort to understand where they were coming from. Tom and Dan, unsurprisingly, grew increasingly frustrated in return, and over time a mutual distrust and low-level animosity took hold.

Early one Friday morning, Dan sat down across from me in the cafeteria at ABC's headquarters on West Sixty-sixth Street. Most days, he and I arrived at the office before everyone else, and we'd often meet in the cafeteria and catch each other up on what was going on. He set his breakfast tray down and said, "Tom is flying out to L.A. today. Do you know why?"

"No," I said. "What's up?"

"He's going to fire Brandon Stoddard."

It didn't completely shock me, but I was surprised that I hadn't heard anything about their plans for replacing him. It was going to be big news in Hollywood that they'd fired the head of ABC Entertainment. "What are you going to do?" I asked.

"I don't know," Dan said. "We're just going to have to figure it out."

Tom fired Brandon on that Friday. Dan flew out to meet him over the weekend, and on Monday evening I got a call from him at home. "Bob, what are you doing?"

"Making dinner for my girls," I said.

"We want you to fly out here tomorrow morning. Can you do that?"

I told him I could, and then he said, "Before you get on the plane, there's something you should know. We want you to run Entertainment."

"Excuse me?"

"We want you to be president of ABC Entertainment. Come out here and we'll talk about it."

I flew out to L.A. the next morning and went straight to meet with them. The struggles with Brandon had become too much, they said. They'd spent the weekend canvassing various people about who should replace him. One thought was to give the job to our head of research, Alan Wurtzel, whom they liked and re-spected. They raised this possibility with Stu Bloomberg, who had been the head of comedy and whom they'd just made head of drama at the network, as well. "You can't do that," Stu told them. "This is a creative job. You can't give it to the head of research!" They then asked Stu, "What do you think of Bob Iger?" He didn't know me well, Stu said, but everyone had been impressed with how I'd handled the Olympic coverage, and from what he knew people liked and respected me.

Stu also told them he would gladly work for me, and that was enough for them. "We want you to do this," Tom said. I was flattered, but I also knew this was a big risk for them. This would be the first time in the history of the company that the person running ABC Entertainment wasn't from the entertainment world. I wasn't sure anyone from outside Hollywood had held that job at any of the networks. "Look, I appreciate your faith in me," I told them. "But I haven't read a script since my TV-writing course in college. I don't know this part of the business."

They responded in their usual fatherly way. "Aw, Bob, you'll be great," Tom said.

Dan added, "We want you to survive here, Bob. We hope when you're done you'll be carrying your shield and not being carried out on it!"

I had dinner that night with Stu Bloomberg and Ted Harbert, the two men who, along with Brandon, were responsible for ABC's prime-time lineup. The plan was that I would run the department and Stu and Ted would split the number two job beneath me. Ted would run programming and scheduling; Stu would run development. They were both seasoned entertainment veterans, and Stu, in particular, had been responsible for a lot of ABC's recent success, including *The Wonder Years* and *Roseanne*. They would have been completely justified in their disdain for the guy who knew nothing about their business but was about to be their boss. Instead, they were two of the most supportive people I've ever worked with, and their support started that first night. I told them over dinner that I needed their help. They knew the business, and I didn't, but our fates were intertwined now, and I hoped they would be willing to be patient with me as I learned on the job. "Don't worry, Bob. We'll teach you," Stu said. "It'll be great. Trust us."

I flew back to New York and sat down with my wife. We'd agreed before I went out there that I wouldn't make any final decision without our talking it through first. This job meant living in L.A., and we had a life we loved in New York. We'd just renovated our apartment; our girls were at a great school; our closest friends were in New York. Susan was an executive producer of news at WNBC and one of those New Yorkers who never want to live anywhere else. I knew this would be hard for her and that in her heart she wouldn't want to go. She was incredibly supportive. "Life's an adventure," she said. "If you don't choose the adventurous path, then you're not really living."

The next day, Thursday, Tom and Dan announced that I would be the new head of ABC Entertainment. Three days later I flew out to L.A. and started the job.

CHAPTER 3

KNOW WHAT YOU DON'T KNOW
(AND TRUST IN WHAT YOU DO)

I T WASN'T QUITE leaping without a parachute, but it felt a lot like free fall at first. I told myself: You have a job. They're expecting you to turn this business around. Your inexperience can't be an excuse for failure.

So what do you do in a situation like that? The first rule is not to fake anything. You have to be humble, and you can't pretend to be someone you're not or to know something you don't. You're also in a position of leadership, though, so you can't let humility prevent you from leading. It's a fine line, and something I preach today. You have to ask the questions you need to ask, admit without apology what you don't understand, and do the work to learn what you need to learn as quickly as you can. There's nothing less confidence-inspiring than a person faking a knowledge they don't possess. True authority and true leadership come from knowing who you are and not pretending to be anything else.

Luckily, I had Stu and Ted by my side. I was thoroughly dependent on them, especially in those early days. Their first order of business was to schedule what felt like an endless string of breakfast, lunch, and dinner meetings. Back then, the head of any of the three networks was one of the most powerful people in television (a fact that felt surreal to me), but to everyone in the industry, I was a looming question mark. I had no sense of how things were done in Hollywood, and no experience managing relationships with creative people or working with their representatives. I didn't speak their language. I didn't understand their culture. To them I was a suit from New York who suddenly—for reasons that must have seemed baffling—had immense influence over their creative life. So every day I met with the managers and agents and writers and directors and TV stars that Stu and Ted lined up for me. In most of those meetings, I had the distinct sensation of being poked and prodded in an effort to figure out who I was and what the hell I was doing there.

The task was to not let my ego get the best of me. Rather than trying too hard to impress whoever was across the table, I needed to resist the urge to pretend I knew what I was doing and ask a lot of questions. There was no getting around that I was a square peg there. I didn't come up through Hollywood. I didn't have a big personality or any obvious swagger. I barely knew anyone in town. I could be insecure about that, or I could let my relative bland-ness—my un-Hollywood-ness—be a kind of mystery that worked to my advantage while I absorbed as much as I could.

I arrived in L.A. with six weeks left to decide on a lineup for the 1989–90 prime-time season. On my first day in the office, I was handed a stack of forty scripts to read. Each night I'd take them home and dutifully make my way through them, making notes in the margins but struggling to imagine how the script in front of me would translate to the screen, and doubting my ability to judge what was good and what wasn't. Was I even paying attention to the right stuff? Were there things that other people could obviously see that I was missing entirely? The answer, at first, was yes. I'd come in and meet with Stu and others to winnow the pile the next day. Stu could dissect a script so quickly—"His motivations aren't clear at the top of Act 2 . . ."—and I'd look back through the pages on my lap, thinking, *Wait, Act 2? When did Act 1 end?* (Stu would become one of my closest friends. I sometimes wore him down with my questions and inexperience, but he persevered and taught me vital lessons, not just about how to read scripts but about how to interact with creative people.)

I started to realize over time, though, that I'd internalized a lot by watching Roone tell stories all those years. Sports wasn't the same as prime-time TV, but there were important lessons about structure and pacing and clarity that I'd absorbed without even knowing it. In my first week in L.A., I had lunch with the producer and writer Steven Bochco, who had two huge hits for NBC, *Hill Street Blues* and *L.A. Law*, but had recently signed a lucrative ten-series deal with ABC. I mentioned to Steven that I was anxious about reading scripts. I didn't even know the lingo and yet there was pressure to make decisions, quickly, on so many shows. He waved it off in a way that I found comforting coming from someone like him. "It's not rocket science, Bob," he said. "Trust yourself."

At the time, there were several successful shows in ABC's prime-time lineup—*Who's the Boss?, Growing Pains, Roseanne, The Wonder Years*, and *Thirtysomething*. But we were a distant number two to NBC, the network juggernaut. My job was to find a way to narrow that gap. We added more than a dozen new shows that first season, among them *Family Matters* and *Life Goes On* (the first show on television to feature a major character with Down syndrome), and *America's Funniest Home Videos*, which became an immediate, gigantic hit and is now in its thirty-first season.

We also aired Steven's first big success for the network. He'd just delivered the script when I arrived: *Doogie Howser, M.D.*, about a fourteen-year-old doctor juggling his life as both a physician and an adolescent boy. Steven showed me a video of the teenage actor, Neil Patrick Harris, whom he wanted for the lead role. I told him I wasn't sure. I didn't think Neil could carry the show. Very politely and straightforwardly, Steven slapped me down, gently suggesting that

I didn't know a thing. He informed me that it was basically his decision—not just whom to cast, but whether to go forward with the project or not. According to his deal, if we said yes to a project, he got a thirteen-episode commitment. If we said no, we had to pay him a kill fee of $1.5 million. Saying yes to this show was one of my first program decisions, and thankfully Steven was right about Neil. *Doogie Howser, M.D.* had four strong seasons for ABC and marked the beginning of a long collaboration and friendship with Steven.

THERE WAS ANOTHER, much bigger risk we took that first season. Based on a literal back-of-a-napkin pitch at a restaurant in Hollywood, ABC's head of drama had given the go-ahead to a pilot from David Lynch, by then famous for his cult films *Eraserhead* and *Blue Velvet,* and the screenwriter and novelist Mark Frost. It was a surreal, meandering drama about the murder of a prom queen, Laura Palmer, in the fictional Pacific Northwest town of Twin Peaks. David directed the two-hour pilot, which I vividly remember watching for the first time and thinking, *This is unlike anything I've ever seen and we have to do this.*

As they did every year, Tom and Dan and a few other executives came out that spring for pilot season. We screened *Twin Peaks* for them, and when the lights came up, the first thing Dan did was turn around and look at me and say, "I don't know what that was, but I think it was really good." Tom was much less taken than Dan, and the other New York–based executives in the room agreed. It was too weird, too dark, for network TV.

I had such respect for Tom, but I also knew this show was important enough to fight for. There were changes taking place that we had to face. We were now competing with the edgier programming available on cable TV, and with the new upstart Fox Network, not to mention the growth of videogames and the rise of the VCR. I felt that network television had become boring and derivative, and we had the chance with *Twin Peaks* to put something on

TV that was utterly original. We couldn't just fall back into our same old stance while everything changed around us. It was the Roone lesson all over again: Innovate or die. Eventually, I convinced them to let me screen the pilot for a younger, more diverse audience than a group of older guys from ABC in New York. The test audiences didn't exactly support putting the show on network television, particularly because it was so different; but it was just that—its being *different*—that motivated us to give it the green light and make seven episodes.

I decided to put it on in midseason, in the spring of 1990 rather than the fall of '89. Each season we hold back shows as midseason replacements for the inevitability of a few failing shows. There's a bit less pressure on those replacement shows than the ones that launch in the fall, and it seemed like the best strategy for *Twin Peaks*. So we put it into production, to air in the spring, and in the intervening months rough cuts of the first few episodes began to come in. Although he'd given me permission to go ahead months earlier, Tom watched a couple of them and wrote me a letter that said, "You can't air this. If we put it on television, it will kill our company's reputation."

I phoned Tom and said we had to air *Twin Peaks*. By that point, there was already a tremendous buzz in and outside of Hollywood that we were doing this. There was even an article on the front page of *The Wall Street Journal* about this buttoned-up guy at ABC who was taking huge creative risks. Suddenly I was getting calls from Steven Spielberg and George Lucas. I visited Steven on the set of *Hook,* which he was directing at the time, and George at his Skywalker Ranch. They were both interested in talking about what they might do for ABC. That notion, that directors of that caliber would be interested in making television shows, was unheard of until we started making *Twin Peaks*. (Two years later, in 1991, George delivered *The Young Indiana Jones Chronicles,* which lasted for two seasons.)

I told Tom, "We're getting unbelievable praise from the creative community for taking this risk. We have to air this." To Tom's credit, that's what won him over. He was my boss, and he could have said, "Sorry, I'm overruling you." But he understood the value of our winning over creative people in Hollywood, and he accepted my reasoning that this was a risk worth taking.

We promoted the show on the Academy Awards in late March and aired the two-hour pilot on Sunday, April 8. Nearly thirty-five million people—about a third of TV watchers at the time—tuned in. We then scheduled it for Thursdays at 9:00 P.M., and within weeks *Twin Peaks* became the most successful program we'd put in that time slot in four years. It was on the cover of *Time*. *Newsweek* described it as being "like nothing you've seen in primetime—or on God's earth." I went to New York that May for the up-fronts, the big spring gathering where networks preview upcoming series for advertisers and the press, and had to go onstage to talk about ABC. "Every once in a while a network executive takes a big risk," I said, and immediately the crowd broke into a standing ovation. It was the most exhilarating thing I'd ever felt in my career.

The wave of euphoria broke almost immediately. Within six months, *Twin Peaks* went from cultural phenomenon to frustrating disappointment. We'd given David creative freedom, but as we got toward the end of the first season, he and I became locked in an ongoing debate about audience expectations. The entire show hinged on the question of who killed Laura Palmer, and I felt David was losing sight of that, laying breadcrumbs in a way that felt random and unsatisfying.

David was and is a brilliant filmmaker, but he was not a television producer. There's an organizational discipline that running a show requires (delivering scripts on time, managing a crew, making sure everything moves forward according to schedule) that David simply didn't have. There's a storytelling discipline, too. With a film, you need to get people in for two hours and give them a good experience and hope that they leave the theater engaged and enthralled. With a television series, you have to keep them coming back, week after week, season after season. To this day, I love and respect David, and will forever be in awe of his work, but the fact that he didn't have a television producer's sensibility resulted in storytelling that was too open-ended.

"You need to resolve the mystery, or at least give people some hope that it will be resolved," I said. "It's beginning to frustrate the audience, including me!" David felt the mystery wasn't the most important element of the show; in his ideal version, we'd never find out who the killer was, but other aspects of the town and its characters would emerge. We went around and around until, finally, he agreed to reveal the killer partway through season two.

After that, the storytelling became a mess. There was no engine propelling the story after the mystery was resolved. Making matters worse, there wasn't enough discipline in the production process, which led to confusion and delays. It became obvious to me that David, as brilliant as he was, should not run the show, and I debated firing him and bringing in a group of experienced television showrunners to take it over. I concluded it was a no-win situation, and we would be vilified if we fired David Lynch. Instead, we moved *Twin Peaks* to Saturday night, in part to take pressure off its need to perform, and when its ratings dropped precipitously, David blamed me publicly. I'd given it a death sentence, he said, first by pushing for a resolution to the mystery, then by putting it on a night when nobody would watch it.

Looking back on it now, I'm not convinced I was right. I was applying a more traditional television approach to the storytelling, and David may have been ahead of his time. Deep down, I felt David was frustrating the audience, but it may well be that my demands for an answer to the question of who killed Laura Palmer threw the show into another kind of narrative disarray. David might have been right all along.

Managing creative processes starts with the understanding that it's not a science—everything is subjective; there is often no right or wrong. The passion it takes to create something is powerful, and most creators are understandably sensitive when their vision or execution is questioned. I try to keep this in mind whenever I engage with someone on the creative side of our business. When I am asked to provide insights and offer critiques, I'm exceedingly mindful of how much the creators have poured themselves into the project and how much is at stake for them.

I never start out negatively, and unless we're in the late stages of a production, I never start small. I've found that often people will focus on little details as a way of masking a lack of any clear, coherent, big thoughts. If you start petty, you seem petty. And if the big picture is a mess, then the small things don't matter anyway, and you shouldn't spend time focusing on them.

Of course, no two situations are alike. There's a big difference between giving feedback to a seasoned director like J.J. Abrams or Steven Spielberg and someone with much less experience and confidence. The first time I sat down with Ryan Coogler to give him notes on *Black Panther*, I could see how visibly anxious he was. He'd never made a film as big as *Black Panther*, with a massive budget and so much pressure on it to do well. I took pains to say very clearly, "You've created a very special film. I have some specific notes, but before I give them to you, I want you to know we have tremendous faith in you."

This is all a way of stating what might seem obvious but is often ignored: that a delicate balance is required between management being responsible for the financial performance of any creative work and, in exercising that responsibility, being careful not to encroach on the creative processes in harmful and counterproductive ways. Empathy is a prerequisite to the sound management of creativity, and respect is critical.

REMARKABLY, THE DEMISE of *Twin Peaks* wasn't our biggest failure that season. In the spring of 1990, I gave the green light to *Cop Rock,* a show that would become the butt of late-night jokes and take a permanent place on lists of the worst TV shows of all time. But I stand by the decision to this day.

In one of our earliest meetings, Steven Bochco told me that in addition to *Doogie Howser*, he had another idea: a police drama set to music. He'd been approached by a Broadway producer interested in turning *Hill Street Blues* into a musical, which for various reasons he couldn't do. But the idea had stuck with him—not to make a cop musical for Broadway, but to make a cop musical for TV. He'd bring it up periodically, and I'd deflect the idea. I wanted a cop show from Steven, but I didn't want a musical. That spring, though, still basking in the glow of that first season of *Twin Peaks*, I finally came around. "You know what?" I told him. "Why not? Let's try it."

The show took place in the LAPD and in all respects it operated like a normal, well-plotted police procedural—except that in moments of high drama characters would burst into song: blues songs, gospel songs, big ensemble numbers. I sensed from the moment I saw the pilot that it wasn't going to work, and would possibly be legendarily bad, but I also thought there was a chance I could be wrong. I admired Steven's talent so much, and in any case I figured if I was going to be in, I needed to be all in.

Cop Rock premiered in September 1990. Normally, when shows first aired, I'd ask our head of research in New York to call me in L.A. with the overnight ratings. This time I told him, "If the ratings are good, call. If they're bad, just send a fax." At 5:00 A.M., I woke to the sound of the fax machine humming, then closed my eyes and went back to bed.

The reviews were not, in fact, universally terrible. I remember one complimented the show's "audaciousness." Others said that if you stripped away the music, you were left with a great Steven Bochco police drama. Most of the rest said it was an embarrassment. We pulled it in December of that year, after eleven episodes. Steven threw a wrap party on the lot, to celebrate and mourn the end of the show together. At the end of his remarks, he said, "Well, it ain't over till the fat lady sings," and over our heads soared a corpulent, singing woman on a flying trapeze.

I got up and addressed the cast and crew. "We tried something big and it didn't work," I said. "I'd much rather take big risks and sometimes fail than not take risks at all."

That's genuinely how I felt at the time. I didn't regret trying it. And it's how I felt a few months later when we pulled the plug on *Twin Peaks*. I didn't want to be in the business of playing it safe. I wanted to be in the business of creating possibilities for greatness. Of all the lessons I learned in that first year running prime time, the need to be comfortable with failure was the most profound. Not with lack of effort but with the unavoidable truth that if you want innovation—and you should, always—you need to give permission to fail.

Steven and I shared the flop that was *Cop Rock* together. We had a sense of humor about it, and I made a point to never distance myself from the decision to put it on the air. It felt like a much-higher-stakes version of the lesson I'd learned in that room at ABC Sports years before. You can't erase your mistakes or pin your bad decisions on someone else. You have to own your own failures. You earn as much respect and goodwill by standing by someone in the wake of a failure as you do by giving them credit for a success.

Once the *Cop Rock* wounds had healed a bit, Steven told me that he wanted to make what he called "the first R-rated show in TV history." I said, "Steven, you did *Hill Street Blues* and *L.A. Law* for NBC. Where is that for us? I get a police show and it's *Cop Rock*. And now you want to do something that will send advertisers running for the hills?" What I didn't appreciate is how much Steven felt that he'd already done all that other stuff and was driven to do something different—and how much he was responding to the shifting landscape of television. He felt HBO was going to be eating our lunch soon because their shows' creators didn't have to comply with prudish network censors or worry about offending advertisers. So he pitched *NYPD Blue* as the first R-rated drama on network TV.

I agreed with Steven about the changing nature of television and the stodginess of the networks, but I also knew there was no way I could get permission to put an R-rated show on TV. The sales guys told me that, and I told Steven, and for a while we both walked away from the idea. I did believe, though, that we could do something that stretched the boundaries but wasn't quite R-rated, and Steven eventually got intrigued by that idea. "If we were to do that," he said, "what would it look like?"

He and I consulted with the censors and came up with a template for what we could and could not do on a "PG-13" show. We made a glossary of all the words that were technically inbounds. (*Asswipe* was okay; *asshole* was not. You could use *prick* to describe a person but not a body part.) We pulled out a notebook and drew stick figures, basically, of naked people, figuring out what angles would reveal enough but not too much.

The next step was to sell it to Dan Burke. Dan flew out to L.A., and the three of us had lunch near Steven's office. We showed him our glossary and our stick figures and explained why this show was important to us. "You guys can do this," Dan finally said. "But when the shit hits the fan, and it's going to hit the fan, my skirt isn't wide enough for *you*"—he pointed at me—"to hide behind."

It was another example of my being willing to take risks in part because of the faith Dan and Tom placed in me. They gave me this job, and I'd delivered quickly, and that gave me an enormous amount of latitude with them. I couldn't do whatever I wanted, but I had the freedom to exercise a considerable amount of authority. It's a trust that Brandon Stoddard, my predecessor, never earned. He refused to respect them, and therefore they didn't respect him, which in turn meant they were determined to tell him no when he fought for things he wanted.

After we got Dan's approval, there was a long, painstaking development period, in which Steven pushed in one direction and ABC's standards-and-practices folks pushed back, until compromises were finally reached. The show premiered in the fall of 1993, a full season after we'd initially intended to put it on the air. The American Family Association called for a boycott; many advertisers refused to buy spots; more than 50 of our 225 affiliates preempted the first episode. But the critical reception was extraordinary, and in its second season it was among the top ten shows on TV. It would become a mainstay of prime time for a dozen years, winning 20 Emmys and being regarded as one of the best dramas ever created for the network.

During my stint running prime time, we ended up number one with the coveted 18–49 demographic four out of five years. We even unseated Brandon Tartikoff, who'd kept NBC atop the Nielsen rankings for sixty-eight straight weeks. (Brandon called to congratulate me when the rankings came out showing ABC on top. He was a classy guy, and he'd done something that no one will ever do again. "I feel a little sad about it," I told him. "It's like Joe DiMaggio's streak coming to an end.")

Our success was a team effort, always, but it was also the first success I experienced in my career that was publicly ascribed to me. On the one hand, it felt odd that I was getting credit for things that other people made. I'd come to Entertainment knowing nothing about the job, and this group of incredibly talented people shared everything they knew with me. They worked hard and weren't threatened by the fact that I'd become their boss. Because of their generosity, we succeeded together, and yet the credit was largely given to me.

I think it's also fair to say, though, that we wouldn't have gone to number one in prime time without my running it. Dan and Tom's faith gave me the courage to take big risks; and if I had a strength, it was my ability to urge creative people to do their best work and take chances, while also helping them rebound from failure. It's always a collective effort, but my years running Entertainment gave me a new appreciation for what it takes to get a group of talented people to produce at the highest level.

Finding that balance between accepting credit for real achievements and not making too much of the hype from the outside world has only gotten more necessary during my years as CEO. I often feel guilty in front of other people with whom I work, when so much attention and credit is being directed toward me. It manifests itself in strange ways. I'm often in meetings with someone from outside the company and that person will look only at me, even though I'm surrounded by colleagues at the table. I don't know if other CEOs feel this way, but it's embarrassing to me, and in those moments I make a point of directing praise and attention to my coworkers. Similarly, when I'm the one attending a meeting with a group outside of Disney, I make sure to connect and speak with every person at the table. It's a small gesture, but I remember how it felt to be the overlooked sidekick, and anything that reminds you that you're not the center of the universe is a good thing.

OVER THANKSGIVING WEEKEND 1992, Dan Burke called me to say that the president of ABC was retiring. They wanted me to move back to New York and take his place. This wasn't a total surprise. When they'd made me head of Entertainment, Tom and Dan had suggested that, if I did well, they wanted me eventually to run the network. It was a surprise, though, when I asked Dan when they wanted me to start. "January 1," he said, just over a month.

I was happy to be going back, and not just for the job. Earlier that year, Susan and I had separated and she had moved back to New York with our daughters. Susan never liked L.A., and she liked it less once we were apart. New York was where she felt at home, and I couldn't begrudge her that. I flew back as often as I could to see the girls, but it was a terrible year.

On short notice, I sold the house in Los Angeles and packed up my things and moved in to a room at the Mark Hotel on the Upper East Side. And on January 1, at age forty-three, I became president of the ABC television network. I'd known it was coming for some time, but it was still surreal when it happened. My old mentors—

Roone in News, Dennis Swanson in Sports—were now reporting to me. Ted Harbert, who along with Stu Bloomberg had taught me how to be a television executive, took over for me at Entertainment.

Less than a year later, at the end of 1993, Tom Murphy called me into his office. "Dan's going to retire in February," he said. "I need you to take his job."

"I can't do it," I said. "I've barely started this job. Who will run the network? You gotta wait." As much as my instinct was to say yes to every opportunity, this felt too fast.

Eight months later, Tom came to me again. "I need you in that job," he said. "I need help running the company." In September 1994, I became president and COO of Capital Cities/ABC, a year and nine months after becoming president of the network. It was a dizzying and sometimes destabilizing trajectory. I wouldn't as a rule recommend promoting someone as rapidly as they promoted me, but I will say one more time, because it bears repeating: The way they conveyed their faith in me at every step made all the difference in my success.

Soon after I became Chief Operating Officer, in the spring of 1995, Michael Eisner, the CEO of The Walt Disney Company, began making inquiries into a possible acquisition of Cap Cities/ ABC. It didn't go anywhere initially, and right around that time, Tom told me that he was planning to talk with the board about my succeeding him as CEO. That July, we were in Sun Valley, Idaho, for the annual Allen & Company conference. I was standing in a parking lot talking with Tom, and I could see Warren Buffett, our largest shareholder, and Michael Eisner talking nearby. They waved for Tom to come over, and before he walked away, I said, "Do me a favor. If you decide to sell to Michael, give me some warning, okay?"

It didn't take long. A few weeks later, Michael reached out to Tom formally to begin the negotiation for Disney to buy Capital Cities/ABC.

CHAPTER 4

ENTER DISNEY

S O MUCH HAS been said and written about Disney's acquisition of us that I have little to add, except from my own unique
perspective, given my position at ABC and the fact that I was told
at the time that it was of critical importance to Michael Eisner that
I sign a five-year contract to remain with the combined company.
Michael had been Disney's CEO since 1984, and he'd been running the company without a number two for more than a year, after
his COO Frank Wells died in a helicopter crash in the spring of
1994. If this deal went through, Disney would nearly double in
size, and Michael knew he couldn't integrate the two companies
and run the newly combined entity on his own. It was a lot for me
to absorb. One day I was in line to become the next CEO of Cap
Cities/ABC; the next I was being asked to run the media division
of Disney for at least five years. While the latter was an intriguing
job, objectively, it felt at the time like a bitter pill to swallow.

I knew if I agreed to stay on, it would likely require moving
back to Los Angeles, and I didn't want to do that. I hated the
thought of being away from my daughters again, and my aging

parents were on Long Island, and I wanted to remain close to them. I was also now engaged to Willow Bay, whom I had started dating a little more than a year earlier. Willow had her own great job in New York, anchoring the weekend edition of *Good Morning America*, subbing for the weekday host Joan Lunden during the week, and being groomed as her successor. I didn't want to be apart from her, and I didn't want to ask her to give up her job so she could come across the country with me.

So, on one side of the scale, the personal reasons for walking away were piled fairly high. On the other side, the professional reasons for staying were stacked just as tall. I didn't know Michael well, but I liked and respected him. We had overlapped briefly at ABC years before, but I was a low-level employee then and our paths never crossed. Years later, he and Jeffrey Katzenberg, whom Michael brought in to run Walt Disney Studios after he became CEO, had tried to hire me when I was running ABC Entertainment. That he was now saying the deal wouldn't happen without me suggested that one day he might ask me to fill the role of COO that had been empty since Frank Wells's death. I've generally tried over the years to keep my eye on the job I have and not the jobs I might someday have, but the thought that I might have a shot at running Disney one day was hard to ignore.

Willow was unequivocally supportive. She said I had nothing to lose and a lot to possibly gain by staying, and that she trusted that she and I could figure out whatever we needed to figure out. I sought some wisdom from Tom Murphy, too. Tom was conflicted (he wanted to deliver me to Michael as part of the deal), but he was also capable of separating out his interests, and he'd always been a good sounding board for me. I knew he was being genuine when he said, "Pal, if you play your cards right, one day you will run that company."

Disney and Capital Cities/ABC agreed to financial terms on a Friday afternoon. While there were some finer points still to be hashed out, the only major issue left unresolved was whether I was staying or going. That same night, Willow and I had scheduled a dinner with the Jesuit priest who was going to marry us. (I'm Jewish and Willow's Catholic, so we'd enlisted both Father Ghirlando and a Jewish cantor from New Jersey to officiate our wedding.) There I was, a divorced Jewish guy hoping to impress the priest who would perform our service, and every couple of minutes I had to stand up and excuse myself from the table to take calls regarding the deal. I began to worry about seeming disrespectful to Father Ghirlando, so I finally apologized for the interruptions and said, "I know I'm Jewish, but I need to ask you for 'priest-client' confidentiality."

"Of course," he said.

"We're about to announce the biggest deal in entertainment history, and I'm trying to make a decision on whether to stay on with the company or not. That's what all of these calls are about."

Father Ghirlando didn't offer any clerical wisdom, but he did bless whatever decision I was about to make. We continued talking about our wedding service, but every time I excused myself to take another call, Father Ghirlando seemed mildly thrilled, knowing that he was hearing about one of the biggest acquisitions in the history of American business before the rest of the world.

On Tom Murphy's recommendation, I hired a lawyer named Joe Bachelder, and on Saturday morning I went to Joe's office in midtown Manhattan and told him that this needed to be resolved fast. I was leaning toward staying, so now I was basically sending Joe in to do battle with Disney's general counsel, Sandy Litvack, to work out a deal that felt right to me. The following night, ABC and Disney board members convened at the offices of Dewey Ballantine, the firm representing Disney. It was a tense situation. While the boards were hashing out the specifics of this mega-merger, Sandy Litvack was complaining that the entire thing was going to blow up because Joe was being too tough. At one point Michael Eisner pulled Tom Murphy aside and begged him to intervene and get me to agree to the deal Disney was offering. Michael then confronted me himself a little later. "Bob," he said, "it's easier to negotiate this $19.5 billion deal than it is to figure out yours. Will you please just say yes?"

The final sticking point was the matter of whom I would be reporting to. Joe was pushing for a formal agreement that I would report directly to Michael, and Michael refused. He wanted the freedom to name a president, someone who would exist between the two of us, and he wanted to make sure that I understood he could do that. While I would have liked him to say that I was formally his number two, I appreciated how direct Michael was with me. I finally told Joe to accept later that night. I was hoping for a path to possibly becoming CEO one day (understanding that nothing is ever guaranteed), but it wasn't the right time to fight for that. I wanted the merger to go well, and I wanted to make sure the Capital Cities team was treated well by Disney. Without me there, I was fairly certain they would get subsumed by Disney in potentially dispiriting ways.

We all convened the next morning at the crack of dawn at ABC's headquarters on Sixty-sixth Street. The plan was for us to make the announcement, do a press conference in one of ABC's studios (TV-1, where one of the 1960 Kennedy-Nixon debates took place), and then Michael and Tom would walk next door to TV-2 to do an interview on *Good Morning America*, which was airing live. It truly would be breaking news. No one at ABC News had been told in advance that a deal was imminent. Coincidentally, Willow was filling in for Joan Lunden that day. When Charlie Gibson, her co-anchor, noticed the commotion in the studio next door, he asked her, "On a scale of one to ten, how would you rate what is happening next door?" Willow, who of course knew what was up but was sworn to secrecy, responded, "I'd give it a twelve, Charlie."

My five-year extension was announced along with the deal. Afterward, I immediately convened a meeting of all of the top Cap Cities/ABC executives. None of them saw this coming, and they were still in shock. There were people around the table who had worked for Tom and Dan for their entire careers, and they were looking at me asking, "What happens now? What do we do?"

I spoke as frankly as I could. Disney was a very different corporate culture than ours, but Tom had the interests of the entire company at heart when he agreed to the deal. It was going to be a difficult transition, though; there was no way around that. I wanted people to understand that I knew how unsettling it was. The corporate culture we were all used to was about to end. Disney was more aggressive, more creative, more a creature of Hollywood than the company we'd all worked for. I was in a position to make the transition easier, though, and I wanted them to know they could rely on me if they needed my help.

As for the deal itself, a lot of people were shocked at the $19.5 billion price tag; others thought Tom could have held out longer and sold for much more. It's impossible to say. It turned out to be a bargain for Disney, though; that much is certain. Michael never got much credit for having the guts it took to make that deal, but it was an enormous risk, and it paid off for years to come. The acquisition gave Disney the scale to remain independent when other entertainment companies were coming to the painful realization that they were too small to compete in a changing world. The assets Disney acquired in the merger—especially ESPN—drove growth for years and were a vital buffer for nearly a decade as Disney Animation struggled with a series of box-office disappointments.

A COUPLE OF weeks after we announced the deal, I flew to Aspen to spend a weekend with Michael and his wife, Jane, at their place in Snowmass. I was stunned by how beautiful it was, a giant log cabin designed by the architect Bob Stern, who was also a member of the Disney board, nestled in a valley surrounded by Aspen's peaks. Everything about the place exuded great taste.

Disney had done due diligence about the assets they purchased, but there was no way they could understand all of the complexities of the company they were about to own. I arrived carrying numerous binders, each detailing the many businesses of Capital Cities, including ABC, its television stations, ESPN, a sprawling radio business, a big publishing business with newspapers and magazines, other cable channels, and a collection of other small businesses. "Your team did your assessment quickly," I told him, "so there's a lot you don't know."

For the next two days, I walked Michael through every aspect of our company. He may have been thinking he was buying a television company, but it was so much more complex than that. There was everything from ESPN's rights deals to upcoming negotiations between ABC and the NFL. I gave him a breakdown of our radio business, which ranged from country to talk to WABC, and talked about dealing with a talk radio host who'd said something controversial and incendiary on the air. There were delicate issues around Barbara Walters's contract, which was about to expire, and the intricacies of managing a network news business. The complexities went on and on. I wanted Michael to understand the reality, and I also wanted him to know that I had it covered.

Michael was clearly rattled. He was only fifty-two at the time, but he'd undergone a heart bypass operation a year earlier, and Jane kept a watchful eye on his diet and schedule and exercise routine. I wasn't aware at the time of how much she had been urging him to change his lifestyle, and how much anxiety this acquisition was causing her. She wanted him to work less, and there I was sitting in their home telling him, "This is going to be a much bigger lift than you're aware of, and there's a much greater urgency to solve some of these problems than you know."

At the end of the weekend, Michael drove me to the airport. Along the way, we stopped to meet Michael Ovitz and his family, who had a home nearby. Jane, Michael, and the Ovitz family had plans to go for a hike. I wasn't aware that the two families were close, but I could see that afternoon that there was a chemistry between them. Ovitz had recently tried to leave CAA, the business he cofounded and turned into the world's most powerful talent agency, to run Universal Studios. That hadn't panned out, and he was looking to start a new chapter of his career in Hollywood. As I left for the airport and my flight back to New York, it dawned on me that Michael might be considering him for the number two position at Disney.

A week later that suspicion was confirmed. Michael called and said, "Your briefing was eye-opening. It certainly won't be easy to manage this new company." Jane was concerned, too, he said. Then he addressed the Ovitz question directly. "When we made the deal, I left open the possibility of bringing in someone else between us." Yes, I said, I knew nothing was guaranteed. "Well, I wanted you to know that I'm hiring Michael Ovitz, and he's going to be your boss."

Ovitz was going to be president of the Walt Disney Company, not chief operating officer. As corporate hierarchies go, that meant that he was my boss, but he wasn't necessarily Michael's preordained successor. I felt a moment of disappointment, but I also appreciated that Michael had been straight with me during the negotiation and candid with me now. He didn't try to sugarcoat it or pretend the arrangement was something it was not. I was forty-four at the time and I still had a lot to learn, and in any event, there was nothing to be gained by getting off to a bad start with either of them. I wanted to make things work. After the announcement about Michael Ovitz, I said to a reporter from *The New York Times*, "If Mike Eisner thinks this is the right thing for the company, then I trust his instincts." The day the quote appeared in the *Times*, I was informed by an executive at Disney that Michael disliked being referred to as "Mike." I hadn't even started yet and I'd already committed my first faux pas.

I soon learned that others had much stronger feelings about the Ovitz hire than I did. I was told that Joe Roth, the chairman of the studio, was irate, and that Sandy Litvack and Steve Bollenbach,

Disney's chief financial officer, were unhappy with the new corporate structure and had refused to report to Ovitz. From three thousand miles away in New York, I could already feel the resentment building at "Disney Corporate." Hiring Michael Ovitz had generated internal strife from the moment it was announced, but I had no idea how tense things were going to get.

FOR THE NEXT several months, while we all waited for regulatory approval from the FCC, I commuted to Los Angeles on a weekly basis, getting to know the various Disney executives who would soon be my colleagues. Willow and I also knew we'd have no chance for a honeymoon once the deal closed, so we radically shortened our engagement and got married in early October 1995.

We spent our honeymoon in southern France, and were staying at the posh Grand-Hotel du Cap-Ferrat when a gigantic box arrived filled with Disney merchandise: matching Mickey Mouse pajamas, bride and groom Mickey hats, Donald Duck slippers. There was so much stuff, and it was so over the top, that we didn't know what to do with it all. We decided to leave it there when we left, thinking maybe someone would get a kick out of it or have kids who might like it, but to this day a part of me is embarrassed at the thought of the staff there coming into our room after we checked out and seeing all of the Mickey Mouse paraphernalia. I remember looking at it all and saying to Willow, "I work for a very different company now." (In fact, in all the years I worked for him, I rarely saw Michael Eisner wearing a tie that wasn't a Mickey tie. All the senior leadership were encouraged to wear them, too, though I acted as if I'd never gotten that particular memo.)

There were more significant differences than the branded attire. The whole culture operated differently. Tom and Dan were warm, accessible bosses. If you had a problem, they opened their doors to you. If you needed advice, they offered it selflessly. As businessmen, they were intensely focused on managing expenses and increasing earnings, and they surrounded themselves with executives who could work for them forever as long as they adhered to the same principles. They also believed in a decentralized corporate structure. If you stuck to your budget and behaved ethically, Tom and Dan gave you room to operate with independence. Other than a CFO and a general counsel, there was no corporate staff, no centralized bureaucracy, and very little interference with the business units.

Disney was the opposite of all that. In their earliest days running the company, Michael and Frank Wells had formed a central corporate unit called Strategic Planning, populated by a group of aggressive, well-educated executives (they all had MBAs, many from Harvard and Stanford). They were steeped in analysis and adept at providing the data and "insight" Michael needed to feel secure in every business move the company made, while he made all of the creative decisions himself. They had significant power over the rest of the company, and they wielded it with impunity over all of the senior leaders who ran Disney's various business units.

I arrived at Disney about halfway through Michael's twenty-one-year tenure as CEO. He was one of the most celebrated and successful CEOs in corporate America, and his first decade had been extraordinary. He aggressively expanded Disney's theme parks and resorts and introduced a far more profitable pricing strategy. He launched the cruise-ship business, which was relatively small compared to other businesses but also solidly profitable. Throughout the late '80s and early '90s, Disney Animation produced hit after hit: *The Little Mermaid, Beauty and the Beast, Aladdin,* and *The Lion King.* These led to an explosion in Disney's consumer-products business, with revenue coming from Disney stores and licensing and all forms of global merchandise distribution. The Disney Channel, which they launched in the United States, quickly became a success, and Walt Disney Studios, which was responsible for the live-action films, released a string of commercial hits.

As we joined the company, though, cracks were beginning to show. The void left by Frank Wells's death led to intense acrimony between Michael and Jeffrey Katzenberg, who claimed much of the credit for the success of Animation during Michael's first decade. Jeffrey resented that Michael didn't promote him after Frank Wells's death. Michael in turn resented that Jeffrey was pressuring him to do so. In 1994, not long after his open-heart bypass surgery, Michael forced Jeffrey to resign, which resulted in a very public, very acrimonious, and expensive legal battle. On top of those struggles, Disney's Animation unit began to falter. The next several years would be punctuated by a slew of expensive failures: *Hercules, Atlantis, Treasure Planet, Fantasia 2000, Brother Bear, Home on the Range,* and *Chicken Little.* Others—*The Hunchback of Notre Dame, Mulan, Tarzan,* and *Lilo and Stitch*—were modest successes, but none came close to the creative or commercial successes of the prior decade. To his credit, Michael had the wisdom during this period to enter into a relationship with Pixar that resulted in some of the greatest animated films ever made.

From the beginning, the Disney team—mostly the guys from "Strat Planning," as they were called—took advantage of us as the newcomers to the company. It wasn't that everything they did was bad, it was just the opposite of what those of us who'd worked for Tom and Dan were used to. They were a completely centralized, process-oriented company, and we instinctively bristled at the way they operated. They had also never acquired a big company before, and they'd given very little thought as to how to do it with sensitivity and care. Disagreements that could have been handled with diplomacy were instead done with a tone that was often authoritative and demanding. They acted as if, because they'd bought us, we were expected always to bend to their will. It didn't sit well with a lot of the former Cap Cities people. I was high enough up that I was protected, but a lot of people below me were worried about what was going to happen to them, and I spent a ton of time and energy soothing anxieties and intervening in struggles on their behalf.

I also had my own run-ins. Soon after the acquisition, Disney wisely divested our entire newspaper business, years before the bottom fell out of that industry. But we held on to some magazines, including the fashion magazine *W*. Shortly after the deal, the editor and publisher of *W* mentioned to me that Jane Pratt, the founder of *Sassy* magazine and an early contributor to VH-1 and MTV, had an idea for "a hip *Cosmopolitan*" called *Jane*.

Jane came in and pitched the idea, which I liked because it could connect us to a younger, less stodgy demographic. I reviewed a business plan that made sense to me and I gave the team the green light. I soon got a call from Tom Staggs, who would later be my CFO and worked then in Strat Planning. Tom was contacting me on behalf of his boss, Larry Murphy, who ran the entire Strategic Planning unit. He sheepishly told me that Larry didn't allow any of Disney's businesses to expand, invest, or attempt to start anything new without a thorough analysis by his group. Once they did the analysis, they'd bring their recommendation to Michael.

I could tell Tom wasn't comfortable being the messenger, so I politely said that he should tell Larry that I was going forward with this and didn't need his input.

That quickly led to a call from Larry, who wanted to know what the hell I was doing. "You're creating this magazine?"

"Yes."

"Do you know how much it's going to cost?"

"Yes."

"And you think it's a good idea?"

"Yes."

"We don't work that way at Disney," he said.

In the end, Larry allowed the venture to go forward. He was reluctant to pick a fight with me so soon after I'd joined the company, but the signal was clear that from then on there would be no freelancing at Disney.

In fairness, it was a *small* idea, and arguably not worth the time and investment (though we ended up selling *W* and *Jane* to Si Newhouse at Condé Nast and made a profit on the transaction). But there's a way to convey that while also conveying that you trust the people who work for you, and preserving in them an entrepreneurial spirit. Dan Burke taught me that exact lesson early on in a way that couldn't have been more opposite from the Strat Planning approach. I can't recall exactly what it was in response to, but in one of our conversations about some initiative I was considering, Dan handed me a note that read: "Avoid getting into the business of manufacturing trombone oil. You may become the greatest trombone-oil manufacturer in the world, but in the end, the world only consumes a few quarts of trombone oil a year!" He was telling me not to invest in projects that would sap the resources of my company and me and not give much back. It was such a positive way to impart that wisdom, though, and I still have that piece of paper in my desk, occasionally pulling it out when I talk to Disney executives about what projects to pursue and where to put their energy.

WHILE I WAS trying to adapt to the new culture at Disney, I was also watching the rapid disintegration of the relationship between my new boss, Michael Ovitz, and Michael Eisner. It was painful to witness, and it was taking place before the eyes of a lot of people at the company.

Michael Ovitz's tenure officially began in October 1995, and from the beginning it was clear that he was the wrong guy in the wrong place at the wrong time. He had left CAA and had lost out on a bid to run Universal. You could sense how important it was to him to remain atop the Hollywood pyramid, and the offer to be

Michael Eisner's number two was the life preserver he thought he needed.

But the process of making decisions at an agency is nothing like the process at a large corporation, especially a highly structured place like Disney. Rather than helping Michael run a complicated collection of businesses, which is a big part of the role of a number two, Ovitz came with a thousand ideas, most involving the giant personalities that he had relationships with. As co-head of CAA, a privately held agency, he was used to showing up with a ton of ideas that could immediately be acted upon, and he assumed he could do the same here. He was the quintessential agent, and he was used to always being accessible for clients, often dropping everything he was doing in order to be available for them. Those habits did not work for Disney. He wanted to offer people like Tom Clancy, Magic Johnson, Martin Scorsese, and Janet Jackson (and many more) omnibus deals that would span Disney's businesses. He was constantly pitching these people on what Disney could do for them. Deals like this might sound great in a press release, but they rarely turn out well. They need a senior executive to act as a sponsor, putting in the time and energy necessary to shepherd each aspect of the deal through every business and every initiative. They also send a signal to the talent that they have carte blanche, and at places like Disney, where every idea is carefully vetted, this can be a disaster.

I was working out of New York, but flew to L.A. every week for Michael Eisner's Monday staff lunches, which gave me a front-row seat on the whole debacle. Ovitz would show up with his energy and ideas, and it was clear to everyone around the table that Michael Eisner, who knew better, had little interest in them. Michael would then dutifully run through our business updates and new strategies, and Ovitz, feeling disrespected, would aggressively tune out and broadcast his lack of interest. The whole team saw this happen, in meeting after meeting. The body language alone was painful to witness, and the discomfort started to affect the entire senior management team. When the two people at the top of a company have a dysfunctional relationship, there's no way that the rest of the company beneath them can be functional. It's like having two parents who fight all the time. The kids feel the strain, and they start to reflect the animosity back onto the parents and vent it at each other.

I tried to be polite with Ovitz through it all and respect that I had a direct reporting relationship to him. I made an attempt to educate him on the businesses that reported to me, often giving him briefing reports to help him better understand the particulars of network television ratings or ESPN distribution deals or talent contracts, but each time he was either dismissive of the information or distracted by phone calls. Once, he took a call, in my office, from President Clinton, talking with him for forty-five minutes while I sat outside. A call from Tom Cruise interrupted another meeting. Martin Scorsese ended a third, just minutes after it started. Meeting after meeting was either canceled, rescheduled, or abbreviated, and soon every top executive at Disney was whispering behind his back about what a disaster he was. Managing your own time and respecting others' time is one of the most vital things to do as a manager, and he was horrendous at it.

With his ideas going nowhere and Michael Eisner essentially icing him out of any significant role at the company, Ovitz became angry and embarrassed. Even if he'd been given the authority to genuinely function in his role, though, I think he still would have failed at Disney, because he was just not wired for corporate culture. I would give him a stack of materials in advance of a meeting, and the next day he'd come in not having read any of them and say, "Give me the facts," then render a fast opinion. There was no sense that he was acting fast because he'd processed all the information. The opposite was the case. He was covering up for not being prepared, and in a company like Disney, if you don't do the work, the people around you detect that right away and their respect for you disappears. You have to be attentive. You often have to sit through meetings that, if given the choice, you might choose not to sit

through. You have to learn and absorb. You have to hear out other
people's problems and help find solutions. It's all part of being a
great manager. The problem was, Michael Ovitz wasn't a manager,
he was still an agent. He knew that business better than anyone,
but that's not the business we were in.

IN APRIL 1996, Michael Eisner visited me in my office in New
York. He walked in and closed the door and said, "I know it's not
working with Michael. It was a disaster to hire him." He knew that
other executives, like Joe Roth, the head of Disney Studios, were
talking about quitting because they were so frustrated, and he
pleaded with me not to do that. I wasn't planning to quit. I didn't
like it—my first six months at Disney were the most dispiriting and
unproductive of my career—but I was still new to the company,
and because I was based in New York, I wasn't exposed to the pain
quite as much as others were. Mostly what I thought was, this is a
difficult problem for Michael to deal with, and I don't want to add
to his strain.

"I don't know exactly when I'm going to do it," Michael said to
me. "But I'm going to fire him." He asked me not to discuss it with
anyone, and I gave him my word. I was never sure who else he told,
but I expected Michael would say something to Ovitz within weeks
of that discussion. Instead, months dragged on, and the tension
and the dysfunction grew even worse. Everyone—the two of them,
all of the senior leadership, the entire staff who worked for Ovitz—
was unhappy. It was time to stop the bleeding.

Finally, in December, more than eight months after he told me
he was going to do it, Michael Eisner fired Michael Ovitz and
ended this painful chapter in the history of the company (though
the pain lingered on in the form of shareholder lawsuits over the
$100 million–plus severance package Ovitz received). I now have a
cordial relationship with Michael Ovitz. He's been generous about
Disney's success during my time as CEO, and when I look back on

it, I think of him not as a bad guy but as a participant in a big mistake. The culture shift was just too big a leap for him.

He and Michael both wanted it to work, each for his own powerful reasons. Michael expected that Ovitz would come in and know how to do the work, and Ovitz had no idea what kind of adjustments he'd need to make to succeed within the culture of a giant, publicly traded company.

They should both have known that it couldn't work, but they willfully avoided asking the hard questions because each was somewhat blinded by his own needs. It's a hard thing to do, especially in the moment, but those instances in which you find yourself hoping that something will work without being able to convincingly explain to yourself *how* it will work—that's when a little bell should go off, and you should walk yourself through some clarifying questions. What's the problem I need to solve? Does this solution make sense? If I'm feeling some doubt, why? Am I doing this for sound reasons or am I motivated by something personal?

CHAPTER 5

SECOND IN LINE

F OR THE NEXT three years, Michael ran the company without a number two. Our relationship grew closer in the wake of Ovitz's leaving, but I also sensed from time to time a wariness on Michael's part, that he felt I had an eye on his job and could never fully trust me. It resulted in a kind of ongoing approach and avoidance. Michael would bring me in on decisions at times and confide in me, and then suddenly he would go cold and keep me at arm's length.

It was true that I'd stayed on after the acquisition in part because I thought I might have a shot at running the company one day, but that didn't mean I was angling for Michael's job. It meant I was committed to doing my own job as best I could, and to learning as much as I could about all aspects of the company. As had been the case throughout my career, if the time came when Michael was ready to step down, I wanted to be ready when the opportunity arose.

I've been asked a lot over the years about the best way to nurture ambition—both one's own and that of the people you manage. As a leader, you should want those around you to be eager to rise up and take on more responsibility, as long as dreaming about the job they want doesn't distract them from the job they have. You can't let ambition get too far ahead of opportunity. I've seen a lot of people who had their sights set on a particular job or project, but the opportunity to actually get that thing was so slim. Their focus on the small thing in the distance became a problem. They grew impatient with where they were. They didn't tend enough to the responsibilities they did have, because they were longing so much for something else, and so their ambition became counterproductive. It's important to know how to find the balance—do the job you have well; be patient; look for opportunities to pitch in and expand and grow; and make yourself one of the people, through attitude and energy and focus, that your bosses feel they have to turn to when an opportunity arises. Conversely, if you're a boss, these are the people to nurture—not the ones who are clamoring for promotions and complaining about not being utilized enough but the ones who are proving themselves to be indispensable day in and day out.

As with so many things, Tom and Dan were perfect models in this regard. They were invested in my growth, they conveyed how much they wanted me to succeed, and they cleared a path for me to learn what I needed to know in order to move up and eventually run the company. At every stage I worked hard to absorb as much as I could, knowing that if I performed, they had larger plans in place. As a result, I felt profoundly loyal to them.

The dynamics between a CEO and the next person in line for his or her job are often fraught, though. We all want to believe we're irreplaceable. The trick is to be self-aware enough that you don't cling to the notion that you are the only person who can do this job. At its essence, good leadership isn't about being indispensable; it's about helping others be prepared to possibly step into your shoes—giving them access to your own decision making, identifying the skills they need to develop and helping them improve, and, as I've had to do, sometimes being honest with them about why they're not ready for the next step up.

Michael's relationship with me played itself out in complicated ways. Sometimes I felt he was questioning my abilities; other times he was generous and encouraging and leaned on me to take work off his plate. A high point in our relationship came in late 1998, when Michael came to my office in New York and told me he wanted me to create and run a new international organization. I was chairman of the ABC Group at the time, which meant I was running the ABC network and ESPN, as well as all of Disney TV. This was going to be a huge lift on top of those responsibilities, but I was eager to do it and grateful that Michael had turned to me.

Disney was surprisingly parochial back then. We had offices all over the world, from Latin America to India to Japan, but we didn't have a coherent global strategy or even structures in place that made sense. In Japan, for instance, we had a studio office in one part of Tokyo, a consumer-products business in another, a TV business somewhere else. None of them spoke with another. There was no coordination around back-office functions like accounting, say, or IT. That kind of redundancy existed everywhere. More important than that, though, we didn't have people in any of our territories whose job was to manage our brand in that place and look for unique opportunities. It was all a very passive, Burbank-centric approach.

Michael saw the problem and knew that it needed to change. He knew we needed to grow internationally. Years earlier, he'd set his sights on building a theme park in China. Frank Wells, Michael's number two for the first decade that he ran Disney, had made some overtures to Chinese officials in the early '90s, but he'd never made much progress. From those initial meetings, though, China was aware that we were interested in a park there, and they'd recently signaled that they wanted it to happen.

I was one of the few Disney executives with international experience, from my time working for ABC Sports and *Wide World of*

Sports, and I was the only one who knew anything about China, having managed to get some ABC children's programming on the air there in the pre-Disney days. So Michael made me president of Walt Disney International and tasked me not just with forming an international strategy but with finding a place to build a theme park in China.

We had an initial discussion about where, and for a combination of factors—weather, population, available land—we soon concluded that Shanghai was the only workable location. In October 1998, as Willow was entering her ninth month of pregnancy with our first child, I traveled to Shanghai for the first time for Disney and was taken around and shown three pieces of property. "You can have any one of these," the Chinese officials said, "but you need to decide quickly."

We settled on a property in Pudong, outside of downtown Shanghai, although on our first visit to what was a small farming village on the outskirts of a then-rising city, it wasn't exactly easy to envision a Disney castle in the middle of a fully developed Disneyland. Canals ran throughout the village, with little children and stray dogs walking about. Small vegetable patches were sprinkled among ramshackle houses and occasional general stores. Bicycles far outnumbered cars, and what we would consider "modernity" was nowhere in sight. It was, however, perfectly situated between Shanghai's soon-to-be-opened international airport and what would become "downtown" to one of the world's largest and most vibrant cities. Thus began what would become an eighteen-year journey, which would bring me back to that same spot more than forty times.

MEANWHILE, IN MY other domain, ABC entered the early stages of what would be a long downward slide. The hit shows we'd developed back when I was running prime time had gotten long in the tooth, and we'd become complacent and unimaginative in our development process. *NYPD Blue* was still in the top 20, and we had a couple of others—*Home Improvement, The Drew Carey Show*—that did well. But the rest of our lineup, with the exception of the perennial juggernaut that is *Monday Night Football*, was largely uninspiring.

We were briefly saved in 1999 when we launched *Who Wants to Be a Millionaire*, which we'd initially said no to and then reconsidered when the creator came back to us with Regis Philbin as host. It turned out to be a godsend at the time, and later a crutch. Its numbers were astounding when it first aired, not just for a game show but for any show. That first season, it pulled in about thirty million viewers per night, three nights a week, numbers that were all but inconceivable at that point in network TV. It was number one in the ratings for the '99–2000 season, a network savior, but it couldn't totally mask our deeper problems.

There was one other bright spot that year. In the middle of 1998, I'd begun thinking in earnest about our coverage of the upcoming millennium. I felt strongly that people around the world would be fascinated with this moment, and that the entire company, led by ABC News, should turn its attention and resources to it. Eighteen months in advance, I called a meeting with the senior executives from News, Entertainment, and Sports and told them what I envisioned—that we would provide wall-to-wall, twenty-four-hour coverage as midnight moved across the globe and each time zone rang in the new millennium. I remember saying enthusiastically that we should "own the event," then looking at Roone sitting silent and expressionless across the table. He clearly hated the idea. The meeting ended, and I pulled him aside. "Do you think I'm crazy?" I asked.

"How are we going to make a calendar change visually interesting for twenty-four hours?" he said.

I could have answered in any number of ways (it was actually an interesting challenge), but something in Roone's tone and body language told me his problem wasn't really with the visuals. It was that he was being asked to execute a big idea that wasn't his, by the guy who used to say "How high?" when Roone said "Jump."

I'd been Roone's boss since 1993, when Tom and Dan made me president of the network. We'd worked well together over those years. He was proud that I'd risen to the top of the company, but he still thought of me as his understudy—that I'd cut my teeth under him and I was his ally in the front office who would protect him from corporate meddling and allow him to do his thing. I was less blindly devoted to Roone than he wanted to believe, but there was no harm in his thinking it, and no real reason for me to ever disabuse him of the notion. He was at his best when his ego was least threatened.

But I also needed him to execute the thing I was asking him to execute. It's a tricky thing, moving people over to your side and enlisting their enthusiastic engagement. Sometimes it's worth talking through their reservations and patiently responding to their concerns. Other times you simply need to communicate that you're the boss and you want this done. It's not that one approach is "nice" and the other isn't. It's just that one is more direct and nonnegotiable. It really comes down to what you believe is right for the moment—when a more democratic approach is useful both in getting to the best outcome and in building morale, and when you have enough certainty in your opinion that you're willing to be an autocrat even in the face of disagreement.

In this case, I absolutely believed I was right, and I wasn't going to let anyone, even the vaunted Roone Arledge, dissuade me. Of course he could have easily sabotaged it, undermining it through lack of effort and enthusiasm and communicating that to his people. Like many people I've worked or negotiated with over the years, Roone didn't respond well if he felt he was being big-footed. So I resorted to a kind of "soft autocracy," showing respect but also communicating that this was going to happen no matter what.

"Roone," I said, "if there was ever an idea that people would assume came from you, this is it. It's big and bold. It could be impossible to execute, but when has that ever stopped you?"

I wasn't exactly sure if it was the idea he didn't like, or if at that point he just didn't feel he had the energy for a big production like this. But I knew he couldn't walk away from a challenge, so I was playing to his pride to get him on board. He didn't say anything, but he smiled and nodded, as if to say *Okay, I got it*.

In the end, we created something that will go down as a great achievement. It took months of prepwork by Roone's team to get it done, and he came in at the end, as he had countless times, and lifted the whole thing to another place. Peter Jennings anchored our millennium coverage from Times Square. We were there on the scene when the clock struck midnight in Vanuatu, in the first time zone to welcome the new millennium. Over the next twenty-four hours we were live from China and Paris and Rio de Janeiro, from Walt Disney World and Times Square and finally from Los Angeles before we went off the air. Peter was brilliant, sitting in a tuxedo in a studio overlooking the thousands of party-goers below, guiding viewers through this experience shared by everyone around the globe, which would never happen again in any of our lifetimes. No network committed as many resources as we did, and no one came close to the size of our audience.

I visited the studio a few times throughout that day. It was clear early in the broadcast that our coverage was going to be a huge success, and you could feel the excitement in the studio as the day went on. The most satisfying moment for me came as I watched Roone presiding over the whole production, sending instructions out to the teams in the field, talking into Peter's earpiece to introduce a story line into the coverage, calling for different camera angles and anticipating transitions. It felt like watching the master conductor I'd first laid eyes on a quarter of a century earlier at the Frank Sinatra concert in Madison Square Garden.

About twenty hours into the day, I met him in the control room.

He had a huge smile on his face and grabbed my hand and gave it a long, warm shake. He was proud of himself. He was proud of me. He was grateful that I'd given him the chance to do this. He was nearly seventy years old at that point, and this was the last big event he would produce in a lifetime of them.

Two years later, Roone would die after a protracted battle with cancer. The week before he passed, I was in New York for Thanksgiving weekend, and that Saturday night I was home watching the USC–Notre Dame game on ABC. My phone rang at 10:00 P.M., and when I answered, the ABC operator said, "Mr. Iger, Roone Arledge is calling for you." If you had the number and it was an emergency, you could call the ABC switchboard and an operator would track down the person you needed to talk to. Roone still had the number, and something urgent was on his mind.

The operator connected us. "Roone?"

"Bob, are you watching?"

"The football game?"

"Yes, the football game! Have you noticed the audio is all off?"

The announcers weren't making any sense, he said. It was all gibberish. I was aware that Roone's condition had worsened recently and that he'd been hospitalized. I knew he must have been hallucinating, but some old, sentimental sense of duty kicked in. Roone was saying something was wrong, and I had to try to make it right.

"Let me check, Roone," I said. "I'll call you back."

I called the control room and asked if there were any complaints about the audio. "No, Bob. Nothing" was the response I got from ABC's Master Control Center in New York.

"Can you call the switchboard and check if they're hearing anything?"

After a few moments I heard back: "Nope. Nothing."

I called Roone. "I just checked with the control room. They made sure there's nothing wrong." Before we could linger on what he thought he was hearing, I asked, "How are you doing, Roone?"

His voice was a whisper. "I'm in Sloan Kettering Hospital," he said. "How do you think I'm doing?"

I asked if he was seeing visitors, and the next day I went to see him. When I walked into his room, he was lying in bed, and I knew the moment I saw him that he wouldn't live much longer. There was a figure-skating competition on the television, and he was watching intently. I went over and stood near him. He looked up at me, and then at the skater onscreen. "It's not the same as it used to be," he said. "Is it?"

I don't know if he was thinking back to those days when we could go anywhere and do anything, and there were no executives haranguing him about the money he was spending. Or the days when he was a legend in the room and no one would dare to doubt his authority. Or maybe it was more existential than that. The business had changed beneath him. The world had changed. He didn't have much time left. I looked down at him in bed and I knew this would be the last time I saw him. "No, Roone," I said. "It's not what it used to be."

OUR FORTUNES AT ABC went downhill after the bright spot of our millennium coverage. *Millionaire* was still popular in 2000–01, but not nearly as big as it had been the season before. We could see the diminishing returns, but we didn't have good shows in development. Rather than making major changes in order to revitalize Entertainment, we leaned harder on this one show to carry us. We put it on five times a week as a way of competing against NBC, which was prospering with its "Must See TV" Thursday night, and CBS, which had found its legs again with *Survivor* and *CSI*.

In a matter of a couple of years, we'd slipped from being the most-watched network on television to the last of the "big three," and we were barely holding on to that as Fox continued to grow. I take some of the blame for that. I was running ABC, and I supported putting *Millionaire* on several nights a week. It was an easy fix for ABC's troubles, but when it started to sink, our deeper problems were laid bare.

By late 1999, the strain of running the company on his own was taking a toll on Michael. He was growing more isolated and insecure, more distrustful and critical of the people around him. He knew he needed someone to help shoulder the burden, and he was feeling pressure from the board to signal that, after sixteen years at the top, he was at least beginning to think about succession. It wasn't an easy thing for him to do. After the Ovitz fiasco, Michael was wary of naming a second in command. He recognized that he couldn't keep things going as they were, but he didn't want to deal with the complications of dividing responsibility and sharing decision making and having to involve someone else in his various goings on.

Michael's reluctance to name a number two had consequences throughout the company. It was clear he needed help, but because he wasn't filling the number two position, others moved in to try to occupy the void. Sandy Litvack, our general counsel, was promoted to vice chairman and began to see himself as a de facto COO. Strat Planning, which was now being run by Peter Murphy (no relation to Larry Murphy, his predecessor), got involved in more day-to-day decision making rather than looking at long-term strategy. There was a landgrab for authority and a blurring of boundaries and responsibilities, which had destructive effects on company morale.

For months, Michael was hot and cold toward me. He'd depend on me, and I'd think it was just a matter of time before he named me COO. Then he'd keep me at arm's length, and I'd be back to feeling unsure about the future. In August of '99, I took my first-ever two-week vacation, renting a house on Martha's Vineyard with Willow and our now almost two-year-old son, Max. Tom Murphy called me on the first night of our vacation. He'd been at a dinner in Los Angeles with Michael and a few other Disney board members the night before, and in a discussion about succession, Michael said that I would never be his successor. Tom was "horrified," as he put it to me, especially since he'd exhorted me to stay years earlier during the merger negotiations. "Pal," he said now, "I hate to give you bad news, but you need to leave Disney. Michael doesn't believe in you and he told the board you cannot succeed him. You need to quit."

I was devastated. Over the last several years, I'd dealt with the constant frustration and distraction of having to report to Michael Ovitz. I'd worked incredibly hard to integrate ABC into Disney, making sure that our people were valued and respected and helping to initiate an assimilation process that hadn't been thought through on the Disney side. I'd designed and implemented an entire international structure for the company, which required being away from my family for trip after trip, traveling constantly for over a year. Through it all, I'd always been a defender of and a loyalist to Michael, and now I was being told again, twenty-five years after my first boss had told me back in 1975—I "wasn't promotable."

I told Tom I wasn't going to quit. I was due a bonus at the end of the year, which I wasn't going to walk away from. If Michael was going to fire me, I needed to hear it from him directly. I hung up the phone and gathered my composure. I decided not to tell Willow while we were away. She was a prominent anchor on CNN at that point, cohosting *Moneyline,* an hour-long financial-news program. Her career was soaring, but the job was intense, and on top of the professional demands on her she somehow had been able to find the time and energy to be a wonderful mother to Max. She needed a break, and so I kept all that I was feeling to myself until we were back home in New York.

Then I waited for the shoe to drop. In September, I was at the headquarters in Burbank when Michael asked to see me. I was certain it was the end, and I walked into his office steeling myself for the blow that was coming. I sat down across from him and waited. "Do you think you're ready to move to L.A. permanently and help me run the company?" he asked.

It took me a moment to absorb what he was saying. I was confused, and then relieved, and then unsure that this was something I could trust. "Michael," I finally said, "do you have any idea how inconsistent you've been with me?" He was asking me to move my family out to California and for Willow to give up a huge job, not four weeks after telling a table full of people that I would never be his successor. "You have to be straight with me about what this is," I said.

His reaction was more candid than I expected. He said he wasn't sure I would want to move back to L.A., so that was a concern. The bigger issue, though, was that if he named me COO, he'd be "competing with myself," he said. I assumed he meant that the board would have someone to turn to if they wanted to replace him, but I was never really certain.

"Michael," I said, "I have no intention of gunning for your job or doing anything to undermine you." I told him I would love to have the chance to run the company someday, but I didn't see that happening in the near future. "I've never imagined you leaving," I said. "And I can't imagine the board wanting you to leave." It was true, I couldn't. We weren't in the smoothest waters, but at that point, there wasn't a crisis of confidence around Michael. He was still one of the most respected CEOs in the world.

The meeting ended inconclusively. Michael didn't offer me a title. He didn't put any formal plan in motion. I went back to New York and waited to hear more, but it didn't come up again until a month later. We were attending the London premiere of the stage production of *The Lion King*, and Michael suggested that I fly back to L.A. with him to talk about my future. I was scheduled to fly to China from London, however, and so we agreed I'd come to L.A. a few weeks later to hash out the details.

In early December, Michael finally made a proposal for me to become president and chief operating officer and a member of the Disney board. This was an undeniable vote of confidence, and came as something of a shock, given the conversation with Tom a few months earlier.

I quickly negotiated a deal on my own with Sandy Litvack, who in addition to his quasi-COO role was still our general counsel. Sandy wasn't happy about my ascendancy. The day before the announcement, he called me to change the agreement. I'd be executive vice president rather than president and COO, he said, and the board seat would be eliminated. I told Sandy it was president, COO, and a member of the board or nothing. He called me back an hour later to confirm all three, and we announced the next day.

Professionally, it was an extraordinary opportunity. There was no guarantee that I'd someday become CEO, but at least I had a chance to prove myself. Personally, it was another difficult move. My parents were in their late seventies by then and needed more help than ever. My daughters were twenty-one and eighteen years old, and I didn't want to live on the other side of the country from them again. CNN agreed to let Willow anchor her show from L.A., focusing on the technology and entertainment industries, but it was a difficult thing to make work. Though Willow was incredibly supportive, as she has been every step of the way, it wasn't lost on me that here I was, a decade later, asking another wife to sacrifice her own career in some way in order for us to move to Los Angeles in the service of mine.

I also could not have anticipated in a million years what was to come—for Disney, for Michael, and for me. As is so often the case in life, the thing I'd been striving toward was finally here, and now the hard times were about to begin.

CHAPTER 6

GOOD THINGS CAN HAPPEN

'VE OFTEN SAID that Michael "re-founded" Walt's company. When he took over Disney in 1984, its glory days were a distant memory. The company had been struggling since Walt died in 1966. Walt Disney Studios and Animation were in terrible shape. Disneyland and Walt Disney World were still popular, but they were also responsible for nearly three-quarters of the company's income. In the last two years before Michael came on, Disney's net income fell by 25 percent. In 1983, the corporate raider Saul Steinberg tried to take Disney over, the latest in a series of takeover attempts that the company barely survived.

The next year, Roy Disney, Walt's nephew, and Sid Bass, Disney's largest shareholder, brought in Michael as CEO and chairman and Frank Wells as president to reverse the company's fortunes and maintain its independence. (Michael had been running Paramount, and Frank was the former chief of Warner Bros.) They then hired Jeffrey Katzenberg, who'd worked under Michael at Paramount, to run Disney Studios. Together, Jeffrey and Michael revitalized Disney Animation, which restored the brand's popularity and spawned huge growth in consumer products. They also invested more attention and resources in the Disney-owned Touchstone Films, which then produced several live-action, non-G-rated hits like *Ruthless People* and *Pretty Woman*.

Michael's biggest stroke of genius, though, might have been his recognition that Disney was sitting on tremendously valuable assets that they hadn't yet leveraged. One was the popularity of the parks. If they raised ticket prices even slightly, they would raise revenue significantly, without any noticeable impact on the number of visitors. Building new hotels at Walt Disney World was another untapped opportunity, and numerous hotels opened during Michael's first decade as CEO. Then came the expansion of theme parks, with the opening of MGM-Hollywood Studios (now called Hollywood Studios) in Florida and Euro Disney (now Disneyland Paris) outside of Paris.

Even more promising was the trove of intellectual property—all of those great classic Disney movies—just sitting there waiting to be monetized. They began selling videocassettes of the classic Disney library to parents who'd seen them in the theater when they were young and now could play them at home for their kids. It became a billion-dollar business. Then came the Cap Cities/ABC acquisition in 1995, which gave Disney a big television network, but, most important, brought in ESPN and its nearly hundred million subscribers at the time. All of this illustrated that Michael was a remarkably creative thinker and businessman, and he turned Disney into a modern entertainment giant.

After he made me number two, we divided our responsibilities, giving him primary oversight of the Walt Disney Studios, as well as Parks and Resorts, while I concentrated on the media networks, consumer products, and Walt Disney International. Other than Animation, which he didn't really let me in on, Michael gave me access to much of his thinking and decision making. It's not an exaggeration to say that he taught me how to *see* in a way I hadn't been able to before. I had no experience with the creative process that went into building and running a theme park, and had never spent time visually imagining a visitor's experience. Michael walked through the world with a set designer's eye, and while he wasn't a natural mentor, it felt like a kind of apprenticeship to follow him around and watch him work.

In my time as Michael's number two, we opened Disney's Animal Kingdom in Florida and Hong Kong Disneyland and California Adventure in Anaheim. I walked miles upon miles with him in advance of the opening of those parks—and in existing parks, too—getting a sense of what he saw and what he was constantly looking to improve. He would walk down a path and look out into the distance and immediately identify nuances, like landscaping that wasn't lush enough, or fences that encroached on important views, or buildings that seemed either out of place or out of style.

These were great teaching moments for me. I learned so much about how to manage the business, but more important, I learned what the creative and design essence of our parks should be.

Michael would also allow me to accompany him on his many visits to Walt Disney Imagineering, located on a sprawling campus in Glendale, California, just a few miles from our studio lot in Burbank. Imagineering has been the subject of many books and articles, and the simplest way I can describe it is that it is the creative and technical heart of everything we build that isn't a film or TV show or consumer product. All of our theme parks and resorts and attractions, cruise ships and real estate developments, all of the live performances and light shows and parades, every detail from the design of a cast member's costume to the architecture of our castles emanates from Imagineering. It is impossible to overstate the creative and technical brilliance of Disney's Imagineers. They are artists, engineers, architects, and technologists, and they occupy a place and fulfill a role that is unmatched anywhere else in the world.

To this day, I find myself awed time and time again by their ability to envision something fantastical and then make it real, often at a scale that is enormous. When I visited Imagineering with Michael, I'd observe him critiquing projects large and small, reviewing everything from storyboards detailing the experience in one of our attractions to the design of a stateroom on a soon-to-be-built cruise ship. He'd hear presentations about upcoming parades, or review the design of the lobby of a new hotel. What struck me, and what was invaluable in my own education, was his ability to see the big picture as well as the granular details at the same time, and consider how one affected the other.

As the scrutiny of Michael intensified in the upcoming years, he would often be accused of being an oppressive perfectionist and micromanager. For his part, he'd say, "Micromanaging is underrated." I tend to agree with him, but to a point. Thanks to my years working for Roone Arledge, I didn't need to be convinced that the success or failure of something so often comes down to the details. Michael often saw things that other people didn't see, and then he demanded that they be made better. That was the source of so much of his and the company's success, and I had immense respect for Michael's tendency to sweat the details. It showed how much he cared, and it made a difference. He understood that "great" is often a collection of very small things, and he helped me appreciate that even more deeply.

Michael was proud of his micromanagement, but in expressing his pride, and reminding people of the details he was focused on, he could be perceived as being petty and small-minded. I once watched him give an interview in the lobby of a hotel and say to the reporter, "You see those lamps over there? I chose them." It's a bad look for a CEO. (I should confess that I've caught myself—or have been caught—doing the same thing a few times. Zenia Mucha has said to me, in a way only she can: "Bob, you know you did that, but the world doesn't need to know, so shut up!")

In early 2001, every media and entertainment company was feeling the ground shifting beneath its feet, but no one was sure which way to run. Technology was changing so fast, and the disruptive effects were becoming more obvious and anxiety-provoking. In March of that year, Apple released its "Rip. Mix. Burn." campaign, telling the world that once you purchased music, it was yours to duplicate and use as you wish. A lot of people, including Michael, saw that as a mortal threat to the music industry, which would soon threaten the television and movie industries. Michael was always a staunch defender of copyrights, often speaking out on the issue of piracy, and the Apple ad really bothered him—so much so that he targeted Apple publicly, testifying before the Senate Commerce Committee that Apple was flagrantly disrespecting copyright law and encouraging piracy. This didn't sit well with Steve Jobs.

It was an interesting time, and marked what I saw as the beginning of the end of the traditional media as we knew it. Of great interest to me was the fact that almost every traditional media company, while trying to figure out its place in this changing world, was operating out of fear rather than courage, stubbornly trying to build a bulwark to protect old models that couldn't possibly survive the sea change that was under way.

There was no one who embodied that change more than Steve Jobs, who in addition to running Apple was the CEO of Pixar, our most important and most successful creative partner. In the mid-'90s, Disney had made a deal with Pixar to coproduce, market, and distribute five of their films. *Toy Story* was released in 1995 under a previous deal. It was the first full-length digitally animated feature film—a seismic creative and technological leap—and it grossed nearly $400 million worldwide. *Toy Story* was followed by two more successes: *A Bug's Life,* in 1998, and *Monsters, Inc.,* in 2001. Taken together, those three movies grossed well over a billion dollars worldwide and established Pixar, at a time when Disney Animation was beginning to falter, as the future of animation.

Despite the artistic and financial success of Pixar's films, tension built up between the two companies (mostly, between Michael and Steve). When the original deal was made, Pixar was still a startup, and Disney had all the leverage. Pixar gave away a lot in the deal, including ownership over all the sequel rights to their films.

As their success and stature grew, the unequal dynamic between the two companies began to gnaw at Steve, who hated it when anyone tried to push him around. Michael was more focused on the specifics of the deal that had been negotiated, and seemingly unaware or uncaring of Steve's feelings. The situation worsened as *Toy Story 2* was being developed. It was originally supposed to be released straight to video, bypassing movie theaters, but when early iterations of the film demanded more production resources, the two companies concluded it should be released on the big screen first. The movie grossed nearly $500 million worldwide, and then a contractual argument ensued. Pixar argued it should count toward their five-film Disney commitment, and Michael refused, since it was a sequel. This became another bone of contention between Michael and Steve.

As Pixar's reputation and influence grew with each release, so did the tension with Disney. In Steve's mind, he and Pixar deserved more respect from Disney, and he wanted the contract to reflect the shifting leverage. He also thought, because they were eclipsing Disney both creatively and commercially, that Disney should have turned to them for creative assistance. Instead, he felt Michael always treated them as a lesser partner in the relationship, a studio for hire, which he took as a huge slight.

Michael felt equally disrespected. He and others at Disney believed they were much more than just silent partners in the creation of the films, and that Steve never gave Disney the credit it deserved. I wasn't involved at all in the Pixar relationship during my time as COO, but it was clear that Pixar was gaining swagger as Disney was losing it, and these two strong-willed personalities were destined to battle each other for supremacy.

That was the lay of the land throughout much of 2001—our industry changing at blinding speed; tensions between Michael and Steve threatening the future of a vital partnership; a string of box-office failures leading to a public loss of faith in Disney Animation; sinking ratings at ABC; and a board of directors that was just beginning to take note and question Michael's leadership.

Then came September 11, which would change the world and challenge us in ways we never imagined. I was up that morning at the crack of dawn, working out at home, when I looked up at the TV and saw a report that a plane had just flown into one of the Twin Towers. I stopped my workout and went into another room and turned on the television in time to see the second plane hit. Immediately, I called the president of ABC News, David Westin, to determine what he knew and how we were planning to cover these events that were unfolding before our eyes. David had little information, but like all major news organizations, we were scrambling hundreds of people in many directions—to the Pentagon, the White House, lower Manhattan—to try to understand what was happening.

I rushed to my office and called Michael on my way. He hadn't seen the news yet, but as he turned on his television, we shared our concern—that Disney might also be a target. We made the decision to close down Walt Disney World in Orlando immediately and empty the park, and not to open Disneyland at all. I spent the rest of the day coordinating our response on various fronts—spending hours on the phone with ABC News, making sure all of our people were safe, strategizing security in our parks for the days to come, and generally trying to help people keep calm during what was the most unsettling time of our lives.

Among the many ripple effects of the attacks was a global slowdown in tourism that lasted long after September 11. The impact on Disney's business was devastating. The stock market as a whole fell sharply, and Disney lost nearly a quarter of its value within days of the attacks. Then our largest shareholder, the Bass family, were forced to sell a massive amount of Disney stock—135 million shares, worth about $2 billion—to cover a margin call, which precipitated another steep drop in our share price. Companies around the globe would struggle to recover for some time, but our issues were piling up, and this marked the beginning of a long slide into controversy and strife for Disney, and for Michael.

IN MANY WAYS, he handled the trouble to come admirably and stoically, but it was impossible not to fall prey to pessimism and paranoia as the stress became more intense. I would occasionally answer my phone and Michael would be on the line saying that he'd just been in the shower, or on a plane, or in a conversation over lunch, and had become convinced that something we were doing was going to fail, someone was going to overtake us, some deal was going to go south. He would literally say to me, "The sky is falling," and over time a sense of doom and gloom began to permeate the company.

Michael had plenty of valid reasons to be pessimistic, but as a leader you can't communicate that pessimism to the people around you. It's ruinous to morale. It saps energy and inspiration. Decisions get made from a protective, defensive posture.

Michael's natural pessimism often worked for him, up to a point. He was motivated in part out of a fear of calamity, and that often fueled his perfectionism and his success, although it's not a very useful tool to motivate people. Sometimes his concerns were justified, and it was right to address them, but often a kind of free-floating worry had him in its grip. This wasn't Michael's only state. He also had a natural exuberance that was often infectious. But in his later years, as the stress on him steadily increased, pessimism became the rule more than the exception, and it led him to close ranks and become increasingly cloistered.

No one could have handled the stress that Michael was under perfectly, but optimism in a leader, especially in challenging times, is so vital. Pessimism leads to paranoia, which leads to defensiveness, which leads to risk aversion.

Optimism sets a different machine in motion. Especially in difficult moments, the people you lead need to feel confident in your ability to focus on what matters, and not to operate from a place of defensiveness and self-preservation. This isn't about saying things are good when they're not, and it's not about conveying some innate faith that "things will work out." It's about believing you and the people around you can steer toward the best outcome, and not communicating the feeling that all is lost if things don't break your way. The tone you set as a leader has an enormous effect on the people around you. No one wants to follow a pessimist.

IN THE YEARS after September 11, two key board members, Roy E. Disney and Stanley Gold, who was Roy's lawyer, began to openly express their lack of faith in Michael's ability to run the company. Roy had a long, complicated history with Michael. He was largely responsible for bringing Michael on as CEO and chairman of the board, and along with all shareholders, he benefited greatly under Michael's leadership. Between 1984 and 1994, Disney's annual profits quadrupled, and its stock price increased 1,300 percent.

Michael went out of his way during those years to be solicitous with Roy and show him deference and respect. This wasn't easy to do. Roy could be very difficult at times. He viewed himself as the keeper of the Disney legacy. He lived and breathed and bled Disney, operating as if any break from tradition was a violation of some sacred pact he'd made with Walt himself (who supposedly never showed his nephew much respect). Roy tended to revere the past instead of respecting it, and as a result he had a difficult time tolerating change of any sort. He hated Michael's acquisition of Capital Cities/ABC, because it meant introducing non-Disney brands into the company's bloodstream. On a lesser but maybe more illustrative note, he got very angry one Christmas season when we decided to sell pure white Mickey Mouse plush dolls in our Disney stores. "Mickey is only these colors, black and white and red and yellow, and that's it!" Roy raged in emails to Michael and me. He wanted the "albino Mickeys," as he called them, taken from the shelves, which we didn't do, but it was a huge distraction.

He also had a drinking problem. We never discussed it at Disney while he was alive, but years later one of his kids spoke openly with me about the problems his parents had with alcohol. Roy and his wife, Patti, could get angry after a few drinks, often resulting in vicious late-night emails (I was on the receiving end of several), focused on mistakes he believed we were making as stewards of the Disney legacy.

As the challenges we were facing grew, Roy became more openly critical of Michael, eventually fully turning on him. In 2002, Roy and Stanley sent a letter to the board demanding that Michael address their concerns, which were numerous: the anemic ratings at ABC; the animus with Steve Jobs and Pixar; disagreements over theme-park strategy; and troubles with what they believed was Michael's problematic micromanaging. Their letter was so specific in its grievances that we had no choice but to take it seriously. It resulted in a full management presentation to the board, addressing each issue and how they would be remedied.

It didn't seem to matter. Roy and Stanley spent the better part of a year actively trying to convince the board to oust him, and in the fall of 2003, Michael finally hit his limit with them. Michael's strategy was to turn to the company's governance guidelines regarding board member tenure, which stipulated that board members had to retire at age seventy-two. The rule had never been applied but Roy was challenging Michael in such extreme ways that he decided to invoke the clause. Rather than telling Roy himself, though, Michael had the chairman of the board's nominating committee inform him that he would not be allowed to stand for reelection and would be retired as of the next shareholders meeting in March 2004.

Our next board meeting was scheduled in New York on the Tuesday after Thanksgiving. On Sunday afternoon, Willow and I were on our way to a museum and had plans for a dinner date that evening, when Michael's assistant summoned me to an emergency meeting at Michael's apartment in the Pierre Hotel on East Sixty-first Street. When I arrived, Michael was holding a letter from Roy and Stanley that had been slipped under his door.

He handed it to me and I began to read. Roy stated in the letter that he and Stanley were resigning from the board. He then went on a blistering, three-page critique of Michael's stewardship of the company. The first ten years had been a success, he acknowledged, but the latter years had been defined by seven distinct failures, which Roy laid out point by point:

1) a failure to bring ABC Prime Time back from its ratings abyss; 2) the "consistent micro-management of everyone around you with the resulting loss of morale throughout this company"; 3) a lack of adequate investment in theme parks—building "on the cheap"—that has depressed park attendance; 4) "the perception by all of our stakeholders . . . that the company is rapacious, soulless, and always looking for the 'quick buck' rather than long-term value, which is leading to a loss of public trust"; 5) a creative brain drain from the company due to mismanagement and low morale; 6) a failure to build good relationships with Disney's partners, particularly Pixar; and 7) "your consistent refusal to establish a clear succession plan."

Roy concluded by writing: "Michael, it is my sincere belief that it is you that should be leaving and not me. Accordingly, I once again call for your resignation and retirement."

There was validity to some of Roy's complaints, but many of them were out of context. It didn't matter. We all knew we were on a very rough road now, and we began to strategize for the inevitable public relations nightmare.

The letter was only the beginning. Roy and Stanley soon launched what they called the "Save Disney" campaign. For the next three months, leading up to the annual shareholders meeting in Philadelphia in March 2004, they publicly criticized Michael at every opportunity. They worked to get other members of the board to turn against him. They set up a "Save Disney" website and they aggressively lobbied Disney shareholders to cast a "withhold" vote at the upcoming meeting and dump him from the board. (If you own stock in the company, you receive a proxy, and every year you can cast a vote in favor of individual board members or you can "withhold" your vote of support, which is the equivalent of a no vote.)

While this was going on, the long-simmering animosity between Michael and Steve Jobs finally boiled over. Disney was trying to extend its five-picture partnership deal with Pixar, but Steve put a new deal on the table that was impossible to accept. Pixar would control production and retain all sequel rights, and Disney would be reduced to a distribution partner. Michael refused; Steve wouldn't budge on any counterproposals. In the middle of the prolonged negotiations, an internal memo that Michael wrote to the board before the release of *Finding Nemo* got leaked to the press. In the memo, Michael said that he wasn't impressed by the early cuts he'd seen, and that Pixar would get a "reality check" on what he believed was their unearned arrogance. If *Nemo* didn't do well, he suggested, that wouldn't necessarily be bad, since Disney would have more leverage in the negotiations.

There was nothing Steve was more averse to than someone trying to use leverage over him. If you tried to do that, he went nuts. Michael, too, was averse to anything he perceived as bullying of him or the company, and the combination of the two of them made an already challenging negotiating process nearly impossible. At some point, Steve referred to Disney Animation's string of "embarrassing duds," and then in January 2004, he made a very public, in-your-face announcement that he would never deal with Disney again. "After ten months of trying to strike a deal, we're moving on," he said. "It's a shame Disney won't be participating in Pixar's future successes." Michael responded by saying it didn't matter, we could make all of the sequels we wanted of the Pixar films we'd released and there was nothing they could do about it.

Then Roy and Stanley got involved and issued a statement of their own, saying, "More than a year ago, we warned the Disney board that we believed Michael Eisner was mismanaging the Pixar partnership and expressed our concern that the relationship was in jeopardy," adding fuel to their argument that Michael had lost control of the company.

In fact, Michael had been right to reject Steve's terms. It would have been fiscally irresponsible to accept the deal Steve proposed. The cost to Disney was too high and the benefits were too low. But the public perception, which was amplified by all of the coverage of the busted negotiations and the rift with Steve Jobs, was that Michael had screwed up badly, and it was a blow to him.

Two weeks later, we convened an investors conference in Orlando. The plan was to reassure industry analysts about the future of the company and counter all of the recent damage. Our first-quarter earnings reports were to be released that day, and the numbers were good. *Finding Nemo* and *Pirates of the Caribbean,* which had come out in May and June the previous year, were both massive hits, and overall our revenue was up 19 percent. It was the first blue sky we'd seen in a while, and we were looking forward to making the case that we were back on track.

Things didn't pan out that way. On a cloudy, cool Florida morning, I left my hotel room at around 7:00 A.M. and was on my way to the conference when I received a call from Zenia Mucha, our chief communications officer. Zenia often makes her points emphatically; in this case emphatic was an understatement. "Comcast has gone hostile!" she hollered into the phone. "Get to Michael's suite now!"

Comcast was the largest cable provider in the country, but Brian Roberts, their CEO, knew that owning Disney would transform them. It would allow them to marry Disney's content with their vast cable distribution network, which would be a potent combination. (They were especially interested in ESPN, which at the time was the highest-priced channel in cable TV.)

A few days earlier, Brian had called Michael and made an offer to buy Disney. Michael told him he wasn't going to engage in negotiations, but if he wanted to make an official offer, the board would be obligated to consider it. "But we're not for sale," Michael said. The rejection resulted in a hostile, unsolicited public offer to the Disney board and its shareholders to acquire Disney for $64 billion, to be paid in Comcast stock. (For every share of Disney stock they owned, shareholders would get .78 a share of Comcast stock.)

When I walked into Michael's suite, the first thing I heard were the voices of Brian Roberts and Steve Burke, Comcast's president, giving a live interview on CNBC. I knew Steve well. He had worked for me for two years, from 1996 to 1998, and had been with Disney for ten years before that, most recently at Disneyland Paris. When Michael replaced him there and brought him back to New York, Steve came to work for me at ABC. He's the eldest son of my old boss, Dan Burke, whom I deeply respected and loved, and while he didn't have Dan's natural warmth, Steve was smart and funny and a fast learner. I taught him a lot about the TV and radio businesses, and he taught me a lot about navigating the ins and outs of Disney.

In 1998, I badly needed someone to take over ABC and free me up to do the other aspects of my job, and I told Steve I was planning to promote him to president of the network. He said that he didn't want to move to L.A. (Michael was planning to move all of ABC to L.A. at the time), and shortly after that, he told us he was leaving Disney for Comcast. I'd invested so much in him, and we'd grown close over those two years, that it felt like a knife in my back. Now here he was on television, twisting it further. When asked what he would do to fix the network, Steve replied, "Bring in better people to run it."

Zenia and Alan Braverman, our general counsel, and Peter Murphy, the head of Strategic Planning, were already there in Michael's suite when I arrived, staring at the TV. We were all caught completely off guard by the takeover bid, and immediately scrambled to formulate a response. We needed to put out a public statement, but first we had to find out where the board stood. At the same time we were trying to figure out what made Brian so certain Disney would sell in the first place? Soon it became apparent that someone, either inside the board or close to it, must have told him that Michael was vulnerable and Disney in such bad shape that if he made an offer, the board would go for it. It would give the board a less confrontational way to get rid of Michael. (Years later, Brian confirmed to me that an intermediary, claiming to represent a board member, encouraged him to bid.)

As we struggled to collect ourselves together, another wave hit that we didn't see coming. A company called Institutional Shareholder Services (ISS) is the biggest company in the world providing proxy and governance advice to investors—largely mid-sized funds—on how they should assess corporate governance and cast their proxy votes. ISS typically influences more than a third of the voting shares in a proxy election, and that morning they issued a public recommendation in support of Roy and Stanley's campaign to vote against Michael. The proxy votes wouldn't be announced until March, but we already knew to expect a large vote of no confidence.

As we left Michael's suite to go to the investors' meeting, we were now facing two massive crises. I remember thinking that it was like we'd entered a conventional war with Roy and Stanley and Steve, and now another party had launched nuclear weapons. We did our best under the circumstances to defend ourselves to the investors, but serious concerns about the future of the company had been raised in very public ways. We held our heads high, touting our recent returns and walking them through our future plans, making the best case we could under the circumstances. It was a tough meeting, though, and there was no way around it: Things were only going to get tougher.

OVER THE NEXT several weeks, Comcast's takeover bid collapsed. Brian Roberts had assumed that Disney's board would jump at his initial offer, and when they didn't, it allowed for a number of other factors to emerge. First, the announcement of our increased earnings resulted in a spike in our stock price, so we immediately became more expensive. Second, Comcast's shareholders reacted negatively to the announcement. They weren't in support of Brian's move, and Comcast's stock price sank fast, diminishing the offer even further and throwing the whole calculus off. Last, influencing all of this was a general public opposition to the deal being expressed to the media: that "Disney" still had emotional resonance as an American brand, and the idea of its being swallowed by a giant cable provider was anathema to consumers. Comcast eventually withdrew its bid.

Michael's troubles weren't going away, however. The following month, three thousand Disney shareholders gathered in Philadelphia for our annual meeting. The night before the meeting, Roy and Stanley and the Save Disney contingent held a big public rally at a downtown hotel. There was a lot of media coverage of the event, in which Roy and Stanley vehemently criticized Michael and called for a change in leadership. At some point Zenia came to me and said, "You have to go out and talk to the press. We need to get our side of the story out." There was no way Michael was going to do it—it would have been too charged and confrontational—so I had to be the one.

Zenia quickly notified some members of the press that I would be coming out to speak with them, and the two of us walked into the lobby of the convention center, where our meeting was to take place the next day. Seventy-five giant, differently designed Mickey Mouse statues had been transported from Orlando for the meeting, and I stood between two of them and took questions for about an hour. I didn't have any notes prepared, and I don't recall the specific questions, though I'm sure they were all about the shareholder meeting, and how we were planning to respond to the criticisms coming from Roy and Stanley. I do recall that it was withering. I defended the company and supported Michael, and I expressed my genuine skepticism about Roy and Stanley's motivations and actions. It was the first time in my career I've ever had to withstand the glare of so much press scrutiny, and while there was no way to reverse the tide that was coming in, I look back on that moment and feel proud for having been able to stand there and hold my ground.

THE NEXT DAY, shareholders started lining up outside the convention center at 5:00 A.M. When the doors opened hours later, thousands of people streamed in, many of whom were sent into a large overflow room to watch on closed-circuit TV. Michael and I made opening remarks; then each of our business-unit leaders gave presentations about the state of their businesses and future plans.

We had agreed to allow Roy and Stanley to each make fifteen-minute statements, but not from the stage. When they went beyond the time limit, we let them finish out of courtesy. Their statements were blistering, and greeted with cheers by many people in the room. After they were done we took questions for an hour. Michael knew it would be an all-out assault from the beginning, but he carried himself through it admirably. He acknowledged many of the difficulties and made his case that our performance and our stock price were improving. He talked about his passion for the company, but it was a foregone conclusion that the day was not going to end well for him.

When the proxy votes were finally tallied, 43 percent of shareholders withheld their support of Michael. It was such a devastating expression of no confidence that we announced the count in raw numbers rather than as a percentage, hoping it might sound less bad. Still, there was an audible gasp in the room when the announcement was made.

The board met in an executive session immediately after the shareholders meeting. They knew they had to do something in response and decided to strip Michael of his role as chairman but let him remain as CEO. George Mitchell, the former Senate majority leader from Maine, was a member of the board, and they unanimously voted for him to replace Michael as chairman. Michael made some effort to convince them otherwise, but he was mostly resigned to the inevitability of it.

There was one final indignity to the day. The news was so big that our own news program, *Nightline,* wanted to devote that night's show to the Save Disney movement and the voting results. We collectively decided that it was in Michael's and the company's best interest to face the music and go on the show to take questions from Ted Koppel, *Nightline*'s anchor, about what it meant for Michael and for the future of Disney. It was incredibly painful for him to be subjected to scrutiny from his own news people, but he did it with a brave face.

The March shareholders meeting and the loss of his chairman's title marked the beginning of the end for Michael, and the reality was beginning to sink in. In early September 2004, he sent a letter to the board announcing that he would step down when his contract expired in 2006. Two weeks later, the board met and accepted Michael's offer. George Mitchell came to me afterward to say they were going to issue a press release announcing that Michael would not renew his contract when it expired, and a search process would commence immediately, with the intention of finding a successor by June 2005. Once they found someone, George told me, they would hasten the transition—in other words, they intended to replace Michael in the fall of 2005, a year before his contract expired.

I asked him what they were planning to say about the search.

"That we're going to look for outside candidates and inside candidates," George said.

"What inside candidates are there other than me?"

"None," he said. "You're the only one."

"Then you need to write that," I said. "I'm the COO, and as of today, you're making Michael a lame duck. I'm going to have to step in and exert a lot more authority." I understood there was no guarantee that I would be Michael's successor, but people in the company needed to know it was at least a possibility.

I felt so much depended on that moment. If the rest of the company didn't believe I was a serious candidate, then I'd have no real authority, and I would be a lame duck right along with Michael. Often people who worry too much about public perception of their power do so because they are insecure. In this case, I needed the board to bestow some degree of power in me if I was going to be able to help run the company through this turbulent time, and if I was going to have any chance of being the next CEO.

"What are you asking?" George said.

"I'm asking you to write in the press release that I'm the only internal candidate."

George understood exactly what I needed and why, and I'll always be grateful for that. It meant I was able to run the company from a position of . . . not exactly strength, but not exactly weakness, either. Even though they'd formally stated that I was a candidate, I don't think anyone on the board, maybe not even George, thought I would get the job, and many of them thought I shouldn't.

There would be a lot of talk during the upcoming months about how Disney's problems could only be solved by a "change agent" from the outside. It's a meaningless phrase and a corporate cliche, but the sentiment was clear. Exacerbating matters was the feeling on the board that their reputation had been sullied, and while it was far less painful to them than what Michael had suffered, they were exhausted from the drama and they needed to send a signal now that things were going to be different. Handing the keys to the guy who'd been Michael's number two through five of the most difficult years in the company's history didn't exactly signal a new day.

CHAPTER 7

IT'S ABOUT THE FUTURE

THE CHALLENGE FOR me was: How do I convince the Disney board that I was the change they were looking for without criticizing Michael in the process? There had been some decisions I disagreed with, and I thought the company was in need of change given all the noise, but I respected Michael and was grateful for the opportunities he'd given me. I'd also been COO of the company for five years, and it would have been hypocritical, transparently so, to lay all of the blame on someone else. Mostly, though, it just wouldn't have been right to make myself look better at Michael's expense. I vowed to myself not to do that.

I spent a few days after the announcement trying to figure out a way to thread that particular needle—how to talk about the past without implicating myself too much in decisions that weren't mine, or swinging too far the other way and joining in a pile-on of Michael. The solution to that predicament came from an unexpected place. A week or so after the board's announcement, I received a phone call from a highly regarded political consultant and brand manager named Scott Miller. Years ago, Scott had done some very useful consulting for ABC, so when he called to say he was in L.A. and asked if he could come see me, I was eager to meet with him.

He arrived in my office a few days later and dropped a ten-page deck in front of me. "This is for you," he said. "It's free." I asked what it was. "This is our campaign playbook," he said.

"Campaign?"

"What you're about to embark on is a political campaign," he said. "You understand that, right?"

In some abstract way, yes, I understood that, but I hadn't been thinking of it in the literal terms Scott meant. I needed a strategy for getting votes, he said, which meant figuring out who on the board might be persuadable and focusing my message on them. He asked me a series of questions: "Which board members are definitely in your corner?"

"I'm not sure any of them are."

"Okay, who's never going to give you a chance?" Three or four names and faces immediately flashed through my mind. "Now, who are the swing voters?" There were a handful whom I thought I might be able to convince to take a flyer on me. "Those are the ones you have to focus on first," Scott said.

He also understood the bind I was in regarding how I talked about Michael and the past, and he'd already anticipated it. "You cannot win this as an incumbent," he said. "You cannot win on the defensive. It's only about the future. It's not about the past."

That may seem obvious, but it came as a revelation to me. I didn't have to rehash the past. I didn't have to defend Michael's decisions. I didn't have to criticize him for my own benefit. It's only about the future. Every time a question came up about what had gone wrong at Disney over the past years, what mistakes Michael made, and why they should think I'm any different, my response could simply and honestly be: "I can't do anything about the past. We can talk about lessons learned, and we can make sure we apply those lessons going forward. But we don't get any do-overs. You want to know where I'm going to take this company, not where it's been. Here's my plan."

"You must think, plan, and act like an insurgent," Scott told me, and your plan should be formed with one clear thought in mind: "This is a battle for the soul of the brand. Talk about the brand, how to grow its value, how to protect it." Then he added, "You're going to need some strategic priorities." I'd given this considerable thought, and I immediately started ticking off a list. I was five or six in when he shook his head and said, "Stop talking. Once you have that many of them, they're no longer priorities." Priorities are the few things that you're going to spend a lot of time and a lot of capital on. Not only do you undermine their significance by having too many, but nobody is going to remember them all. "You're going to seem unfocused," he said. "You only get three. I can't tell you what those three should be. We don't have to figure that out today. You never have to tell me what they are if you don't want to. But you only get three."

He was right. In my eagerness to demonstrate that I had a strategy for solving all of Disney's problems and addressing all of the issues we were confronting, I hadn't prioritized any of them. There was no signaling as to what was most important, no easily digested, comprehensive vision. My overall vision lacked clarity and inspiration.

A company's culture is shaped by a lot of things, but this is one of the most important—you have to convey your priorities clearly and repeatedly. In my experience, it's what separates great managers from the rest. If leaders don't articulate their priorities clearly, then the people around them don't know what their own priorities should be. Time and energy and capital get wasted. People in your organization suffer unnecessary anxiety because they don't know what they should be focused on. Inefficiency sets in, frustration builds up, morale sinks.

You can do a lot for the morale of the people around you (and therefore the people around them) just by taking the guesswork out of their day-to-day life. A CEO must provide the company and its senior team with a road map. A lot of work is complex and requires intense amounts of focus and energy, but this kind of messaging is fairly simple: This is where we want to be. This is how we're going to get there. Once those things are laid out simply, so many decisions become easier to make, and the overall anxiety of an entire organization is lowered.

After the meeting with Scott, I quickly landed on three clear strategic priorities. They have guided the company since the moment I was named CEO:

1) We needed to devote most of our time and capital to the creation of high-quality branded content. In an age when more and more "content" was being created and distributed, we needed to bet on the fact that quality will matter more and more. It wasn't enough to create lots of content; and it wasn't even enough to create lots of *good* content. With an explosion of choice, consumers needed an ability to make decisions about how to spend their time and money. Great brands would become even more powerful tools for guiding consumer behavior.

2) We needed to embrace technology to the fullest extent, first by using it to enable the creation of higher quality products, and then to reach more consumers in more modern, more relevant ways. From the earliest Disney years under Walt, technology was always viewed as a powerful storytelling tool; now it was time to double down on our commitment to doing the same thing. It was also becoming clear that while we were still, and would remain, primarily a content creator, the day would come when modern distribution would be an essential means of maintaining brand relevance. Unless consumers had the ability to consume our content in more user-friendly, more mobile, and more digital ways, our relevance would be challenged. In short, we needed to view technology as more of an opportunity than a threat, and we had to do so with commitment, enthusiasm, and a sense of urgency.

3) We needed to become a truly global company. We were broad with our reach, doing business in numerous markets around the world, but we needed to better penetrate certain markets, particularly the world's most populous countries, like China and India. If our primary focus was on creating excellent branded content, the next step was to bring that content to a global audience, firmly planting our roots in those markets and creating a strong foundation to grow significantly in scale. To continue to create the same things for the same loyal customers was stagnation.

That was the vision. It was about the future, not the past—and the future was about organizing the entire company's mission, all of our businesses, and every one of our 130,000 employees at the time, around these three priorities. Now I just needed to convince ten board members, most of whom had little or no faith in me, that this was the right course for the company and I was the right person for the job.

MY FIRST ALL-ON-ONE interview with the board took place on a Sunday evening in our boardroom in Burbank. They questioned me for two hours, and while they weren't openly combative, they weren't especially warm and friendly, either. They had been under pressure for a long time, and now they were under even more. Their determination to project how seriously they were taking this process was evident in their no-nonsense demeanor. It was clear that my having been on the board myself for five years wasn't going to make the road any smoother.

It so happened that months before I'd committed to participating in a triathlon in Malibu that day, and I didn't want to leave my team in the lurch. So I woke at 4:00 A.M. and drove to Malibu in the dark, rode the eighteen-mile bike leg of the race, then sped home and showered and changed and went to Burbank for my meeting with the board. At the last minute, to keep my energy from slumping during the interview, I devoured a protein bar right before I walked through the door. For the next two hours, my stomach loudly gurgled, and I worried the board was thinking that my GI system was sending a signal to them that I couldn't handle the pressure.

The good news was that this was my first opportunity to show them my plan. I laid out the three core principles, and then I fielded several questions about the poor state of morale within the company. "There is still tremendous passion for the brand," I said. "But my goal is for Disney to be the most admired company in the world, by our consumers and our shareholders and by our employees. That last part is key. We'll never get the admiration or the public unless we get it from our own people first. And the way to get the people working for us to admire the company and believe in its future is to make products they're proud of. It's that simple."

There was another, more practical issue that I mentioned regarding morale. Over the years we'd become a company in which virtually all noncreative decisions were made by the central oversight group, Strategic Planning, that I mentioned earlier. Strat Planning was composed of about sixty-five analysts with MBAs from the best business schools in the country. They occupied the fourth floor of our headquarters, and as the company expanded, Michael depended on them more and more to analyze all of our decisions and dictate the strategies for our various businesses.

In many ways, this made sense. They were very good at what they did, but it created two problems. One was something I alluded to previously, that the centralized decision making had a demoralizing effect on the senior leaders of our businesses, who sensed that the power to run their divisions really resided at Strategic Planning. The other was that their overly analytical decision-making processes could be painstaking and slow. "The world is moving so much faster than it did even a couple of years ago," I said to the board. "And the speed with which things are happening is only going to increase. Our decision making has to be straighter and faster, and I need to explore ways of doing that."

I assumed that if the leaders of our businesses felt more involved in making decisions, that would have a positive, trickle-down effect on the company's morale. I had no idea at the time how dramatic and immediate that effect would be.

THE SIX-MONTH PROCESS that followed that initial interview with the board tested me more than anything in my career. I'd never been more challenged intellectually—in terms of business intelligence, anyway—never done more intensive thinking about how our company operated and what needed fixing, never processed so much information in such a short amount of time. I was doing all of that on top of the day-to-day demands of helping to run the company (Michael was there, but his attention was often understandably elsewhere), and the long, stressful days began to wear on me.

The strain wasn't primarily because of the workload. I've always prided myself on my ability and willingness to put in a greater effort than anyone else. For me, the hardest test by far was managing the public scrutiny and the overtly expressed opinions that I should not be the next CEO. The Disney succession was an important business story, and the reporting around it—What was the board thinking? Who was in the mix? Could the company be righted?—was relentless. The consensus among business analysts and commentators largely echoed the opinions of those board members opposed to me: Disney needed fresh blood, a new perspective. Choosing Iger amounted to a giant rubber stamp of Michael Eisner.

It wasn't just the press, though. Early in the process, Jeffrey Katzenberg met me for breakfast near the Disney lot in Burbank. "You need to leave," Jeffrey told me. "You're not going to get this job. Your reputation has been tarnished." I knew that distinguishing myself from Michael was going to be a struggle, but I hadn't up to that point considered that the outside world perceived me as being tainted. Jeffrey felt a need to disabuse me of that idea. There was no separating me from the mess of the last few years, he said. "You should go do some pro bono work to rehabilitate your image."

Rehabilitate my image? I heard him out and tried to remain calm, but I was stunned, and angry, by Jeffrey's certainty that I was done. Still another part of me wondered if he was right. Maybe I didn't fully comprehend what everyone else around me could see plain as day: that there was no way I was getting this job. Or maybe this was all just Hollywood Kremlinology and the biggest task before me was to continue to make the best case I could make for myself and ignore all of the distractions that I couldn't control.

It's so easy to get caught up in rumor mills, to worry about this person's perception of you or that person's, what someone might say or write about you. It's easy to become defensive and petty and to want to lash out when you feel you're being unfairly misrepresented. I didn't believe I *deserved* this job; I didn't think I was entitled to it, but I did believe I was right for it. Part of proving that was remaining steady in the face of so much publicly expressed doubt. I still recall one headline, in the *Orlando Sentinel,* that said "Eisner's Heir Far from Apparent." Many others expressed similar sentiments, and for a while it seemed that every day someone was writing or talking about what an abdication of responsibility it would be if the board named me CEO. Stanley Gold was quoted in another publication saying I was "a gentleman and a hard-working executive, but most of the Disney board have open questions about whether [I] should succeed Michael." That had an ominous tone to it. There was one board member, Gary Wilson, who not only didn't think I should get the job, but clearly thought he could further his own agenda by baiting me and attempting to humiliate me in our meetings. I had to consistently remind myself that Gary Wilson wasn't my problem. As much as this process was a test of my ideas, it was also a test of my temperament, and I couldn't let the negativity being expressed by people who knew little about me affect the way I felt about myself.

By the end of the process, I would be interviewed fifteen times: that first all-on-one interview; then one-on-one interviews with every member of the board; then follow-up interviews with board members who requested them; then one of the most insulting experiences of my career, an interview with a headhunter named Gerry Roche, who ran a well-known search firm called Heidrick and Struggles.

Gerry had been hired by the board to "benchmark" me against the outside candidates and to help the board field candidates they did not know. When I learned of this, I complained to George Mitchell that it was offensive and that I'd already answered everything that could be asked of me. "Just do it," George said. "The board wants to check off every box."

So I flew to New York for a lunch meeting at Gerry's office. We sat in a conference room, with only water on the table. Gerry held a copy of James Stewart's *DisneyWar,* which had just been published and which investigated—and in several instances reported inaccurately—Michael's years as CEO and mine as COO. The book had Post-it notes on several pages, to mark the passages he wanted to challenge me on. He flipped through the book and asked me a series of questions that had little or nothing to do with me. Thirty minutes into the interview, Gerry's assistant came in with a single brown-bagged lunch, for him, and told him the private jet that was going to take him to a wedding in Florida was leaving soon, and he had to go or he was going to miss it. With that, he got up and left. I never ate, and I walked out of the interview infuriated at the waste of time and the lack of respect.

There was only one time that the stress and frustration truly got to me. It was January 2005, several months into the process, and I'd taken my six-year-old son, Max, to an L.A. Clippers game at the Staples Center. In the middle of the game, my skin began to feel clammy. My chest tightened, and I felt short of breath. Both of my parents had suffered heart attacks at fifty. I was fifty-four at the time and I knew the symptoms. In fact, I'd always lived in fear of having one. Part of me was sure this was it, and another part was sure it couldn't be. I ate well, worked out seven days a week, had regular checkups. I couldn't be experiencing a heart attack, could I? I debated calling for an EMT at the game, but was worried about frightening Max.

Instead, I told him I was feeling sick to my stomach, and we left for home. There was a driving rainstorm in L.A. that afternoon, and I was barely able to see the road. My heart felt like it was getting squeezed by a fist inside my chest. I knew it was foolish to be behind the wheel with my son in the backseat, and I worried that I'd made a terrible mistake. In the moment, though, I could only think that I needed to get home. I pulled into our driveway, Max jumped out of the car, and I immediately phoned my internist, Dennis Evangelatos, then called a friend who came and drove me to Dennis's house. Dennis knew me well and he was aware of the stress I'd been under. He checked my vital signs, then looked me square in the eye and said, "You're having a classic anxiety attack, Bob. You have to get some rest."

It was a relief, but also a worry. I'd always thought of myself as somewhat impervious to stress, able to stay focused and calm in tense situations. The strain of this process was taking a bigger toll than I'd admitted even to myself, much less to my family or close friends, and a bigger toll than it should take. I left Dennis's house and got home and took some time to put everything that was happening into perspective. It was a big job, and a big title, but it wasn't my life. My life was with Willow and my boys, with my girls back in New York, with my parents and my sister and my friends. All of this strain was ultimately still about a job, and I vowed to myself to try to keep that in perspective.

The only time I cracked in front of the board was in my final interview with them. After months of interviews and presentations, they called for one more, a Sunday evening meeting in a hotel conference room in Pasadena. I arrived to learn that they had spent the afternoon at one of the board member's homes interviewing Meg Whitman, the CEO of eBay, who was the other main contender at that point. (The other four had either dropped out or been eliminated.) By then, I had had it with the whole process. I couldn't believe there was anything left that they didn't know, any question that hadn't already been answered thoroughly several times over. I wanted it to come to an end. The company, which had been facing an uncertain future for half a year now—much longer, if you added in the months of turmoil around Michael's future—needed it to come to an end even more. Some members of the board didn't comprehend this, and I had hit the limits of my patience.

Toward the end of that final interview, Gary Wilson, the board member who had been goading me to disparage Michael throughout the entire process, asked me one more time: "Tell us why we should believe that you are different. What do you think Michael did wrong? What would you do differently?" It struck a nerve, and I lashed back at him in front of the rest of the board. "You've asked me the same questions on three prior occasions," I said, struggling to keep myself from hollering. "I find it offensive, and I'm not going to answer it."

Everyone in the room went silent, and the interview came to an abrupt end. I stood up and left without looking any of them in the eye. I didn't shake anyone's hand. I didn't thank them for their time. I'd flunked my self-imposed test to withstand anything they threw at me with patience and respect. That night, George Mitchell and another board member, Aylwin Lewis, each called me at home. "You probably didn't do yourself irreparable harm," George said, "but you didn't do yourself much good, either." Aylwin was harsher. "This wasn't the time to let everyone see you sweat, Bob," he said.

I wasn't happy I'd done it, but I was human. I couldn't take it back at that point, anyway, and I felt my anger was justified. At the end of my conversation with George, I said, "Please just make a decision. It's time. The company is suffering because of all this."

When I look back on that time now, I think of it as a hard-earned lesson about the importance of tenacity and perseverance, but also about the need to steer clear of anger and anxiety over things you can't control. I can't overstate how important it is to keep blows to the ego, real as they often are, from occupying too big a place in your mind and sapping too much of your energy. It's easy to be optimistic when everyone is telling you you're great. It's much harder, and much more necessary, when your sense of yourself is being challenged, and in such a public way.

The succession process was the first time in my career that I had to face that level of anxiety head on. It was impossible to completely filter out the chatter about me or to not be hurt by very public conversations about how ill-suited I was for the job. But I learned, through strong self-discipline and love from my family, that I had to recognize it for what it was—that it had no bearing on who I was—and put it in its proper place. I could control what I did and how I comported myself. Everything else was beyond my control. I didn't maintain that perspective every moment, but to the extent that I was able to, it kept the anxiety from having too strong a hold.

ON A SATURDAY in March 2005, the board convened to make its decision. Most of the members called into the meeting; Michael and George Mitchell were together in a conference room at ABC in New York.

I woke up that morning thinking I might have convinced enough of the "undecided" members of the board to give me the job, but when I thought of all the drama and scrutiny around the process, it felt just as possible that they would go another way, that some of the skeptics would have argued forcefully for a change in the narrative, and they would name an outsider.

I spent the day with my two boys, trying to distract myself. Max and I tossed a ball around, went to lunch, and spent an hour in his favorite neighborhood park. I told Willow that if bad news came, I was getting in my car and taking the cross-country drive that I'd long dreamed of taking. A solo trip across the United States seemed like heaven to me.

As soon as that meeting ended, George Mitchell and Michael called me at home. Willow was with me in the office we shared. The job of CEO was mine, they said; it would be announced the next day. I appreciated that Michael was on the call. I knew it must have been painful for him. He'd poured himself into that job and wasn't quite ready to relinquish it, but if he had to be succeeded by someone, I believe he was happy that that person was me.

I was grateful to George for the way he had treated me throughout the process. If not for him, I don't think I would have gotten a fair shake by the rest of the board.

Mostly, I was thankful for Willow. I couldn't have done it without her faith and wisdom and support. She was rooting for me the whole time, of course, but time after time, she told me this was not the most important thing in my life, in our lives. I knew she was right, but taking her words to heart took work, too, and she helped me do that. Once the call ended, Willow and I sat quietly for a moment, trying to savor it all. I had a mental list of the people I wanted to call right away, and I was fighting the urge to start dialing and instead trying to just be still, to breathe a bit, to let in both the elation and the relief.

Eventually, I called my parents in Long Island. They were proud, if a little incredulous that their son was going to be running the company founded by Walt Disney. Then I called my daughters in New York, and my old Capital Cities bosses, Dan Burke and Tom Murphy. And then I called Steve Jobs. It was an odd call to make, but it felt important to me to reach out to him, in case there might still someday be a chance of salvaging the relationship with Pixar.

I barely knew Steve at that point, but I wanted him to know that it was going to be announced the next day that I was the next CEO of the company. His response was basically "Okay, well, that's cool for you." I told him that I'd love to come see him and try to convince him that we could work together, that things could be different. He was typical Steve. "How long have you worked for Michael?"

"Ten years."

"Huh," he said. "Well, I don't see how things will be any different, but, sure, when the dust settles, be in touch."

PART TWO

LEADING

CHAPTER 8

THE POWER OF RESPECT

THERE WAS A six-month waiting period between my appointment and Michael's exit from Disney. I had plenty to focus on running the company day to day, but I was looking forward to taking a breather and spending some time gathering my thoughts after the long succession process. I figured the clock on my "first 100 days" would start when Michael walked out the door, and until then I could fly somewhat under the radar and be patient and methodical in my plans.

I couldn't have been more wrong. Immediately after the announcement, everyone—the press, the investment community, the rest of the industry, Disney employees—was asking the same thing: What's your strategy for fixing the company and how fast can you implement it? Because of its history, and because Michael had so dramatically transformed it, Disney has always been one of the most scrutinized corporations in the world. The very public struggles we'd endured over the last few years only increased intrigue around who I was and what I was going to do. There were a lot of skeptics who still saw me as a temporary CEO, a short-term patch until the board could identify a star from the outside. Curiosity was high, and expectations were low, and I quickly realized that I needed to define our direction and get some key things done before my tenure officially began.

In week one of my CEO-in-waiting period, I called my closest advisers—Tom Staggs, who was now CFO; Alan Braverman, our general counsel; and Zenia Mucha, our communications chief—into my office and ticked off a list of the most critical things to accomplish in the next six months. "First, we have to try to bury the hatchet with Roy," I said. Roy Disney had felt vindicated to some extent by the fact that Michael was forced to leave, but he was still angry that the board hadn't acted sooner, and he was critical of their decision to give me the job, especially after I'd spoken publicly in Michael's defense. I didn't believe there was much Roy could do practically to undermine me at this point, but I felt it was important for the image of the company not to be in an ongoing battle with a member of the Disney family.

"Second, we have to try to salvage a relationship with Pixar and Steve Jobs." The end of the Pixar partnership was a huge blow to Disney, from both a financial and a public-relations standpoint. Steve was one of the most respected people in the world at that point—in technology and business and culture—and his rejection and withering criticism of Disney was so public that any mending of that fence would be seen as a big early win. Plus, Pixar was now the standard-bearer in animation, and while I didn't yet have a complete sense of just how broken Disney Animation was, I knew that any renewed partnership would be good for our business. I also knew that chances were slim that someone as headstrong as Steve would be open to something. But I had to try.

Last, I needed to begin the process of changing the way we made decisions, which meant restructuring Strat Planning, changing its size, its influence, and its mission. If the first two priorities were largely about how the public perceived us, this one was about

THE POWER OF RESPECT

transforming the perception of the company from within. It would take a while, and there would certainly be anger and resistance to contend with from Strat Planning, but we had to start reconfiguring the apparatus and pushing strategic responsibility back to the businesses sooner rather than later. I hoped that if we could reduce the grip that Strat Planning had over all of our divisions, we would slowly begin to restore the company's morale.

First, though, was the rapprochement with Roy Disney. Before I could even reach out to him, however, the prospects for peace blew up. Within days after the announcement of my promotion was made, Roy and Stanley Gold sued the board for what they said was a "fraudulent succession process." It was an absurd charge—that the fix was in and it was a foregone conclusion that I'd get the job—but it was also going to be a major distraction. I hadn't even begun the job and I already had my first crisis: an ugly, public lawsuit over my legitimacy as CEO.

I decided to call Stanley on my own, not through a lawyer, to see if he would be willing to sit down and talk. Until he and Roy resigned in the fall of 2003, Stanley and I had served on the board together. It was obvious to me over those few years that Stanley didn't respect me, but I thought he would at least be willing to hear me out. He was less emotional and more practical than Roy, and I suspected that I might be able to make him see that a long legal battle with Disney wasn't in anyone's interest. He agreed to talk, and we met at the country club to which he belonged that's not far from the Disney lot.

I began by describing to Stanley the gauntlet I had just endured: the many interviews, the outside search firm, the numerous candidates the board had considered, the six months of incessant public scrutiny. "It was a thorough process," I said. "They devoted a lot of time to their decision." I wanted Stanley to fully grasp that his lawsuit was without merit and not likely to succeed.

He went over all the old ground with me, rehashing yet again the litany of his and Roy's criticisms of Michael and the way the company had been run for the last several years. I didn't debate him, just heard him out, and reiterated that all of that was in the past and that the board's process had been legitimate. Late in the conversation, Stanley became less argumentative. He suggested that a lot of this animosity was because Roy was hurt, despite having preemptively resigned in protest, that Michael was invoking our mandatory board retirement age to push him off the board, which was disrespectful. Roy's relationship with the place he thought of as home had been severed, Stanley said. Roy blamed the board for not listening to him when he'd launched the campaign to unseat Michael in the first place. They'd eventually gotten rid of him, but Roy felt that he, too, had paid an unfair price in all of this.

At the end of our conversation, Stanley said, "If you can come up with any means of bringing Roy back, we'll drop the lawsuit." I never expected him to say that out loud, but I left the meeting and immediately called George Mitchell. George was eager to close this chapter, too, and he implored me to figure out a way to work something out. I called Stanley back and told him I wanted to speak with Roy directly. I wasn't hopeful, but I felt certain that the only way forward was to clear the air face-to-face.

Roy and I met at the same country club. It was a frank and not especially pleasant conversation. I told him I was well aware of his disdain for me, but I asked him to accept the reality that I'd been appointed CEO and that the process wasn't rigged. "Roy," I said, "if I fail, the line of people demanding my head will be a lot longer than you and Stanley."

He made clear that he would gladly continue to wage war with the company if he didn't think it was heading in the right direction, but he also showed a vulnerable side I'd never seen before. Being alienated from the company was painful for him, and the ongoing fight seemed to have worn him out. He'd aged considerably in the two years since he'd left the board, and he struck me as needy and frail in a way he hadn't in the past. I wondered if all of this wasn't a part of some larger psychic struggle. The truth was, it wasn't just

Michael who was at odds with Roy; besides Stanley, not enough people within Disney had given him the respect he felt he deserved, including his long-gone uncle, Walt. I had never had any real connection to Roy, but I detected vulnerability in him now. There was nothing to be gained by making him feel smaller or insulted. He was just someone looking for respect, and getting it had never been especially easy for him. It was so personal, and involved so much pride and ego, and this battle of his had been going on for decades.

Once I saw Roy in that light, I began to think that maybe there was a way to appease him and put this fight to rest. Whatever I did, though, I didn't want to allow him to be too close to me or the company, for fear that he would inevitably try to start an insurgency from within. I also couldn't agree to anything that would be seen as disrespectful toward Michael, or look like a validation of Roy's criticisms of him, so a delicate balance was required. I called Michael and explained my predicament and asked his advice. He wasn't happy to hear that I was offering an olive branch to Roy, but he acknowledged that peace with him was important. "I trust you to do the right thing," he said. "But don't let him in too far."

I contacted Stanley once more and proposed the following: I would give Roy an emeritus role on the board and would invite him to film premieres and theme-park openings and special company events. (He wouldn't attend board meetings, however.) I'd also give him a small consulting fee and an office on the lot so he could come and go and call Disney his home again. In exchange, there would be no lawsuit, no public proclamation of victory, and no more airing of criticisms. I was stunned when Stanley said we should draw up an agreement to be executed within twenty-four hours.

Just like that, a crisis that threatened to loom over my early days as CEO was resolved. Making peace with Roy and Stanley would be viewed by some parties as a kind of capitulation, but I knew the truth, and that was far more valuable than perception.

The drama with Roy reinforced something that tends not to get enough attention when people talk about succeeding in business, which is: Don't let your ego get in the way of making the best possible decision. I was stung when Roy and Stanley sued the board for choosing me as CEO, and I certainly could have gone to battle with them and prevailed, but it all would have come at a huge cost to the company and been a giant distraction from what really mattered. My job was to set our company on a new path, and the first step was to defuse this unnecessary struggle. The easiest and most productive way to do that was to recognize that what Roy needed, ultimately, was to feel respected. That was precious to him, and it cost me and the company so little.

A little respect goes a long way, and the absence of it is often very costly. Over the next few years, as we made the major acquisitions that redefined and revitalized the company, this simple, seemingly trite idea was as important as all of the data-crunching in the world: If you approach and engage people with respect and empathy, the seemingly impossible can become real.

ONCE THE PEACE accord with Roy was signed, my next task was to explore if there was any chance of repairing Disney's relationship with Steve Jobs and Pixar. Two months after I'd called Steve to tell him I'd been named CEO, I reached out to him again. My ultimate goal was to somehow make things right with Pixar, but I couldn't ask for that initially. Steve's animosity toward Disney was too deep-rooted. The rift that had opened between Steve and Michael was a clash between two strong-willed people whose companies' fortunes were going in different directions. When Michael criticized the tech industry for not having enough respect for content, Steve was insulted. When Steve suggested Disney was creatively broken, Michael was insulted. Michael had been a creative executive his whole life. Steve believed that because he ran Pixar, which was the ascendant animation studio, he knew better. When Disney Animation began to slip even further, Steve became more haughty with Michael because he felt we needed him more, and Michael hated that Steve had the upper hand.

I had nothing to do with any of that, but it didn't matter. My asking Steve to just change his mind, after he'd so publicly ended the partnership and excoriated Disney, would be far too simple for him. There was no way it was going to be that easy.

I had an idea unrelated to Pixar, though, that I thought might interest him. I told him I was a huge music lover and that I had all of my music stored on my iPod, which I used constantly. I'd been thinking about the future of television, and it occurred to me that it was only a matter of time before we would be accessing TV shows and movies on our computers. I didn't know how fast mobile technology was going to evolve (the iPhone was still two years away), so what I was imagining was an iTunes platform for television. "Imagine having access to all of television history on your computer," I said. If you wanted to watch last week's episode of *Lost*, or something from the first season of *I Love Lucy*, there it would be. "Imagine being able to watch all of *Twilight Zone* again whenever you wanted to!" It was coming, I was certain of that, and I wanted Disney to be in front of the wave. I figured the best way to do that was to convince Steve of the inevitability of this idea, "iTV," as I described it to him.

Steve was silent for a while, and then he finally said, "I'm going to come back to you on this. I'm working on something I want to show you."

A few weeks later, he flew down to Burbank and came to my office. Steve's idea of small talk was to glance out the window, make a brief comment about the weather, and then immediately start talking about the business at hand, which is exactly what he did that morning. "You can't tell anyone about this," he said. "But what you're talking about with television shows—that's exactly what we've been imagining." He slowly withdrew a device from his pocket. At first glance it looked just like the iPod I'd been using.

"This is our new video iPod," he said. It had a screen the size of a couple of postage stamps, but he was talking about it like it was an IMAX theater. "This is going to allow people to watch video on our iPods, not just listen to music," he said. "If we bring this product to market, will you put your television shows on it?"

I said yes right away.

Any product demo by Steve was powerful, but this was a personal demonstration. I could feel his enthusiasm as I stared at the device, and I had a profound sense of holding the future in my hand. There could be complications if we put our shows on his platform, but in the moment I knew instinctively that it was the right decision.

Steve responded to boldness, and I wanted to signal to him that there could be a different way of doing business with Disney going forward. Among his many frustrations was a feeling that it was often too difficult to get anything done with us. Every agreement needed to be vetted and analyzed to within an inch of its life, and that's not how he worked. I wanted him to understand that I didn't work that way, either, that I was empowered to make a call and that I was eager to figure out this future together, and to do so quickly. I thought that if he respected my instincts and my willingness to take this risk, then maybe, just maybe, the door to Pixar might crack open again.

So I told him again, yes, we were in.

"Okay," he said. "I'll get back to you when there's more to discuss."

That October, five months after that first conversation (and two weeks after I officially became CEO), Steve and I stood on a stage together at the Apple launch and announced that five Disney shows—including three of the most popular on TV, *Desperate Housewives, Lost,* and *Grey's Anatomy*—would now be available for download on iTunes, and for consumption on the new iPod with the video player.

I'd essentially brokered the deal myself, with assistance from Anne Sweeney, who ran ABC. The ease and the speed with which we got it done, combined with the fact that it showed an admiration for Apple and its products, blew Steve's mind. He told me he'd never met anyone in the entertainment business who was willing to try something that might disrupt his own company's business model.

When I walked onstage that day to announce our Apple partnership, the audience was confused at first, thinking, *Why is the new Disney guy up there with Steve? It can only be one reason.* I had no script, but the first thing I said was "I know what you're thinking, but I'm not here for that!" There were laughs and groans. Nobody wished we were making that announcement more than I did.

A FEW DAYS after I got the job in March 2005, a meeting showed up on my calendar about ticket pricing at the theme park we would soon be opening in Hong Kong. The request came from the office of Peter Murphy, the head of Strategic Planning. I called the person who was running Parks and Resorts at the time and asked him whose meeting it was.

"It's Peter's," he said.

"Peter's having a meeting about ticket pricing in Hong Kong?"

"Yes."

I called Peter and asked why.

"We have to make sure they're doing the right thing," he said.

"If they can't figure out what pricing should be, they shouldn't be in their jobs." I said. "But if we believe they should be in their jobs, then they should be in charge of pricing." I had the meeting canceled, and while it wasn't a hugely dramatic moment, it was the beginning of the end of Strat Planning as we'd known it.

Peter has a first-rate mind and an almost unequaled work ethic, and as I've mentioned, Michael had come to depend on him almost exclusively as the company grew. Peter consolidated and protected his burgeoning power. His skill and his intellect often caused him to be disdainful of other senior leaders, and as a result he was feared and disliked by many of them. It was a tense and increasingly dysfunctional dynamic.

As far as I knew, it hadn't always been that way. When Michael and Frank Wells came in to run the company in the mid-'80s, they created Strat Planning to help them identify and analyze a range of new business opportunities. After Frank's death in 1994 and the Cap Cities/ABC acquisition in '95, Michael needed help managing the newly expanded company. In the absence of a clear number two, he leaned heavily on Strat Planning to help him make decisions and steer Disney's various businesses. I recognized the value of their contributions, but I could also see, with each passing year, that they were growing too large and too powerful, and that the more influence they wielded, the more disempowered the people who were running our individual businesses became. By the time Michael named me COO, there were about sixty-five people in Strat Planning, and they'd taken over nearly all of the critical business decisions across the entire company.

All of our senior business leaders knew that strategic decisions about the divisions they ran—Parks and Resorts, consumer products, Walt Disney Studios, and so on—weren't actually theirs to make. Power was concentrated within this single entity in Burbank, and Peter and his people were viewed more as an internal police force than a partner to our businesses.

In many respects Peter was a futurist. He felt our business leaders were old-school managers whose ideas were at best variations on the status quo. He wasn't wrong about that. There were many people at the company at that point who didn't have the analytical skills and aggressive attitude exemplified by Peter and his team. You can't wear your disdain for people on your sleeve, though. You end up either cowing them into submission or frustrating them into com lacency. Either way, you sap them of the pride they take in ork. Over time, nearly everyone abdicated responsibility to d Strat Planning, and Michael was comforted by the ana- or they represented.

To my mind, though, they were often too deliberative, pouring every decision through their overly analytical sieve. Whatever we gained from having this group of talented people sifting through a deal to make sure it was to our advantage, we often lost in the time it took for us to act. This isn't to say that research and deliberation aren't important. You have to do the homework. You have to be prepared. You certainly can't make a major acquisition without building the necessary models to help you determine whether a deal is the right one, but you also have to recognize that there is never 100 percent certainty. No matter how much data you've been given, it's still, ultimately, a risk, and the decision to take that risk or not comes down to one person's instinct.

Peter saw no problem with a system in which he and the analysts who worked for him made so many of the company's decisions. Meanwhile, businesses around us were adapting to a world that was changing at blinding speed. We needed to change, we needed to be more nimble, and we needed to do it soon.

A week or so after that exchange about Hong Kong ticket pricing, I called Peter into my office and told him I was planning to reconstitute Strat Planning. I said I wanted to drastically reduce the size of the group and begin streamlining our decision making by putting more of it in the hands of the business leaders. We both knew that my vision for the group wouldn't be a good fit for him and it didn't make sense for him to stay.

Shortly after that conversation I had a press release drafted saying that Peter was leaving and that Strat Planning was being reformulated, and then I immediately began dismantling the group. I shrank Strat Planning from sixty-five people to fifteen. Tom Staggs, my CFO, had the idea to bring Kevin Mayer, who had once been with the group and left a few years earlier, back to the company to run the newly lean and repurposed team. Kevin would report to Tom, and he and his group would focus on potential acquisitions, with a clear mandate that any acquisitions be in the service of our three core priorities.

CHAPTER 9

DISNEY-PIXAR AND A NEW PATH TO THE FUTURE

THOSE MONTHS SPENT talking with Steve about putting our TV shows on his new iPod began—slowly, tentatively—to open up into discussions of a possible new Disney/Pixar deal. Steve had softened, but only a little. He was willing to talk, but his version of any new agreement was still very one-sided in Pixar's favor.

We parried a few times over what a deal might look like but got nowhere. I asked Tom Staggs to join the discussions and see if he could make progress. We also brought in a go-between from Goldman Sachs, Gene Sykes, whom we trusted and who knew Steve well. We floated a few different ideas to Steve through Gene, but Steve still didn't budge. His resistance wasn't complicated. Steve loved Pixar and he didn't care about Disney, so any agreement he'd deign to consider would have huge upsides for them and come at a steep price for us.

One proposal had us ceding to Pixar the valuable sequel rights to the films we'd already released together, like *Toy Story, Monsters, Inc.,* and *The Incredibles,* in exchange for a 10 percent stake in their company. We'd get board seats, the right to distribute all new Pixar films, and a big press announcement saying that Disney and Pixar would continue as partners. The financial value was weighted heavily toward Pixar, though. They'd get to make original Pixar-branded films and sequels, which they'd own forever, and our role essentially would be to serve as passive distributors. There were a few other similar proposals that I turned down. Tom and I would look at each other after each round of negotiations, and ask ourselves if we were crazy to not just make any deal with Steve, but then we'd quickly conclude that any deal we made had to have long-term value, and an announcement didn't give us that.

The reality was, Steve had all of the leverage in the world. By then, Pixar had become the standard-bearer for inventive, sophisticated animated filmmaking, and he never seemed worried about walking away from us. Our only bargaining chip was that we currently had the rights to make sequels of those earlier films without them, and in fact we'd started to develop some under Michael when talks had broken down two years before. Steve knew we would struggle to make anything genuinely great, though, given the state of Disney Animation, and he almost dared us to try.

ON SEPTEMBER 30, 2005, Michael spent his last day as CEO of the company he'd run for twenty-one years. It was a sad, awkward day. He was leaving with no ongoing connection to Disney—no seat on the board, no emeritus or consulting role. It was about as "cold turkey" as it gets. He was gracious with me, but I could feel the tension between us. As hard as the last few years had been, Michael didn't want to leave, and I found myself at a loss for words.

I met briefly with Zenia Mucha and Tom Staggs and Alan Braverman, and told them that my sense was that it was "better to let him be," so we kept a respectful distance and gave him some privacy to leave on his own terms. Michael's wife, Jane, and one of their sons came for lunch, and later that day he drove off the lot for the last time. I can't imagine what he must have felt. He'd come in two decades earlier and saved the company, and now he was driving away knowing that his era was over and that the place that he had turned into the largest entertainment company in the world would keep going on without him. It's one of those moments, I imagine, when it's hard to know who exactly you are without this attachment and title and role that has defined you for so long. I felt deeply for him, but I knew there was little I could do to make it easier for him.

Three days later, on Monday, October 3, I officially became the sixth CEO of the Walt Disney Company. For the first time in my career, I was reporting only to a board of directors, and after the long succession process and the six-month waiting period, I was about to preside over my first board meeting. In advance of most board meetings, I've asked all of my business heads for an update on their businesses, so that I could inform the board on business performance, important issues, and challenges and opportunities. For my first meeting, though, there was only one item on my list.

In advance of the meeting, I asked our studio head, Dick Cook, and his number two, Alan Bergman, to put together a presentation covering the last ten years of Disney Animation: every film we'd released, what they'd each earned at the box office, and so on. They were both concerned. "It's going to be ugly," Dick said.

"The numbers are horrible," Alan added. "It's probably not the best way for you to start out."

Regardless of how dispiriting or even incendiary the presentation was going to be, I told the studio team not to worry about it. I then asked Tom Staggs and Kevin Mayer to do some research on how our most important demographic, mothers with children under age twelve, viewed Disney Animation versus our competitors. Kevin, too, said that the story wasn't going to be a good one. "That's fine," I told him. "I just want a candid assessment of where we stand."

All of this was in the service of a radical idea, which I hadn't shared with anyone but Tom. A week earlier, I'd said to him, "What do you think about us buying Pixar?"

He thought I was joking at first. When I told him I was serious, he said, "Steve will never sell to us. Even if he would, it won't be at a price we could support, or that the board would support." He was probably right, but I wanted to make the case to the board anyway, and to do so I needed a blunt, detailed presentation about the current state of Disney Animation. Tom was hesitant, in part because he was protective of me and in part because, as CFO, he had a responsibility to the board and our shareholders, which meant not always going along with whatever the CEO had in mind.

MY FIRST BOARD meeting as CEO was an evening meeting, and I and the ten other board members took our places around the long conference table in our boardroom. I could sense the anticipation in the air. For me, it was one of the most momentous meetings of my life. For them, they were hearing from a new CEO for the first time in more than two decades.

The board had been through a lot in the last decade: the painful decision to bring Michael's tenure to an end, the ongoing fight with Roy and Stanley, the hostile takeover attempt by Comcast, the shareholder lawsuit over Michael Ovitz's $100 million–plus severance deal, a legal fight with Jeffrey Katzenberg over the conditions of his exit in 1994. The list went on. They had been subjected to a lot of criticism, and along with me they'd been put under a microscope as the succession and transition unfolded. It was a highly charged environment, because they would soon be judged on their decision to give me the job, and they knew there were still plenty of skeptics. Some of them (two or three, though I'll never be exactly sure who) had been opposed to my appointment altogether, right to the very end. So I stepped into that room knowing that even though the vote had ultimately been unanimous, there were people seated at the table who didn't expect or want me to be there for long.

George Mitchell opened the meeting with a quick, heartfelt

comment about the significance of the moment. He congratulated me for "enduring the process," as he put it, and then turned the floor over to me. I was so filled with restless energy and a desire to get to the heart of the matter right away, that I skipped over the pleasantries and immediately said, "As you all know, Disney Animation is a real mess."

They'd heard this before, but I knew that the reality was far worse than any of them was aware. Before presenting the financials and the brand research we'd prepared, I recalled a moment from just a few weeks earlier, at the opening of Hong Kong Disneyland. It was the last big event Michael presided over as CEO, and several of us had traveled to Hong Kong for the opening ceremonies, which took place on a blinding, 95-degree afternoon. Tom Staggs, Dick Cook, and I were standing together as the opening parade came down Main Street. Float after float passed by us. There were floats carrying characters from Walt's legendary films: *Snow White*, *Cinderella*, *Peter Pan*, and so on. And others with characters from the big hits of Michael's first decade: *The Little Mermaid*, *Beauty and the Beast*, *Aladdin*, and *The Lion King*. And there were floats with characters from the Pixar films: *Toy Story* and *Monsters, Inc.* and *Finding Nemo*.

I turned to Tom and Dick and asked, "Do you guys notice anything about this parade?" Nothing stood out to them. "There are barely any Disney characters from the last ten years," I said.

We could spend months analyzing what had gone wrong, but there it was, right in front of us. The movies weren't good, which meant the characters weren't popular or memorable, and that had significant ramifications for our business and our brand. Disney was founded on creativity, inventive storytelling, and great animation, and very little of our recent films lived up to our storied past.

I finished describing that scene to the board and then turned down the lights. The room got quiet as we projected onto a screen the list of films put out by Disney Animation over the last decade: *The Hunchback of Notre Dame*, *Hercules*, *Mulan*, *Tarzan*, *Fantasia*

2000, Dinosaur, The Emperor's New Groove, Atlantis, Lilo and Stitch, Treasure Planet, Brother Bear, and *Home on the Range.* Some were mild commercial successes; several were catastrophes. None had been met with any critical exuberance. Over that stretch, Animation had lost nearly $400 million. We'd spent well over a billion dollars making those films, and marketed them aggressively, and yet we had little to show for the investment.

Over that same stretch of time, Pixar had produced success after success, both creatively and commercially. Technologically, they were doing things with digital animation that we—Disney!—had only dabbled in. More profoundly, they were connecting in powerful ways to both parents and kids. After painting that bleak financial picture, I asked Tom to present the results of our brand research. Among women with children under twelve, Pixar had eclipsed Disney as a brand mothers thought of as "good for their family." In a head-to-head comparison, Pixar was far more beloved—it wasn't even close. I noticed a few board members murmuring to each other and sensed some anger starting to build.

The board knew Animation had been struggling, and they certainly knew Pixar was on a tear, but the reality had never been presented to them this starkly. They had no idea the numbers were this bad, and they'd never contemplated the brand research. When I was done, a couple of them pounced. Gary Wilson, who'd been my most ardent opponent during the search, said, "You were the COO for five of those years. Aren't you accountable for this?"

There was nothing to be gained from being defensive. "Disney and Michael deserve a lot of credit for creating a relationship with Pixar in the first place," I said. "It wasn't always an easy collaboration, but great things came from it." I said that after the acquisition of ABC, the company became more challenging to manage, and Animation received less attention than it should have. This problem was exacerbated by the revolving door at our studio of senior executives, none of whom had done a particularly good job running the unit. I then reiterated what I'd said many times throughout the succession process: "This can't be about the past. There's nothing we can do about bad creative decisions that were made and disappointing films that were released. But there's a lot we can do to change the future, and we need to start now."

I pointed out to the board that "as Animation goes, so goes the company." In so many respects, Disney Animation *was* the brand. It was the fuel that powered many of our other businesses, including consumer products, television, and theme parks, and over the last ten years, the brand had suffered a lot. The company was much smaller then, before Pixar, Marvel, and Lucasfilm were acquired, so the pressure on Animation to perform, not only on behalf of the brand but to enhance almost all of our businesses, was far more intense. "I feel enormous pressure to figure this out," I said. I knew that shareholders and analysts were not going to give me a grace period, and the first thing they would judge me on was my ability to turn Disney Animation around. "The drum is already beating loudly for me to solve this problem."

I then described what I saw as three possible paths forward. The first was to stick with current management and see if they could turn things around. I quickly expressed my doubts about this option, given what they'd delivered so far. The second was to identify new talent to run the division, but in the six months since being named, I'd scoured the animation and moviemaking world looking for people who could do the job at the level we needed, and I'd come up empty. "Or," I said, "we could buy Pixar."

The response to the idea was so explosive that if I were holding a gavel I would have used it to bring the court to order.

"I don't know if they're for sale," I said. "If they are, I'm certain they'll be wildly expensive." As a public company, Pixar's market cap was somewhere above $6 billion, and Steve Jobs owned half of the company's stock. "It's also highly unlikely Steve would ever want to sell." All of that seemed to bring relief to a few members, but it provoked others toward a lengthy discussion about whether there were any circumstances that would justify our spending billions of dollars to buy them.

"Buying Pixar would allow us to bring John Lasseter and Ed Catmull"—Pixar's visionary leaders, along with Steve Jobs—"into Disney," I said. "They could continue to run Pixar, while simultaneously revitalizing Disney Animation."

"Why can't we just hire them?" somebody asked.

"For one, John Lasseter is under contract at Pixar," I said. "But they're also wedded to Steve and to what they've built there. Their loyalty to Pixar, to its people and its mission, is enormous. It's naïve to think we could hire them." Another member suggested that we just needed to back a truck filled with money up to their doors. "These people can't be bought that way," I said. "They're different."

I immediately sought out Tom and Dick after the meeting, to get their impression of how the presentation had gone. "We didn't think you'd get out of there with your title intact," Tom said. He sounded as though he were kidding, but deep down I knew he wasn't.

When I got home that night, I walked into the house and Willow asked how it went. I hadn't told even her what I'd been planning. "I told them I thought we should buy Pixar," I said.

She, too, looked at me like I was crazy, and then added to the chorus, saying, "Steve will never sell to you." But then she reminded me of something she'd told me not long after I got the job: "The average tenure for a Fortune 500 CEO is less than four years." At the time, it was a joke between us, to make sure the expectations I set for myself were realistic. Now, though, she said it with a tone that implied I had little to lose by acting fast. "Be bold," was the essence of her advice.

As for the board, some were vehemently against the idea and made that very clear, but enough were intrigued that they gave me what I described as a "yellow light": go ahead, explore the idea, but proceed cautiously. Collectively, they concluded it was so unlikely to ever happen that they might as well let us amuse ourselves by exploring it.

The next morning I told Tom to start putting together a thorough analysis of the financials, though I also said there was no rush. I was planning to broach the idea with Steve later that day, and I figured there was a good chance that in a matter of hours the whole thing would be moot. I spent the morning building up the courage to make the call, and finally did so in the early afternoon. I didn't reach him, which was a relief, but as I was driving home from the office at around six-thirty, he returned my call.

This was about a week and a half before our announcement about the video iPod, so we spent a couple of minutes talking about that before I said, "Hey, I have another crazy idea. Can I come see you in a day or two to discuss it?"

I didn't yet fully appreciate just how much Steve liked radical ideas. "Tell me now," he said.

While still on the phone, I pulled into my driveway. It was a warm October evening, and I turned the engine off, and the combination of heat and nerves caused me to break out in a sweat. I reminded myself of Willow's advice—be bold. Steve would likely say no immediately. He might also be offended at what he perceived as the arrogance of the idea. How dare I think Pixar was something Disney could just come along and buy? Even if he told me where I could shove it, though, the call would end, and I'd be left exactly where I already was. I had nothing to lose. "I've been thinking about our respective futures," I said. "What do you think about the idea of Disney buying Pixar?" I waited for him to hang up or to erupt in laughter. The quiet before his response seemed endless.

Instead, he said, "You know, that's not the craziest idea in the world."

I'd so braced myself for rejection that now, even though I knew rationally that there were a million more hurdles between this moment and ever bringing this idea to fruition, I felt a rush of adrenaline that it was even a possibility. "Okay," I said. "Great. When can we talk more?"

PEOPLE SOMETIMES SHY AWAY from taking big swings because they assess the odds and build a case against trying something before they even take the first step. One of the things I've always instinctively felt—and something that was greatly reinforced working for people like Roone and Michael—is that long shots aren't usually as long as they seem. Roone and Michael both believed in their own power and in the ability of their organizations to make things happen—that with enough energy and thoughtfulness and commitment, even the boldest ideas could be executed. I tried to adopt that mindset in my ensuing conversations with Steve.

A couple of weeks after that call in my driveway, he and I met in Apple's boardroom in Cupertino, California. It was a long room, with a table nearly as long down the middle. One wall was glass, looking out over the entrance to Apple campus, and the other featured a whiteboard, probably twenty-five feet long. Steve said he loved whiteboard exercises, where an entire vision—all the thoughts and designs and calculations—could be drawn out, at the whim of whoever held the felt pen.

Not unexpectedly, Steve was the holder of the pen, and I sensed he was quite used to assuming that role. He stood with marker in hand and scrawled PROS on one side and CONS on the other. "You start," he said. "Got any pros?"

I was too nervous to launch in, so I ceded the first serve to him.

"Okay," he said. "Well, I've got some cons." He wrote the first with gusto: "Disney's culture will destroy Pixar!" I couldn't blame him for that. His experience with Disney so far hadn't provided any evidence to the contrary. He went on, writing his cons in full sentences across the board. "Fixing Disney Animation will take too long and will burn John and Ed out in the process." "There's too much ill will and the healing will take years." "Wall Street will

With the cast of *Twin Peaks* in 1990, not long after being promoted from number two at ABC TV to head of ABC Entertainment. The learning curve was steep.
The Walt Disney Company

With Cap Cities CEO Tom Murphy on the day it was announced that we were being acquired by Disney, 1995. *The Walt Disney Company*

With my soon-to-be boss, Disney CEO Michael Eisner, August 1995.
The Walt Disney Company

With Roone Arledge, my mentor from my early days at ABC Sports, 1996. It was Roone who taught me: Innovate or die. *The Walt Disney Company*

On stage in Cupertino with Apple CEO Steve Jobs in 2005 to announce that ABC shows would be carried on the new video iPod, a major breakthrough in our relationship. *Justin Sullivan/Getty Images*

With George Lucas, signing the deal to acquire Lucasfilm—and *Star Wars*—in October 2012. *The Walt Disney Company*

With my old pal Mickey
in Tokyo, 2013.
Bob Iger personal collection

With Willow (in a Yoda dress,
no less!) at the Academy
Awards in 2014.
The Walt Disney Company

On the red carpet with
Willow (this time, no Yoda
dress) at the Academy
Awards in 2015.
The Walt Disney Company

With Walt Disney, the one who started it all, 2016.
The Walt Disney Company

Preparing to give a speech to open Shanghai Disneyland, just after hearing of a tragedy at our park in Orlando.

Bob Iger personal collection

The Castle at Shanghai Disneyland, just prior to opening.

The Walt Disney Company

Backstage at the Bibbidi Bobbidi Boutique with cast and crew, Shanghai Disneyland, 2016. *The Walt Disney Company*

At the official ribbon-cutting ceremony at Shanghai with Wang Yang, CPC Politburo member and State Council vice premier, and Han Zheng, CPC Politburo member and party secretary of Shanghai.

The Walt Disney Company

With Chadwick
Boseman at the
Black Panther
premiere in Los
Angeles, 2018.
*The Walt Disney
Company*

With Rupert Murdoch in London, just before the announcement of our 21st
Century Fox acquisition, December 2017.
The Sun/Arthur Edwards

hate it." "Your board will never let you do it." "Pixar will reject Disney as an owner, as a body rejects a donated organ." There were many more, but one in all cap letters, "DISTRACTION WILL KILL PIXAR'S CREATIVITY." I assumed he meant that the whole process of a deal and the assimilation would be too much of a shock to the system they'd created. (A few years later, Steve would propose shutting down Disney Animation completely and just making animated films at Pixar. Even John Lasseter and Ed Catmull hated the idea, and I rejected it.)

It seemed pointless for me to add to his list, so we moved to the pros. I went first and said, "Disney will be saved by Pixar and we'll all live happily ever after."

Steve smiled but didn't write it down. "What do you mean?"

I said, "Turning Animation around will totally change the perception of Disney and shift our fortunes. Plus, John and Ed will have a much larger canvas to paint on."

Two hours later, the pros were meager and the cons were abundant, even if a few of them, in my estimation, were quite petty. I felt dispirited, but I should have expected this. "Well," I said. "It was a nice idea. But I don't see how we do this."

"A few solid pros are more powerful than dozens of cons," Steve said. "So what should we do next?" Another lesson: Steve was great at weighing all sides of an issue and not allowing negatives to drown out positives, particularly for things he wanted to accomplish. It was a powerful quality of his.

Steve died six years later. I joined the Apple board not long after his death. Every time I went to a meeting there and looked at that gigantic whiteboard, I saw Steve, intense, energetic, engaged, and far more open to the possibility of making this idea (and I suspected many ideas) work.

"I need to visit Pixar," I said. I'd never been there, and toward the end of our contract, things had gotten so bad, there was so little collaboration, that we didn't even know what they were working on. There was one last film for us to distribute, *Cars,* but no one at

Disney had even seen it. We'd heard they were working on a film about rats in the kitchen of a Paris restaurant, which people at Disney had scoffed at. Communication had completely ceased as each company prepared for the final separation.

If I was going to make the case for buying them, though, I needed to know a lot more about how they worked. I wanted to meet the key people, learn about their projects, and get a sense of the company's culture. What did it *feel* like there? What did they do differently from us that led them to consistently create brilliance?

Steve immediately agreed to the visit. He explained to John and Ed that we'd talked, and while he'd committed to nothing, and wouldn't commit to anything without their being on board, he thought it was worth their while to show me around the place. The following week, I showed up at the Pixar campus in Emeryville alone. John's assistant greeted me in the lobby and led me into their cavernous atrium, which Steve had helped design. Dining areas stretch along both sides, and at the far end was the main entrance to their theater. There were people milling about and convening in small groups in a way that reminded me more of a university student union than a film production company. The place was vibrant with creative energy. Everyone seemed happy to be there.

If I had to name the ten best days I've ever had on the job, that first visit to the Pixar campus would be high on the list. John and Ed welcomed me warmly and explained that I would spend the first half of the day meeting with every director, and they would show me elements of the films they were working on—rough cuts of scenes, storyboards, concept art, original scores, and cast lists. Then I would see their new "technology pipeline" and get a sense of how the tech side and the creative side worked together.

John was up first. He showed me a virtually finished cut of *Cars*, and I sat there in the theater mesmerized by the quality of the animation and by how far the technology had advanced since their last release. I remember being awed by the way the light reflected off the metallic paint on the race cars, for instance. These were images

I'd never seen in computer-generated animation. Brad Bird then showed me his work in progress, the scorned "rat movie," *Ratatouille*. It struck me as one of the most thematically sophisticated and narratively original films Pixar had ever made. Andrew Stanton, fresh off of *Finding Nemo*, presented a portion of *Wall-E*, a dystopia about a lonely robot who falls in love with another robot, with a bracing message about the social and environmental perils of consumerism run amok. That was followed by Pete Docter's pitch for *Up*, a love story that grapples with grief and mortality and takes place against the stunning visual backdrop of South America. (Pete would direct *Inside Out* after *Up*.) And Gary Rydstrom pitched a story about species extinction, told through an adventure involving two blue-footed newts. Pixar later abandoned that project, but I loved the sheer level of imagination and intelligence in Gary's presentation. Brenda Chapman showed me *Brave*. Lee Unkrich, who would go on to direct *Toy Story 3* and *Coco*, pitched a movie about pets in an apartment building on the Upper West Side of Manhattan. (*Ratatouille, Wall-E, Up, Toy Story 3, Brave, Inside Out,* and *Coco* would all go on to win Academy Awards for Best Animated Feature Film.)

I then spent a few hours with Ed Catmull and the engineers on the tech side, who described in detail the technological platform that served the whole creative enterprise. I saw firsthand what John described when he'd welcomed me into the building that morning. He said the animators and directors were constantly challenging the engineers to give them the tools with which they could fulfill their creative dreams—to make Paris *feel* like Paris, for instance. And Ed and his team on the engineering side were always building tools on their own, which they then brought to the artists to inspire them to think in ways they hadn't before. "Look at how we can make snow, or water, or mist!" Ed showed me the most sophisticated animation tools ever invented, technological ingenuity that enabled creativity at its highest form. This yin and yang was the soul of Pixar. Everything flowed from it.

I got into my car in the Pixar parking lot at the end of the day and immediately began scribbling notes. Then I called Tom Staggs and said I had to come see him as soon as I landed in L.A. I had no idea if the board would go for it, and I knew that Steve could change his mind on a whim. But I felt breathless as I described to Tom the level of talent and creative ambition, the commitment to quality, the storytelling ingenuity, the technology, the leadership structure, and the air of enthusiastic collaboration—even the building, the architecture itself. It was a culture that anyone in a creative business, in any business, would aspire to. And it was so far beyond where we were and beyond anything we might be able to achieve on our own, that I felt we had to do all we could to make this happen.

When I got back to my office in Burbank, I met immediately with my team. It's an understatement to say they didn't share my enthusiasm. I'd been the only one to see firsthand what the essence of Pixar was, and to them the idea was still too impractical. There were too many risks, they said. The cost would be too great. They worried that I was barely into my tenure as CEO and I was already putting my future—not to mention the company's future—on the line by pursuing this.

This would be a recurring theme in nearly every discussion I had about Pixar. I was told over and over that it was too risky and ill-advised. Many people thought Steve would be impossible to deal with and would try to run the company. I was also told that a brand-new CEO shouldn't be trying to make huge acquisitions. I was "crazy," as one of our investment bankers put it, because the numbers would never work out and this was an impossible "sale" to the street.

The banker had a point. It's true that on paper the deal didn't make obvious sense. But I felt certain that this level of ingenuity was worth more than any of us understood or could calculate at the time. It's perhaps not the most responsible advice in a book like this to say that leaders should just go out there and trust their gut, because it might be interpreted as endorsing impulsivity over thoughtfulness, gambling rather than careful study. As with everything, the key is awareness, taking it all in and weighing every factor—your own motivations, what the people you trust are saying, what careful study and analysis tell you, and then what analysis can't tell you. You carefully consider all of these factors, understanding that no two circumstances are alike, and then, if you're in charge, it still ultimately comes down to instinct. Is this right or isn't it? Nothing is a sure thing, but you need at the very least to be willing to take big risks. You can't have big wins without them.

My instinct about Pixar was powerful. I believed this acquisition could transform us. It could fix Disney Animation; it could add Steve Jobs, arguably the strongest possible voice on issues of technology, to the Disney board; it could bring a culture of excellence and ambition into ours that would reverberate in much-needed ways throughout the company. Ultimately, the board could say no, but I couldn't let go of this out of fear. I told my team that I respected their opinions, and I knew they were looking out for me, which I appreciated, but I thought we had to do this. At the very least I had to exhaust every possible way of making it happen before I gave in.

I called Steve the day after my visit to Emeryville. Before I dialed, I told myself that I should try to contain my enthusiasm. I needed to offer praise, because Steve's pride in Pixar was enormous, but this might be the beginning of a real negotiation, and I didn't want him to feel that I was so desperate for what they had that he could ask for the moon. The moment I got Steve on the phone, any semblance of a poker face collapsed. I couldn't pretend I felt anything other than pure enthusiasm. I described the day to him from beginning to end, and hoped that my honesty would ultimately serve me better than any "shrewd" pretense anyway. It could have seemed like a weakness—if you show that you want something so

badly you'll be made to pay—but in this case the genuine enthusiasm worked. I ended by saying, as if it wasn't already clear, that I
really wanted to try to make this happen.

Steve told me he would seriously consider it only if John and Ed
were on board. After we talked, he contacted them to say that he
was open to a negotiation, and to promise them that he would
never make a deal without their blessing. We planned that I would
meet with each of them again, so I could explain in more detail
what I was imagining and could field any questions they had. Then
they would decide if they were interested in going forward with a
negotiation.

A few days later I flew up to the Bay Area to have dinner with
John and his wife, Nancy, at their home in Sonoma. We had a long,
pleasant conversation and immediate chemistry. I gave them an
overview of my career, the *Wide World of Sports* days and the experience of being acquired by Capital Cities, the years programming
ABC prime time, and finally the Disney takeover and the long
road to becoming CEO. John talked about his days working at
Disney Animation more than two decades earlier, before the Michael era. (He was let go when the powers that be felt there wasn't
a future in computer animation!)

"I know what it's like to be taken over by another company," I
told him. "Even in the best of circumstances, the merger process is
delicate. You can't just force assimilation. And you definitely can't
with a company like yours." I said that even if it isn't purposeful,
the buyer often destroys the culture of the company it's buying, and
that destroys value.

A lot of companies acquire others without much sensitivity regarding what they're really buying. They think they're getting
physical assets or manufacturing assets or intellectual property (in
some industries, that's more true than in others). In most cases,
what they're really acquiring is people. In a creative business, that's
where the value truly lies.

I took pains to assure John that the only way it made sense for

Disney to buy Pixar was if we protected whatever it was that made their culture so unique. Bringing Pixar into our company would be a mammoth transfusion of leadership and talent, and we'd need to do it right. "Pixar needs to be Pixar," I said. "If we don't protect the culture you've created, we'll be destroying the thing that makes you valuable."

John said he was happy to hear that, and then I dropped my grand plan on him. "I'd want you and Ed to run Disney Animation, too."

All these years later, John said he was still smarting at having been fired from Disney, but his respect for the heritage of Disney Animation was powerful. Just as I had an impossible time hiding my enthusiasm from Steve, John had an equally impossible time hiding his at the thought of running Disney Animation. "Well, that would be a dream," he said.

A few days later, Ed Catmull flew down to meet with me in Burbank. (We had dinner at a steakhouse near the Disney lot, though neither of us ate meat.) As with John, I took pains to explain to Ed my philosophy about acquisitions—that the culture they'd built was central to the magic they were able to create, and that I had zero interest in forcing them to be anything other than what they already were. I also talked about the other opportunity that was on the table: that I wanted John and him to revitalize Disney Animation.

If John is all emotion and extroversion, Ed is the photographic negative. He is a quiet, thoughtful, introverted doctor of computer science, who invented much of the technology that made Pixar's digital animation possible. We were far behind Pixar technologically, but there were other tech resources in other parts of Disney that Ed was interested in getting his hands on. In his understated way, he said, "It would be exciting to see what we could do here."

Steve called the next day to say that John and Ed had given him the go-ahead to negotiate with me, and not long after that, I had my second meeting with the Disney board, this time in New York.

I told them about the visit to Pixar and the meetings with John and Ed, and that Steve was willing to negotiate. Tom Staggs, who still had some misgivings, gave a presentation on the potential economics of an acquisition, including the question of issuing more shares and the potential dilution of Disney stock, and his best guess as to how the investment community would react, which was mixed to fairly negative at best. The board listened intently, and while they remained largely skeptical by meeting's end, they gave us permission to negotiate with Steve and come back with something more specific for them to consider.

Tom and I flew straight from our board meeting to San Jose and met with Steve at Apple's headquarters the next day. I knew going in that I didn't want the process to be drawn out. Steve was constitutionally incapable of a long, complicated back-and-forth (the prolonged, acrimonious negotiations with Michael were still fresh in his memory). He was already averse to the way Disney made deals, and I feared that if we got bogged down on any one point, he would sour on the whole thing and walk away.

So as soon as we sat down, I said, "I'll be straight with you. This is something I feel we have to do." Steve agreed that we needed this, but unlike in the past, he didn't use his leverage to demand a wildly impossible number. Wherever we landed was going to be very good for them, but he knew it needed to be in the realm of possibility for us, too, and I think he appreciated my frankness.

Over the course of the next month, Tom and Steve went over the possible financial structure in great detail and arrived at a price: $7.4 billion. (It was an all-stock deal—2.3 Disney shares for each Pixar share, and netted out to $6.4 billion because Pixar had $1 billion in cash.) Even if Steve stopped just short of being greedy, it was still a huge price, and it was going to be a tough sell to our board and to investors.

We also negotiated what we called a "social compact"—a two-page list of culturally significant issues and items that we promised to preserve. They wanted to feel that they were still Pixar, and everything related to protecting that feeling mattered. Their email addresses would remain Pixar addresses; the signs on their buildings would still say Pixar. They could keep their rituals for welcoming new employees and their tradition of monthly beer blasts. A much more sensitive negotiation took place over the branding on films, merchandise, and theme-park attractions. Our research showed that Pixar had eclipsed Disney as a brand—a fact that they were well aware of—but I felt that over time the strongest branding for the Pixar films, especially since John and Ed would now be running Disney Animation, would be Disney-Pixar. Ultimately, that's what we settled on. Pixar's famous "Luxo Junior" animation would still open each of their films, but it would be preceded by the Disney castle animation.

THE CHALLENGE BEFORE me now was convincing our board. I realized my best shot was for them to meet and hear from Steve and John and Ed directly. No one could sell this better than the three of them. So, on a weekend in January 2006, we all convened in a Goldman Sachs conference room in L.A. Several members of the board were still opposed to a deal, but the moment Steve, John, and Ed started talking, everyone in the room was transfixed. They had no notes, no decks, no visual aids. They just talked—about Pixar's philosophy and how they worked, about what we were already dreaming of doing together, and about who they were as people.

John spoke with passion about his lifelong love of Disney and his desire to return Disney Animation to its former glory. Ed gave a cerebral, fascinating dissertation about where technology was heading and what might be possible for both Disney and Pixar. As for Steve, it's hard to imagine a better salesman for something this ambitious. He talked about the need for big companies to take big risks. He talked about where Disney had been and what it needed to do to radically change course. He talked about me and the bond that we'd formed already—with the iTunes deal, but also in the ongoing discussions about preserving Pixar's culture—and his desire to work together to make this crazy idea a success. For the first time, watching him speak, I felt optimistic that it might happen.

The board was scheduled to meet for a final vote on January 24, but word of a possible deal soon leaked out. Suddenly I was receiving calls from people urging me not to do it. Among them was Michael Eisner. "Bob, you can't do this," he said. "It's the stupidest thing in the world." It was the same list of concerns. It was too expensive, too risky. Bringing Steve into the company would be a disaster. "You can fix Animation," Michael said. "You don't need them to do it. They're one failure away from being an average performer." He even called Warren Buffett, thinking that if Warren thought it was a dumb investment, he would be able to sway the people he knew on the Disney board. Warren didn't weigh in, so Michael called Tom Murphy, to see if he would say something, and then he reached out to George Mitchell and asked if he could address the board directly himself.

George called me and told me about the request. "George," I said, "you're not going to let him do it, are you? At this point?" Michael had been out of the company for four months. His connection with Disney had ended on his last day at work. I knew it was difficult for Michael, but I was offended by his meddling. It was something he would never have tolerated when he was CEO.

"It's cheap," George said. "Just let it happen. We show him respect, we hear him out, then you make your case." This was quintessential George. After years in the Senate, including a stint as majority leader, and after helping to broker peace in Northern Ireland, he was the consummate statesman. He genuinely felt Michael deserved the respect, but he also knew Michael could be a rogue element here, influencing the board from outside, and it was better to let him come in and talk, giving me the chance to immediately issue a rebuttal in the same room. It's the only thing George ever did as chairman that rankled me, but there was nothing I could do but trust in his instincts.

On the day the board was set to vote, Michael came in and made his case. It was the same one he'd made with me—the price tag was too high, Steve was difficult and imperious and would demand control, Animation was not beyond repair. He looked at me and said, "Bob can fix Animation." I said, "Michael, *you* couldn't fix it, and now you're telling me that I can?"

Before the meeting, George came into my office and said, "Look, I think you're going to get this. But it's not a done deal. You have to go in there and pitch your heart out. You have to do the equivalent of pounding your fists on the table. Show your passion. Demand their support."

"I thought I'd already done all that," I said.

"You have to do it one more time."

I entered the boardroom on a mission. I even took a moment before I walked into the room to look again at Theodore Roosevelt's "The Man in the Arena" speech, which has long been an inspiration: "It is not the critic who counts; not the man who points out how the strong man stumbles, or where the doer of deeds could have done them better. The credit belongs to the man who is actually in the arena, whose face is marred by dust and sweat and blood." My face wasn't quite marred by dust and sweat and blood, and the Disney boardroom wasn't the harshest of arenas. But I had to go in there and fight for something I knew was a risk. If they said yes, and it worked, I'd be a hero for changing the fortunes of the company. If they said yes, and it didn't work, I wouldn't be long in the job.

I spoke with as much fire as I could muster. "The future of the company is right here, right now," I said. "It's in your hands." I repeated something I'd said back in October, in my first board meeting as CEO. "As Disney Animation goes, so goes the company. It was true in 1937 with *Snow White and the Seven Dwarfs* and in

1994 with *The Lion King,* and it's no less true right now. When Animation soars, Disney soars. We have to do this. Our path to the future starts right here, tonight."

When I was done, George began the voting process, calling on each member in alphabetical order to vote aloud and offering them a chance to speak if they wanted to. The room went very quiet. I recall making eye contact with Tom Staggs and Alan Braverman. They were confident we would get the vote, but now I wasn't sure. After all the board had been through over the past few years, it seemed likely that risk aversion could rule the day. The first four members voted yes, and the fifth also voted yes but added that he was doing so only out of support for me. Of the remaining five, two voted against, bringing the final tally to nine for and two against. The deal was approved.

There was a brief discussion about whether another vote should be taken to make it unanimous, but George quickly shut that down, arguing that the process had to be transparent. Someone worried about the public perception of a less-than-unanimous vote, but I said that I didn't care. All anyone had to know was that the Disney board approved it. The vote did not have to be made public, and if anyone asked whether it was unanimous, we should respond with the truth. (Years later, Michael admitted to me that he was wrong about Pixar, which was gracious of him.)

ON THE DAY of the announcement, Alan Braverman, Tom Staggs, Zenia Mucha, and I traveled to Pixar's headquarters in Emeryville. Steve, John, and Ed were there, and the plan was to release the announcement right after the stock market closed at 1 P.M. PST, then hold a press conference and a town hall meeting with Pixar's employees.

Just after noon, Steve found me and pulled me aside. "Let's take a walk," he said. I knew Steve liked to go on long walks, frequently with friends or colleagues, but I was surprised at the timing and suspicious about his request. I turned to Tom to ask what he thought Steve wanted, and we guessed either he want to back out or he wanted something more.

I looked at my watch as Steve and I left the building. It was now 12:15. We walked for a while and then sat on a bench in the middle of Pixar's beautiful, manicured grounds. Steve put his arm behind me, which was a nice, unexpected gesture. He then said, "I'm going to tell you something that only Laurene"—his wife—"and my doctors know." He asked me for complete confidentiality, and then he told me that his cancer had returned. He'd been diagnosed with a rare form of pancreatic cancer a few years earlier, and after an operation he had declared that he was completely cured. But now it was back.

"Steve, why are you telling me this?" I asked. "And why are you telling me now?"

"I am about to become your biggest shareholder and a member of your board," he said. "And I think I owe you the right, given this knowledge, to back out of the deal."

I checked my watch again. It was 12:30, only thirty minutes before we were to announce the deal. I wasn't sure how to respond, and I was struggling to process what I'd just been told, which included asking myself whether what I now knew would trigger any disclosure obligations. Did I need to tell our board? Could I ask our general counsel? He wanted complete confidentiality, so it would be impossible to do anything except accept his offer and back away from a deal I wanted badly, and we needed badly. Finally I said, "Steve, in less than thirty minutes we are set to announce a seven-plus billion dollar deal. What would I tell our board, that I got cold feet?" He told me to blame him. I then asked, "Is there more that I need to know about this? Help me make this decision."

He told me the cancer was now in his liver and he talked about the odds of beating it. He was going to do whatever it took to be at his son Reed's high school graduation, he said. When he told me that was four years away, I felt devastated. It was impossible to be having these two conversations—about Steve facing his impending death and about the deal we were supposed to be closing in minutes—at the same time.

I decided to reject his offer to cancel the deal. Even if I took him up on it, I wouldn't have been able to explain why to our board, which not only had approved it, but had endured months of my pleas to do so. It was now ten minutes before our release was to go out. I had no idea if I was doing the right thing, but I'd quickly calculated that Steve was not material to the deal itself, although he certainly was material to me. Steve and I walked in silence back to the atrium. Later that day I spoke with Alan Braverman, whom I trusted like a brother, and told him what Steve had told me. He endorsed the decision I'd made, which came as a great relief. That night I took Willow into my confidence, too. Willow had known Steve for years, since long before I knew him, and instead of toasting what had been a momentous day in my early days as CEO, we cried together over the news. No matter what he told me, no matter how resolved he would be in his fight with cancer, we dreaded what was ahead for him.

The Pixar deal was announced at 1:05 PST. After Steve and I addressed the press, we both stood on a platform in the cavernous Pixar atrium, John and Ed at our side, in front of almost a thousand Pixar employees. Before I spoke, someone gave me a Luxo lamp as a present to commemorate the moment. Extemporaneously, I thanked the group and told them I was going to use it to illuminate our castle. It has ever since.

CHAPTER 10

MARVEL AND MASSIVE RISKS THAT MAKE PERFECT SENSE

THE PIXAR ACQUISITION served our urgent need to revitalize Disney Animation, but it was also the first step in our larger growth strategy: to increase the amount of high-quality branded content we created; to advance technologically, both in our ability to create more compelling products and to deliver those products to consumers; and to grow globally.

Tom Staggs, Kevin Mayer, and I had a list of "acquisition targets" that we believed could help us fulfill those priorities, and we decided to focus first on intellectual property. Who possessed great IP that could have applications across the full range of our businesses? Two companies came immediately to mind: Marvel Entertainment and Lucasfilm. We had no idea if either might be for sale, but for a variety of reasons (among them that I believed it would be very hard to convince George Lucas to sell the company he'd built himself and relinquish control of the *Star Wars* legacy), we put Marvel at the top of our list. I wasn't steeped in Marvel lore, but you didn't have to be a lifelong reader of the comics to know it was a trove of compelling characters and stories that would plug easily into our movie, television, theme-park, and consumer-products businesses. There were other companies on our list, but none were as valuable as Marvel and Star Wars.

The approach wasn't without complications. For one, Marvel was already contractually bound to other studios. They had a distribution agreement with Paramount for multiple upcoming films. They'd sold the *Spider-Man* rights to Columbia Pictures (which eventually became Sony). *The Incredible Hulk* was controlled by Universal. *X-Men* and *The Fantastic Four* belonged to Fox. So even if we could acquire everything that wasn't tied up by other studios, it wasn't as pure an IP acquisition as we would ideally have liked. We wouldn't have all the characters under one umbrella, which would potentially cause some brand confusion and some licensing complications down the road.

The larger obstacle, though, was that the person who ran Marvel, Ike Perlmutter, was a mystery to us. Ike was a legendarily tough, reclusive character, former Israeli military, who never appeared in public or allowed pictures of himself to be taken. He had made a fortune by buying up the debt of distressed companies and then using it to take control of them. And he had a reputation for being penurious to the extreme. (There are stories of Ike pulling paper clips out of trash cans.) Beyond that, we knew very little about him. We had no idea how he'd respond to our overtures, or if he'd respond at all when we reached out to him.

Ike's connection to Marvel Comics went back to the mid-'80s, when Marvel's then owner, Ron Perelman, acquired part of ToyBiz, a company that Ike owned along with a partner named Avi Arad. Throughout the comic-collecting boom of the late '80s and early '90s, Marvel was hugely profitable. Then the boom ended, and losses started piling up. There were financial restructurings and a bankruptcy filing, and finally a long power struggle between Perelman; the investor Carl Icahn, who'd become Marvel's chairman; and Ike and Avi Arad. In 1997, Ike and Arad wrested control of the company away from both Perelman and Icahn. The next year, they fully merged ToyBiz and Marvel to form Marvel Enterprises, which eventually became Marvel Entertainment.

By 2008, when we began looking into them in earnest, Marvel was a publicly traded company, with Ike as its CEO and controlling shareholder. We spent about six months trying to get a meeting with him and got nowhere. You'd think it wouldn't be that difficult for the CEO of one company to arrange a meeting with another, but Ike didn't do anything that he didn't want to do, and because he was so secretive, there were no direct channels to him.

If he was going to give us the time of day, it would be because someone he trusted vouched for us. We did have one connection. A former Disney executive named David Maisel had joined Marvel to help them get into the movie business. David and I always got along, and he checked in from time to time to see if there was anything we could do together. He'd pushed me several times to consider becoming the distributor of the films Marvel was embarking on, but I wasn't interested in just being a distributor. I told David I wanted to meet with Ike, and asked if he had any advice. He said he would try to arrange something, and that he thought it was a great idea, but he made no promises and urged patience.

Meanwhile, Kevin Mayer couldn't stop fantasizing about what Disney could do if we added Marvel. Kevin is as intense and laser-focused as anyone I've ever worked with, and when he sets his sights on something of value, it's very hard for him to accept my advice to "be patient," and so he harangued me on a near-daily basis to find some way to get to Ike, and I told him we needed to wait and see what David could do.

Months went by. Intermittently, David would reach out with the same message—nothing yet, keep waiting. And then, finally, he called one day in June 2009 and said Ike was willing to meet. David never explained why things had changed, but I suspect he told Ike we had some interest in possibly acquiring Marvel, and that intrigued him.

A few days after we got the word from David, I went to meet

Ike at the Marvel offices in midtown Manhattan. As with John and Ed at Pixar, I wanted him to feel that I was there out of respect, so I went to New York expressly to meet with him and showed up by myself, not with a team of Disney executives. Marvel's offices confirmed Ike's reputation. They were spartan. His own office was tiny and unadorned: a small desk, some chairs, small tables and lamps. No expensive furniture or sweeping view, very little on the walls. You'd never know that it belonged to the CEO of an entertainment company.

Ike was noticeably wary of me, but he wasn't cold or uninviting. He had a wiry frame and a powerful handshake. When I sat down he offered me a glass of water and a banana. "From Costco," he said. "My wife and I shop there on weekends." I didn't know how much David had told him about me or what I wanted to talk about, but you can't meet someone and then right after the niceties say you want to buy his company. So while I suspected Ike knew there was likely only one reason I was in his office, we first chatted about where we each came from and our respective businesses. He asked specifically about the Pixar purchase, and I told him about integrating them into Disney in a way that allowed them to maintain their unique culture. It was at that point that I explained why I was there and raised the notion of doing something similar with Marvel.

Ike didn't leap at it, but he didn't reject it, either. We talked for another half hour, and then he suggested we meet later that night at the Post House, a steak place he liked in the East Sixties. Our dinner conversation was long and wide-ranging. I learned about the various businesses Ike had run, and about his life in Israel before coming to America. He was as tough and proud as advertised, and I didn't press too hard on the idea of a possible sale—just enough to share my vision for how Marvel could be part of a bright future at Disney. Toward the end of the meal, he told me, "I need to think about it," and I said I'd check in with him tomorrow.

When I called the next day, Ike told me that he still had doubts, but he was intrigued. Ike's a shrewd businessman, and he stood to make a lot of money from a sale to Disney, but he'd also taken control of Marvel when it was in trouble and had turned it around. I think the notion that some other CEO would just come in and buy it up didn't sit easily with him, even though he knew he'd make a fortune off of it.

Ike and I are very different people, and we've had our disagreements over the years since the acquisition of Marvel, but I genuinely respected where he'd come from in his life. He'd arrived in the United States with next to nothing, and by virtue of his own smarts and tenacity had become wildly successful. I wanted him to understand that I appreciated who he was and what he'd done, and that he and his company would be in good hands. However, Ike would never fit easily into a corporate structure or respond well to what he perceived as Hollywood slickness, so if he was going to be comfortable with selling to Disney, he had to feel like he was dealing with someone who was being authentic and straight with him, and who spoke a language he understood.

Luckily for me, Willow happened to be in New York on business that week, and so I suggested to Ike that he and his wife join us for dinner. Willow doesn't often attend business dinners with me, but her understanding of business, her resumé, and her ease with people make her a secret weapon. We met again at the Post House—at the same table Ike and I had sat at a few nights earlier. Ike's wife, Laurie, is a smart, energetic person (who happens to be a competitive bridge player), and she and Willow made the conversation easy and relaxed. There wasn't any business talk, it was just a chance to give them a sense of who we were and what was important to us, and for us to get a sense of who they were, too. Ike didn't say it outright, but I felt confident by the end of the night that he was warming to the idea.

THIS WASN'T THE first time Marvel had been on Disney's radar. Early in my time working for Michael, I attended a staff lunch in which he floated the idea of acquiring them. A handful of executives around the table objected. Marvel was too edgy, they said. It would tarnish the Disney brand. There was an assumption at the time—internally, and among members of the board—that Disney was a single, monolithic brand, and all of our businesses existed beneath the Disney umbrella. I sensed Michael knew better, but any negative reaction to the brand, or suggestion that it wasn't being managed well, he took personally.

Among other things, Disney had a successful but often strained partnership with Miramax, run by Bob and Harvey Weinstein, which Michael had acquired in 1993. (The partnership was dissolved in 2005, when Michael was still CEO, and seven years later we sold the entire business.) Miramax released around three hundred films over those years. Many were critically successful and profitable, but many others lost money. There were intense fights with the Weinsteins over budgets and struggles over the content of films, particularly Michael Moore's documentary *Fahrenheit 9/11*, which Michael Eisner didn't want Disney to distribute. There was one problem after another, and while there were Academy Award winners, it was never easy with them. One example occurred in 1999, when Miramax launched *Talk* magazine, which was a huge money loser. They committed to the magazine with Tina Brown, before Michael had a chance to bless it, and it was a debacle from the beginning. I never had anything to do with the Miramax relationship, but I saw how it took a toll on Michael, internally and publicly. Fighting with Harvey and Bob Weinstein was a constant source of stress, on top of dealing with the board's opinion that Miramax was fiscally irresponsible. As the pressure increased on him in the last few years, I watched Michael grow weary and wary. So when he got pushback from some executives over the Marvel idea, his default was not to force the issue. It wasn't that long ago that he'd made the ABC deal, after all, so there was no great urgency to acquire another company.

My highest priority when I took over as CEO had been to revive the Disney brand by reviving Animation. Now that John and Ed were in place, that problem was well on its way to being solved. Once Disney Animation was solid, I was open to other acquisitions, even if they weren't obviously "Disney." In fact, I was much more conscious of not wanting to play it safe. We'd taken a huge risk with the Pixar acquisition, and it would have been easy to hold our cards for a while rather than pushing for more growth. Three years after Pixar became part of Disney, though, the sands were shifting even more dramatically under the entire entertainment business, and it was important for us to keep thinking ambitiously, to capitalize on our momentum and expand our portfolio of branded storytelling.

If anything, when it came to Marvel, I had the opposite worry of those who were wary of acquiring a company that was decidedly edgier than Disney: not what Marvel would do to Disney, but how loyal Marvel fans would react to their being associated with us. Would we possibly destroy some of their value by acquiring them? Kevin Mayer's team researched that question, and after several conversations with Kevin, I felt comfortable we could manage the brands respectfully and separately, that they could exist side by side and neither would be negatively affected by the other.

Some of Ike's key creative people were understandably anxious about being acquired, too. I invited several of them out to Burbank and met with them myself, describing my own experiences with the Capital Cities and Disney acquisitions and assuring them that I knew what it felt like to be swallowed up by another company. I uttered the same sentence to them that I had repeated multiple times during my negotiations with Steve and John and Ed: "It doesn't make any sense for us to buy you for what you are and then turn you into something else."

ONCE IKE MADE clear that he was willing to enter into a more serious negotiation, Tom Staggs, Kevin Mayer, and their teams began the exhaustive process of assessing Marvel's current and potential value, as a stand-alone company and as part of Disney, in order to arrive at an offer that made sense. It involved a full accounting of their assets and liabilities and contractual obstacles, as well as their personnel and the issues of assimilating them into our company. Our team constructed a multiyear scenario of potential movie releases with projected box-office estimates. They also built into the model what we could do to grow the business within Disney—in our theme parks and publishing and consumer products businesses.

Since the Pixar deal, with Steve as a board member and our largest shareholder, whenever I wanted to do something big, I talked it over with him, to get his advice and support before taking it to the full board. Steve's voice mattered in our boardroom; they had such respect for him. Before we went any further in the negotiations, I went up to Cupertino and had lunch with Steve and walked him through Marvel's business. He claimed to have never read a comic book in his life ("I hate them more than I hate videogames," he told me), so I brought my encyclopedia of Marvel characters with me to explain the universe to him and show him what we would be buying. He spent about ten seconds looking at it, then pushed it aside and said, "Is this one important to you? Do you really want it? Is it another Pixar?"

Steve and I had become good friends since we'd made the Pixar deal. We socialized on occasion and talked a few times a week. We vacationed at adjacent Hawaiian hotels a few times and would meet and take long walks on the beach, talking about our wives and kids, about music, about Apple and Disney and the things we might still do together.

Our connection was much more than a business relationship. We enjoyed each other's company immensely, and we felt we could say anything to each other, that our friendship was strong enough that it was never threatened by candor. You don't expect to develop such close friendships late in life, but when I think back on my time as CEO—at the things I'm most grateful for and surprised by—my relationship with Steve is one of them. He could criticize me, and I could disagree, and neither of us took it too personally. Plenty of people warned me that the worst thing I could do was let Steve into the company, that he would bully me and everyone else. I always said the same thing: "How can Steve Jobs coming into our company not be a good thing? Even if it comes at my expense? Who wouldn't want Steve Jobs to have influence over how a company is run?" I wasn't worried about how he would act, and I was confident that if he did do something that was out of line, I could call him out on it. He was quick to judge people, and when he criticized, it was often quite harsh. That said, he came to all the board meetings and actively participated, giving the kind of objective criticism you'd expect from any board member. He rarely created trouble for me. Not never but rarely.

I once gave him a tour of a hotel in Orlando called "Art of Animation." It's a huge hotel, three thousand rooms, priced more affordably than many of our hotels. I was proud of its quality for the price, and when Steve came down for a board retreat shortly after it opened, I took him to see it. We walked into the hotel, and Steve looked around and proclaimed, "This is crap. You're not faking anybody."

"Steve," I said, "this is for people who want to come to Disney World with their kids and can't afford to spend hundreds of dollars a night on a room. It's ninety bucks, and it's a decent, nice, clean, pleasant place."

"I don't get it," he barked. Most people would have appreciated the quality and the care we'd taken to design it, but Steve wasn't most people. He was looking at it through his own lens.

"It's not for you," I said. "I'm sorry that I showed it to you." I was a little mad at his snobbery, but I also knew that was just who he was. He built things of the highest quality, not necessarily afford-able to all, but he never sacrificed quality in order to attain afford-ability. I never showed him anything like that again.

When *Iron Man 2* came out, Steve took his son to see it and called me the next day. "I took Reed to see *Iron Man 2* last night," he said. "It sucked."

"Well, thank you. It's done about $75 million in business. It's going to do a huge number this weekend. I don't take your criticism lightly, Steve, but it's a success, and you're not the audience." (I knew *Iron Man 2* was nobody's idea of an Oscar winner, but I just couldn't let him feel he was right all of the time.)

Not long after that, at the 2010 Disney shareholders meeting, Alan Braverman, our general counsel, came up to me and said, "We have a huge no vote on four board members."

"How huge?"

"Over a hundred million shares," he said.

I was baffled. Normally, there might be a 2 to 4 percent no vote at the most. A hundred million shares was way beyond that. Some-thing was off. "A hundred million shares?" I said again. The com-pany was doing quite well by then and our board members were well respected. There'd been no public criticism that I knew of, no warnings that something like this might come up. It didn't make any sense. After a minute, Alan said, "I think it might be Steve." He had all those shares, and he voted against four of his fellow board members. This was one day before we revealed the vote. An-nouncing that four board members had received a gigantic with-hold vote would be a public-relations nightmare.

I called Steve. "Did you vote against four board members?"

"I did."

I said, "First of all, how can you do that without talking to me about it? It's going to stick out like a sore thumb. I don't know how I'll explain it publicly, and I don't know how I'm going to explain it to them. It's going to eventually come out that it was you. Plus, they're four good board members! Why are you voting against them?"

"I think they're a waste of space," he said. "I don't like them." I started to defend them, then immediately realized that wasn't going to work with Steve. I wasn't going to convince him he was wrong. "What do you want me to do?" he finally said.

"I need you to change your vote."

"I can change my vote?"

"Yes."

"Okay, I'll change my vote because it is important to you. But I'm telling you, I'm voting against them next year."

He never ended up doing that. By the time the next shareholders meeting came around, he was terribly ill and focused on other things. With these few exceptions, Steve was a wonderful, generous business partner and wise counsel.

When it came to the Marvel question, I told him that I wasn't sure if it was another Pixar, but they had great talent at the company, and the content was so rich that if we held the IP, it would put some real distance between us and everyone else. I asked him if he'd be willing to reach out to Ike and vouch for me.

"Okay," Steve said. "If you think it's right, then I'll give him a call." He never would have invested in such a company himself, but he trusted and wanted to help me more than he hated comic books and superhero movies. The next day, he called and talked with Ike for a while. I think even Ike was impressed, and flattered, to be getting a call from Steve Jobs. Steve told him that the Pixar deal far exceeded his expectations, because I'd lived up to my word and respected the brand and the people.

Later, after we'd closed the deal, Ike told me that he'd still had his doubts and the call from Steve made a big difference to him. "He said you were true to your word," Ike said. I was grateful that Steve was willing to do it as a friend, really, more than as the most influential member of our board. Every once in a while, I would say to him, "I have to ask you this, you're our largest shareholder," and he would always respond, "You can't think of me as that. That's insulting. I'm just a good friend."

ON AUGUST 31, 2009, a few months after my first meeting with Ike, we announced we were buying Marvel for $4 billion. There were no leaks in advance, no speculation in the press about a possible acquisition. We just made the announcement, then prepared for the backlash: Marvel is going to lose its edge! Disney is going to lose its innocence! They spent $4 billion and they don't have *Spider-Man*! Our stock fell 3 percent the day we announced the deal.

Not long after the announcement, President Obama hosted a small luncheon with a group of business leaders in the Rose Garden. Brian Roberts from Comcast was there, and Alan Mulally from Ford, and a handful of others. We ate and chatted about our various businesses, and the president mentioned he was a big Marvel fan. Afterward, Brian and I shared a car from the White House. "Where do you see the value with Marvel?" he asked during the ride. I said there was an endless supply of IP. "Aren't they all spoken for?" Some of them were, I said, but there are a lot more. Brian then told me he'd been talking with Jeff Immelt, the CEO of General Electric, which owned NBCUniversal at the time. (Before long, Comcast would buy NBC from them.) Jeff had apparently told Brian that our Marvel deal confounded him. "Why would anyone want to buy a library of comic book characters for $4 billion?" he'd said. "It makes me want to leave the business."

I smiled and shrugged. "I guess we'll see," I said. I wasn't worried about what other CEOs would say. We'd done our homework. We knew that time would prove that the brands could easily coexist, and we knew there was a depth to the Marvel universe that most people weren't aware of. During our research, we'd put together a dossier that contained a list of about seven thousand

Marvel characters. Even if we couldn't obtain *Spider-Man* or the rights controlled by other studios, we'd still have more than enough to mine. The content was there, and the talent was there. (In fact, the Marvel Studios talent, led by Kevin Feige, described their long-term vision for what would become the Marvel Cinematic Universe, or MCU. There was a lot of work ahead of them, but the plan Kevin laid out, including a plan for intertwining characters across multiple films well into the next decade, seemed brilliant to me.)

We assimilated Marvel quickly and easily. Ike kept running the business (which included their publishing, television, and movie divisions, among other things) from New York. Kevin Feige worked from Manhattan Beach and continued to report to Ike. Early on, this structure seemed to work, at least on the surface. The movies were successful, and it was apparent fairly soon after the acquisition that unless we made some egregious unforced errors or were blindsided by some unforeseen outside event, Marvel was going to be worth far more than we'd anticipated.

As we came to understand more closely how Marvel worked, we became aware of a problematic dynamic between the New York office—Marvel's home base—and the film-making business that Kevin oversaw in California. The movie business can be both thrilling and maddening. It doesn't operate like other traditional businesses. It requires making bet after bet based on nothing but instinct. Everything is a risk. You can have what you think is a great idea and the right team assembled, and things can still get derailed for a whole host of reasons that are often beyond your control. A script doesn't come together, a director has bad chemistry with his or her team or has a vision for a film that runs contrary to yours, a competitive movie comes out that upends your expectations. It's easy to get swept up in the glamour of Hollywood and lose all perspective; and it's equally easy to feel contempt for it and lose all perspective. I've seen both occur many times.

Whatever the case, I was detecting a growing tension between the Marvel team in New York and Kevin's team in L.A. The New York office was overseeing the film studio's budget—and therefore experiencing the anxiety over costs and risks—but they were also removed from Hollywood culture and perhaps less sensitive to the challenges of the creative process. Putting pressure on movie executives, particularly creative producers, to make better films for less money isn't necessarily a terrible approach. Any studio has to be aware of the economic realities of the business: production costs do sometimes get out of hand; hard lines do sometimes have to be drawn when it comes to negotiating contracts; there's an endless litany of financial decisions that have to be attended to in order to guard against losing money on a film. It's a fine line, though, and I've often observed how the business side can sometimes put too many demands on the creative process, and be too indifferent to the pressures that the filmmakers are under, and that strain ends up doing more harm than good.

Kevin is one of the most talented film executives in the business, but my sense was that the strained relationship with New York was threatening his continued success. I knew I had to intervene, and so in May 2015, I made the decision to split Marvel's movie-making unit off from the rest of Marvel and bring it under Alan Horn and the Walt Disney Studios. Kevin would now report directly to Alan, and would benefit from his experience, and the tensions that had built up between him and the New York office would be alleviated. The transition wasn't an easy one, but ultimately it defused what could have become an untenable situation.

FIRING PEOPLE, OR taking responsibility away from them, is arguably the most difficult thing you have to do as a boss. There have been several times when I've had to deliver bad news to accomplished people, some of whom were friends, and some of whom had been unable to flourish in positions that I had put them in. There's no good playbook for how to fire someone, though I have my own internal set of rules. You have to do it in person, not over the phone and certainly not by email or text. You have to look the person in the eye. You can't use anyone else as an excuse. This is you making a decision about them—not them as a person but the way they have performed in their job—and they need and deserve to know that it's coming from you. You can't make small talk once you bring someone in for that conversation. I normally say something along the lines of: "I've asked you to come in here for a difficult reason." And then I try to be as direct about the issue as possible, explaining clearly and concisely what wasn't working and why I didn't think it was going to change. I emphasize that it was a tough decision to make, and that I understand that it's much harder on them. There's a kind of euphemistic corporate language that is often deployed in those situations, and it has always struck me as offensive. There's no way for the conversation not to be painful, but at least it can be honest, and in being honest there is at least a chance for the person on the receiving end to understand why it's happening and eventually move on, even if they walk out of the room angry as hell.

In fact, Alan Horn was now the head of Disney Studios as a result of my having fired his predecessor, Rich Ross, whom I'd put into the job right after we'd made the Marvel deal. At the time, I'd thought I was making a bold, unconventional choice. Rich didn't have movie experience, but he'd been tremendously successful running the Disney Channel. He'd launched several franchise shows and coordinated the success of those brands across our divisions. He'd expanded our children's TV business into markets all over the world, but I'd underestimated how hard a leap it would be to run the studio, in part because I still didn't fully appreciate the complexities of the movie business myself. I was eager to make a bold choice, and while Rich didn't have any experience navigating the close-ranked culture of Hollywood, I thought he could bring a different and necessary set of skills to the job.

I've made some big personnel mistakes over the years, and this was one of them. I'd always been grateful that Tom Murphy and Dan Burke had bet on my ability to succeed in one business because I'd succeeded in another. I made that same gamble with Rich, but the transition was just too tough for him, and once he got underwater, he never stopped struggling. After a couple of years we had too few films in the pipeline. Various powerful partners, inside and outside Disney, had lost faith in Rich and were openly complaining about doing business with him. (Ike was one of Rich's most vocal detractors.) As I looked at the studio, very little was going right, and it was clear that my instinct wasn't going to work out. Rather than putting more effort into making it work, or becoming defensive about having done it, I needed to contain the damage, learn from my missteps, and move on, quickly.

At some point in Rich's brief tenure as chairman of Disney Studios, Bob Daly, who was then co-chair of Warner Bros., called me and said I should talk to Alan Horn about serving as an adviser to Rich. Alan had been pushed out as president and COO of Warner Bros. He was sixty-eight at that point, and though he was responsible for several of the biggest films of the past decade, including the Harry Potter franchise, Jeff Bewkes, Time Warner's CEO, wanted someone younger running his studio.

Alan was still contractually bound to Warner Bros. when Bob raised the possibility of his serving as Rich's mentor, but a year later, when it was clear to everyone in the industry that Rich wasn't long for the job, Bob called me again and urged me to consider Alan. I didn't know Alan well, but I respected his work, and I respected what he stood for, inside and outside the industry. I was also aware that the forced retirement had been humiliating for him.

I asked him to breakfast and explained that I needed to replace Rich soon. It was clear over the course of that and two subsequent meetings that Alan wanted to prove he had another chapter in him, but he was also wary of trying something and having it go awry and adding one more sour note to the end of his career. The last thing he needed, he said, was to go to another place and have it not work out.

"I can't afford another mistake, either," I told him. Over the next several months, Alan and I discussed the possibility of his becoming our new studio head. One of the questions was what my involvement in his business would be. I told him that no one at the company could approve huge projects without me. "The head of Parks and Resorts can't build a two-hundred-million-dollar ride without my approval," I said. "The same goes for movies." Though things had ended badly at Warner Bros., Alan was used to having more or less complete autonomy. Even if he wanted to be involved in the movie business, Jeff Bewkes was three thousand miles away in New York. "I'm thirty feet away," I told Alan. "And I care about this, a lot. You need to know before you make a decision that I'll definitely be involved in your business. Ninety-nine percent of the time you'll be able to make what you want to make, but I can't give you total freedom."

Alan eventually agreed, and in the summer of 2012 he came on as the head of Disney Studios. What I saw in him wasn't just someone who at this late stage in his career had the experience to reestablish good relations with the film community. He also had something to prove. He was galvanized, and that energy and focus transformed Disney Studios when he took over. As I write this, he's now past seventy-five and is as vital and astute as anyone in the business. He's been successful in the job beyond all of my hopes. (Of the nearly two dozen Disney films that have earned more than $1 billion at the box office, almost three-quarters of them were released under Alan.) And he's a decent, kind, forthright, collaborative partner to everyone he works with. Which is another lesson to be taken from his hiring: Surround yourself with people who are good in addition to being good at what they do. You can't always predict who will have ethical lapses or reveal a side of themselves you never suspected was there. In the worst cases, you will have to deal with acts that reflect badly on the company and demand censure. That's an unavoidable part of the job, but you have to demand honesty and integrity from everyone, and when there's a lapse you have to deal with it immediately.

THE ACQUISITION OF Marvel has proved to be much more successful than even our most optimistic models accounted for. As I write this, *Avengers: Endgame,* our twentieth Marvel film, is finishing up the most successful opening weeks in movie history. Taken together, the films have averaged more than $1 billion in gross box-office receipts, and their popularity has been felt throughout our theme-park and television and consumer-products businesses in ways we never fully anticipated.

But its impact on the company and on popular culture has gone far beyond the box office. Since 2009, Kevin and Alan and I and a few others have met quarterly to plot out future Marvel releases. We discuss projects that are well into production, and others that are specks of an idea. We mull potential characters to introduce, consider sequels and franchises that we might add to the expanding Marvel Cinematic Universe. We consider actors and directors and think about how the various stories can be cross-pollinated.

I often resort to reading my handy Marvel encyclopedia before these meetings, to immerse myself in the depths of the characters and see if any spark my curiosity enough to push them into development. Back when Kevin was still reporting to Ike and studio decisions were being made by the Marvel team in New York, I raised the issue of diversity in one of these meetings. Marvel films so far had been built largely around characters who were white and who were men. When I said that I thought we should be changing that, Kevin agreed, but was worried that members of the Marvel team in New York would be skeptical. I called the team to discuss my concerns. One of them told me, "Female superheroes never drive big box office." Their other assumption was that international audiences wouldn't want to watch black superheroes.

I didn't believe that those old "truisms" were actually true, and so we started to discuss what characters we could introduce in their own films. Kevin mentioned Black Panther, who was about to be written into the *Captain America: Civil War* script, and Alan and I were both intrigued. Chadwick Boseman, who'd received considerable acclaim for playing Jackie Robinson in *42*, was going to be cast as Black Panther. He was such a magnetic, compelling actor, and I could easily see him in a leading Marvel role.

Around the same time, Dan Buckley, who runs Marvel's television and comic book businesses, told me that the writer Ta-Nehisi Coates, who I felt was one of the most important voices in contemporary American literature, was writing a Black Panther comic for us. I asked Dan to send it to me and was amazed by the elegant storytelling and the way Ta-Nehisi had added such depth to the character. I devoured the comic, and before I even finished it had placed *Black Panther* on the list of must-do Marvel projects in my mind.

The Marvel skeptics in New York weren't the only ones who felt that a black-led superhero movie couldn't perform at the box office. There's a long-held view in Hollywood that films with predominantly black casts, or with black leads, will struggle in many international markets. That assumption has limited the number of black-led films being produced, and black actors being cast, and many of those that have been made had reduced budgets to mitigate the box-office risk.

I've been in the business long enough to have heard every old argument in the book, and I've learned that old arguments are just that: old, and out of step with where the world is and where it should be. We had a chance to make a great movie and to showcase an underrepresented segment of America, and those goals were not mutually exclusive. I called Ike and told him to tell his team to stop putting up roadblocks and ordered that we put both *Black Panther* and *Captain Marvel* into production.

Ike heeded my requests. We put *Black Panther* into development immediately, and *Captain Marvel* followed soon after. Both movies defied every preconceived notion of what they would do at the box office. As I write this, *Black Panther* is the fourth-highest-grossing superhero film of all time, and *Captain Marvel* the tenth. Both have earned well over $1 billion. Both were extraordinarily successful internationally. What they've achieved culturally, though, is even more significant.

The experience of watching *Black Panther* with the crowd of people that packed the Dolby Theatre for the premiere will remain one of the most memorable moments of my career. Until then, I'd only seen it during screenings at my house or with a small group at the studio. I knew we had something special, but you're never quite sure how something is going to be received. Still, I couldn't wait to share it with the world, and to see and feel their reaction to it. That night the energy in the room was electric long before the lights went down. You could feel the anticipation that something unprecedented was about to happen, something historic, and the film more than exceeded those expectations.

Afterward, I received more calls and notes than I'd ever received about anything I'd been associated with in my career. Spike Lee and Denzel Washington and Gayle King reached out. I'd had a production assistant deliver a copy of the film to President Obama, and when I spoke with him after, he told me how important he believed the film was. Oprah sent a note calling it "a phenomenon in every way" and adding, "It makes me tear up to think that little black children will grow up with that forever."

There may be no product we've created that I'm more proud of than *Black Panther*. After its opening week, I felt the need to share my pride of the film and sent this note out to everyone in the company:

Dear Fellow Employee,

It's hard not starting with "Wakanda forever," as we share great news about *Black Panther*!

Marvel's *Black Panther* is a masterpiece of movie making, a film that succeeds on multiple levels, touching hearts and opening minds . . . all while entertaining millions of people and far exceeding the loftiest box office projections. This groundbreaking movie opened to a record-breaking $242 million in domestic box office over the holiday weekend, and delivered the second-highest four-day opening in movie history. Worldwide box office to date is more than $426 million, and the movie has yet to open in a number of major markets.

Black Panther has also become an instant cultural phenomenon, sparking discussion, causing reflection, inspiring people young and old, and breaking down age-old industry myths.

As CEO of this phenomenal company, I receive a lot of feedback about what we create. In the 12 years I've had this role I have never seen such an overwhelming outpouring of genuine excitement, praise, respect, and gratitude as I've seen for *Black Panther*. . . . It speaks to the importance of showcasing diverse voices and visions, and how powerful it is for all sectors of our society to be seen and represented in our art and entertainment. The movie's success is also a testament to our company's willingness to champion bold business and creative initiatives, our ability to execute an innovative vision flawlessly, and our commitment to bringing extraordinary entertainment to a world that is hungry for heroes, role models, and unbelievably great storytelling.

CHAPTER 11

STAR WARS

I WOULD HAVE LIKED for Steve to have seen what our invest-ment in Marvel turned into. He probably would have never cared much for the movies (although I think he would have appreciated how *Black Panther* and *Captain Marvel* flew in the face of industry shibboleths), but he would have been proud that he'd been instru-mental in bringing Ike around, and that the brand had flourished so much under Disney.

With every success the company has had since Steve's death, there's always a moment in the midst of my excitement when I think, *I wish Steve could be here for this.* It's impossible not to have the conversation with him in my head that I wish I could be having in real life.

In the summer of 2011, Steve and his wife, Laurene, came to our house in L.A. to have dinner with Willow and me. He was in the late stages of cancer by then, terribly thin and in obvious pain. He had very little energy, and his voice was a low rasp. But he wanted to spend an evening with us, in part to toast what we'd done years ago. We sat in our dining room and raised glasses of wine before dinner. "Look what we did," he said. "We saved two companies."

All four of us teared up. This was Steve at his warmest and most sincere. He was convinced that Pixar had flourished in ways that it never would have had it not become part of Disney, and that Disney had been reenergized by bringing on Pixar. I couldn't help but think of those early conversations and how nervous I was to reach out to him. It was only six years ago, but it seemed like another lifetime. He'd become so important to me, professionally and personally. As we toasted, I could barely look at Willow. She had known Steve much longer than I had, going way back to 1982, when he was one of the young, brash, brilliant founders of Apple. Now he was gaunt and frail and in the last months of his life, and I knew how much it pained her to see him that way.

He died on October 5, 2011. There were about twenty-five people at his burial in Palo Alto. We gathered in a tight square around his coffin, and Laurene asked if anyone wanted to say anything. I hadn't prepared to speak, but the memory of that walk we took on Pixar's campus years earlier came to mind.

I'd never told anyone other than Alan Braverman, our general counsel, and Willow, because I needed to share the emotional intensity of that day with my wife. I thought the moment captured Steve's character, though, so I recalled it there at the cemetery: Steve pulling me aside; the walk across campus; the way he put his arm around me and delivered the news; his concern that I should have this intimate, terrible knowledge, because it might affect me and Disney and he wanted to be fully transparent; the emotion with which he talked about his son and his need to live long enough to see him graduate from high school and begin his life as an adult.

After the funeral, Laurene came up to me and said, "I've never told my side of that story." She described Steve coming home that night. "We had dinner, and then the kids left the dinner table, and I said to Steve, 'So, did you tell him?' 'I told him.' And I said, 'Can we trust him?'" We were standing there with Steve's grave behind us, and Laurene, who'd just buried her husband, gave me a gift that I've thought about nearly every day since. I've certainly thought of Steve every day. "I asked him if we could trust you," Laurene said. "And Steve said, 'I love that guy.'"

The feeling was mutual.

WHEN I WENT up to Cupertino to talk with Steve about Marvel, he asked if I was looking at anything else. I mentioned Lucasfilm, and he said, "You should just call George." Steve had bought Pixar from George Lucas, and he and George had been close for years. "You never know," he said. "George might be interested. The two of us should go to his ranch and have lunch with him one day."

We never did make that lunch. Steve soon became too sick, and his involvement in Disney's business waned. But Lucas had been at the top of our acquisition list ever since we'd completed the Marvel deal, and I'd been thinking about how to approach George in a way that wouldn't offend him with the suggestion that he sell *us* the marvelous worlds that he'd created.

Michael Eisner had made a licensing agreement with George back in the mid-'80s to build *Star Wars*- and *Indiana Jones*–themed attractions at our parks. And in May 2011, we were reopening the *Star Wars* attractions (Star Tours, they're called) in Disney World and Disneyland after a yearlong refurbishing. I knew George was going to Orlando to rededicate the attraction as a favor to the company and his friends in Imagineering, and I decided to join him. With the occasional exception, I normally leave the opening of new attractions to the head of Parks and Resorts, but I thought this might give me a chance to at least float the idea with George and get some sense of whether he'd ever consider selling to us.

Our relationship went back to my days running ABC Entertainment. After the success of *Twin Peaks*, some of the most respected directors in Hollywood started expressing interest in making television series with us. I met with George and he pitched an idea for a show that would follow a young Indiana Jones as he traveled around the world. "Each episode will be a history lesson," George said. Indy would interact with historical figures like Churchill and Freud and Degas and Mata Hari. I gave him a very fast yes, and in 1992, we put *The Young Indiana Jones Chronicles* on Monday nights as a lead-in to *Monday Night Football*. The show opened to big numbers, but over time the audience lost interest in the historical lessons, and ratings fell. But George had delivered everything he'd said he would, and I felt that because of that, and because this was George Lucas, it deserved a second season and another chance to catch on with viewers. It never did, but George had been grateful at the time that I'd given the show that chance.

On the day of the rededication of Star Tours in Orlando, I set up a breakfast with him at the Brown Derby, which was near the attraction in our Hollywood Studios Park. The restaurant doesn't normally open before lunch, but I asked them to set up a table just for us, so we would have privacy. When George and his fiancée, Mellody Hobson, arrived, they were surprised to see that no one was there but me. We sat down and had a lovely breakfast, and about halfway through it I asked George if he'd ever thought about selling. I tried to be clear and direct without offending him. He was sixty-eight years old at the time, and I said, "I don't want to be fatalistic, George, and please stop me if you would rather not have this conversation, but I think it's worth putting this on the table. What happens down the road? You don't have any heirs who are going to run the company for you. They may control it, but they're not going to run it. Shouldn't you determine who protects or carries on your legacy?"

He nodded as I talked. "I'm not really ready to sell," he said. "But you're right. And if I decide to, there isn't anyone I want to sell to but you." He recalled *Young Indiana Jones* and how much he appreciated that I'd given the show a chance even when it didn't have the ratings. And then he brought up what we'd done with Pixar, which at some point Steve must have spoken to him about. "You did that right," he said. "You took care of them. If I get around to it, you're the only call I'll make."

He said something else that I kept in mind in every subsequent conversation we had: "When I die, the first line of my obituary is going to read '*Star Wars* creator George Lucas . . .'" It was so much a part of who he was, which of course I knew, but having him look into my eyes and say it like that underscored the most important factor in these conversations. This wasn't negotiating to buy a business; it was negotiating to be the keeper of George's legacy, and I needed to be ultra-sensitive to that at all times.

Much to the chagrin of Kevin Mayer and some others at Disney, who were lusting after Lucasfilm because, like Marvel and Pixar before it, it fit so perfectly into our strategy, I decided not to reach out to George after our discussion in Florida. If the conversation went forward, it would have to be because he decided he wanted it. I had such respect and affection for George, and I needed him to know this was in his hands. So we waited. About seven months after that breakfast, George called me and said, "I'd like to have lunch to talk more about that thing we talked about in Orlando."

We met for lunch at Disney in Burbank, and I let George lead the conversation. He quickly got down to business and said he'd been thinking about our conversation and was ready to get serious about selling. Then he said he wanted "the Pixar deal." I was thrilled he was open to exploring an acquisition, but I understood what he meant by the Pixar deal, and it was immediately clear that the negotiation wasn't going to be easy. We already sensed Lucasfilm was potentially quite valuable for us, but it wasn't worth $7.4 billion, at least not based on our analysis at that point. When we were pursuing Pixar, there were six movies already in varying stages of production, and a general sense of when they would be released. That meant they would generate revenue and profits quickly. Pixar also came with a big group of world-class engineers, seasoned directors, artists and writers, and a real production infrastructure. Lucas had many talented employees, particularly on the tech side, but no directors other than George, and no film development or production pipeline, as far as we knew. We'd done some work trying to figure out their value, and Kevin and I had discussions about what we might pay, but because they weren't a publicly traded company, their financial information wasn't accessible and there was a lot we didn't know or couldn't see. Our analysis was built on a set of guesses, and from those we tried to build a financial model—valuing their library of films and television shows; their publishing and licensing assets; their brand, which was dominated by *Star Wars;* and their special effects business, Industrial Light and Magic, which George had founded years earlier to provide the dazzling special effects for his films.

We then projected what we might do if we owned them, which was pure conjecture. We guessed we could produce and release a *Star Wars* film every other year in the first six years after acquiring them, but it would take us time to get started, since we didn't detect that anything was in development. This analysis took place in early 2012, so we estimated our first *Star Wars* release would be in May 2015, if we could acquire them quickly. Other films would follow in 2017 and 2019. Then we estimated what the global box office of the films would bring in, which was even more conjecture, since the last *Star Wars* film, *Revenge of the Sith,* was released in 2005, seven years earlier. Kevin gave me a collection of reviews from all of the previously released films and a rundown of what they earned, and we settled on at least a billion dollars in global box office for our first three films.

Next, we tackled their licensing business. *Star Wars* remained very popular with kids, particularly young boys, who were still assembling Lego Millennium Falcons and playing with lightsabers. Adding that licensing business to our consumer products business would be quite valuable, but we had no access to the actual revenue being generated from licensing. Lastly, we considered what we might do at our theme parks, given the fact that we were already paying Lucasfilm for the rights to the Star Tours attractions in three of our locations. I had big dreams about what we might build, but we decided to ascribe little or no value to them because there were too many unknowns.

In George's mind, Lucasfilm was as valuable as Pixar, but even from our relatively uninformed analysis they weren't. They might be someday, but it would take years of work to get it there, and we'd still have to make great films. I didn't want to offend him, but I didn't want to lead him on, either. The worst thing you can do when entering into a negotiation is to suggest or promise something because you know the other person wants to hear it, only to have to reverse course later. You have to be clear about where you stand from the beginning. I knew if I misled George, simply to begin the bargaining process, or to keep the conversation going, it would ultimately backfire on me.

So I said right away, "There's no way this is a Pixar deal, George." And I explained why, recalling my visit to Pixar early on, and the richness of creativity that I discovered.

He was momentarily taken aback, and I thought the discussions might end right there. Instead, he said, "Well, then, what do we do?"

I told him we needed to look closely at Lucasfilm and we needed his cooperation. We'd sign a confidentiality agreement, and we would do it in a way that wouldn't raise too many questions within his company. "We just need your CFO or someone who knows the financial structure to walk us through it," I said. "I have a small team that will go in there and do it quickly. We'll keep it very quiet. Other than a few people, your employees won't know that we're snooping around."

Typically, the price we pay for assets doesn't vary much from what we believe the value to be in the first place. It's often possible to start low and hope to pay far less than what you're valuing an asset at, but in the process you risk alienating the person you're negotiating with. "I don't mess around when it comes to these

things," I told George. We would quickly arrive at a number that
we believed his company was worth—and one that I believed I
could sell to the board, to our shareholders, and to Wall Street—
and whatever that number was, I said, "I'm not going to come in
low and negotiate toward the middle. I'm going to do it the way I
did it with Steve."

George allowed us the access we needed, but at the end of that
process we still found ourselves struggling to settle on a firm valu-
ation. A lot of our concern had to do with how to assess our own
ability to begin making good movies—and quickly. We hadn't
begun to form a long-term creative vision because we had no creative people assigned to the task. We had nothing, really, which
meant there was a lot of creative risk, and hitting the schedule we'd
set for ourselves—and which our financial analysis was based on—
would be daunting and maybe impossible.

I eventually called George and told him we had narrowed it
down to a price range, and we still needed time to home in on a
specific price. It would be between $3.5 billion and $3.75 billion.
George had come way down from his "Pixar price," but I could tell
he was not going to accept anything lower than Marvel. I met with
Kevin and his team and we looked at our analysis again. We didn't
want to falsely raise our box office estimates, but even at the top
end of the range I'd given George, there was some room for us to
pay more, though it would put a lot more pressure on the timing
and performance of the films. Could we make three in six years?
These were *Star Wars* films, and we would have to be very careful.
Ultimately, Kevin and I decided we could afford $4.05 billion, or
slightly above what we paid for Marvel, and George immediately
agreed.

Then the more difficult negotiations began over what George's
creative involvement would be. In Pixar's case, the entire acquisition was predicated on John and Ed's continued involvement not
just with Pixar but with Disney Animation. John became chief cre-

ative officer, but he still reported to me. With Marvel, I'd met with Kevin Feige and the rest of their team and I knew what they had in the works, and we'd begun collaborating closely to determine the future of Marvel films. With Lucas, there was only one person with creative control—George. He wanted to retain that control without becoming an employee. It would have been a dereliction of my responsibilities to spend more than $4 billion and then say, essentially, *This is still yours. Go ahead and make whatever movies you want to make on whatever timeline you can make them.*

Few people in the film business commanded as much respect as George. *Star Wars* had only ever been his. No matter how much he understood intellectually that he was selling the company and it didn't make sense that he would retain creative control, his entire self was wrapped up in the fact that he was responsible for what was perhaps the greatest mythology of our time. That's a hard thing to let go, and I was deeply sensitive to that. The last thing I wanted to do was insult him.

I also knew we couldn't spend this money and do what George wanted, and that saying that to him would put the whole deal at risk. That is exactly what happened. We agreed to a price quickly, but then we negotiated back and forth for several months over what his role would be. It was difficult for him to cede control of the ongoing *Star Wars* saga, and it made no sense for us not to have it. We went over and over the same ground—George saying he couldn't just hand over his legacy, me saying we couldn't buy it and not control it—and twice walked away from the table and called the deal off. (We walked the first time and George walked the second.)

At some point in the process, George told me that he had completed outlines for three new movies. He agreed to send us three copies of the outlines: one for me; one for Alan Braverman; and one for Alan Horn, who'd just been hired to run our studio. Alan Horn and I read George's outlines and decided we needed to buy them, though we made clear in the purchase agreement that we would not be contractually obligated to adhere to the plot lines he'd laid out.

It was an upcoming change in capital gains laws that eventually salvaged the negotiations. If we didn't close the deal by the end of 2012, George, who owned Lucasfilm outright, would take a roughly $500 million hit on the sale. If he was going to sell to us, there was some financial urgency to come to an agreement quickly. He knew that I was going to stand firm on the question of creative control, but it wasn't an easy thing for him to accept. And so he reluctantly agreed to be available to consult with us at our request. I promised that we would be open to his ideas (this was not a hard promise to make; of course we would be open to George Lucas's ideas), but like the outlines, we would be under no obligation.

On October 30, 2012, George came to my office, and we sat at my desk and signed an agreement for Disney to buy Lucasfilm. He was doing everything he could not to show it, but I could tell in the sound of his voice and the look in his eyes how emotional it was for him. He was signing away *Star Wars*, after all.

A FEW MONTHS before we closed the deal, George hired the producer Kathy Kennedy to run Lucasfilm. Kathy had cofounded Amblin Entertainment along with her husband, Frank Marshall, and Steven Spielberg, and had produced *E.T.* and the *Jurassic Park* franchise and dozens of critical and commercial hits. It was an interesting move on George's part. We were on the verge of buying the company, but he suddenly decided who was going to run it and ultimately produce the upcoming films. It didn't upset us, but it did come as a surprise, just as it surprised Kathy to learn that the company she was agreeing to run was about to be sold! Kathy is a legendary producer, and she has been a great partner, and this was one final way for George to put someone in whom he trusted to be the steward of his legacy.

The deal closed at the end of 2012, and Kathy, Alan, and I began searching for a creative team. We eventually convinced J.J. Abrams to direct our first *Star Wars* movie and hired Michael Arndt, who'd written *Toy Story 3* and *Little Miss Sunshine,* to write the script. J.J. and I had dinner soon after he decided to take on the project. We'd known each other from back in the ABC days—he'd made *Alias* and *Lost* for us, among other things—and it was important to me to sit down and acknowledge what we both knew, that the stakes on this project were higher than anything either of us had ever done before. I joked at some point during dinner that this was a "$4 billion movie"—meaning that the whole acquisition depended on its success—which J.J. later told me wasn't funny at all.

I know how he appreciated that I had as much skin in this one as he did, though, and we could share the burden of what it meant to be responsible for the first *Star Wars* film not made by George Lucas. In all of our interactions, from initial conversations about how the myth should unfold to visits to the set and the editing room, I tried to communicate to J.J. that I was a *partner* in the project and not just a CEO putting pressure on him to deliver a great film and a big box office success. There was more than enough pressure to go around for both of us, and I wanted him to feel that he could call me at any moment to discuss any problem he was wrestling with, and that I would call him with ideas that I had. I was a resource for him, and a collaborator, but not someone who needed to put my stamp on this film out of vanity or title or obligation. Luckily, we have similar sensibilities and tastes, and we mostly agreed on what was problematic and what was working. Over the lengthy development and production process, in Los Angeles, and then at the Pinewood Studios in London, in Iceland, in Scotland, and in Abu Dhabi, J.J. proved to be a great collaborator and never lost sight of the enormity of the project or the tremendous burden it carried—with George, with *Star Wars* fans, with the press, and with our investors.

There's no rule book for how to manage this kind of challenge, but in general, you have to try to recognize that when the stakes of a project are very high, there's not much to be gained from putting additional pressure on the people working on it. Projecting your anxiety onto your team is counterproductive. It's subtle, but there's a difference between communicating that you share their stress— that you're in it *with* them—and communicating that you need them to deliver in order to alleviate your stress. No one on this project needed reminding of what was at stake. My job was to not let us lose sight of our ambition when we confronted creative and practical obstacles, and to help us get to solutions in the best possible way. Sometimes that meant allocating more resources, sometimes it meant talking through new drafts of a script, or watching endless dailies and numerous cuts of the film. Often it just meant reminding J.J. and Kathy Kennedy and Alan Horn that I believed in all of them and there were no better hands for this film to be in.

That's not to say it was a smooth ride from the start. Early on, Kathy brought J.J. and Michael Arndt up to Northern California to meet with George at his ranch and talk about their ideas for the film. George immediately got upset as they began to describe the plot and it dawned on him that we weren't using one of the stories he submitted during the negotiations.

The truth was, Kathy, J.J., Alan, and I had discussed the direction in which the saga should go, and we all agreed that it wasn't what George had outlined. George knew we weren't contractually bound to anything, but he thought that our buying the story treatments was a tacit promise that we'd follow them, and he was disappointed that his story was being discarded. I'd been so careful since our first conversation not to mislead him in any way, and I didn't think I had now, but I could have handled it better. I should have prepared him for the meeting with J.J. and Michael and told him about our conversations, that we felt it was better to go in another direction. I could have talked through this with him and possibly avoided angering him by not surprising him. Now, in the first meeting with him about the future of *Star Wars*, George felt betrayed, and while this whole process would never have been easy for him, we'd gotten off to an unnecessarily rocky start.

THERE WERE OTHER struggles on top of George's feelings about the film. Michael wrestled with the screenplay for months, and eventually J.J. and Kathy made the decision to replace him with Larry Kasdan, who'd co-written *The Empire Strikes Back* and *Return of the Jedi* with George (as well as *Raiders of the Lost Ark* and *The Big Chill* and many others). Larry and J.J. completed a draft fairly quickly, and we began shooting in the spring of 2014.

We'd originally planned to release the movie in May 2015, but because of those early script delays and some other complications later on, we didn't release it until December. This moved it out of our 2015 fiscal year and into our 2016 fiscal year. My presentation to the board prior to the acquisition, and our disclosures to investors assuring them that we would begin to see a return on investment in 2015, turned out not to be true. Hundreds of millions of dollars moved out of one fiscal year and into the next. This was not a huge deal, but it had to be dealt with.

One of the biggest mistakes that I've seen film studios make is getting locked into a release date and then letting that influence creative decisions, often rushing movies into production before they're ready. I've tried hard not to give in to calendar pressures. It's better to give up a release date and keep working to make a better movie, and we've always tried to put quality before everything else, even if it means taking a short-term hit to our bottom line. In this case, the last thing we wanted to do was put out a movie that didn't live up to the expectations of *Star Wars* fans. The *Star Wars* fan base is so passionate, and it was vital that we give them something they loved and felt worthy of their devotion. If we didn't get that right on our first *Star Wars* film, we'd suffer a breach of trust with our audience that would be very hard to recover from.

Just prior to the global release, Kathy screened *The Force Awak-*

ens for George. He didn't hide his disappointment. "There's nothing new," he said. In each of the films in the original trilogy, it was important to him to present new worlds, new stories, new characters, and new technologies. In this one, he said, "There weren't enough visual or technical leaps forward." He wasn't wrong, but he also wasn't appreciating the pressure we were under to give ardent fans a film that felt quintessentially *Star Wars*. We'd intentionally created a world that was visually and tonally connected to the earlier films, to not stray too far from what people loved and expected, and George was criticizing us for the very thing we were trying to do. Looking back with the perspective of several years and a few more *Star Wars* films, I believe J.J. achieved the near-impossible, creating a perfect bridge between what had been and what was to come.

On top of George's reaction, there was a lot of speculation in the press and from die-hard fans about how we were going to "Disney-fy" *Star Wars*. As with Marvel, I made the decision not to put "Disney" anywhere in the film credits or the marketing campaigns, and to not in any way change the *Star Wars* logo. "Disney-Pixar" made sense from an animation-branding perspective, but Lucas fans needed to be reassured that we, too, were fans first, respectful of the creator and looking to expand on his legacy, not usurp it.

Even though he had issues with the film, I thought it was important for George to be at the *Force Awakens* premiere. He didn't want to come at first, but Kathy, with the help of George's now-wife, Mellody Hobson, convinced him it was the right thing to do. Among the last things we negotiated before the deal closed was a non-disparagement clause. I asked George to agree that he wouldn't publicly criticize any of the *Star Wars* films we made. When I brought it up with him, he said, "I'm going to be a big shareholder of the Walt Disney Company. Why would I disparage you or anything you do? You have to trust me." I took him at his word.

The question now was how to handle the premiere. I wanted the world to know that this was J.J.'s movie, and Kathy's movie, and it was our first *Star Wars* movie. It certainly was by far the biggest film we'd released since I became CEO. We held a gigantic premiere in the Dolby Theatre, where the Academy Awards take place. I went onstage first, and before I brought J.J. and Kathy out with me, I said, "We're all here because of one person, who created the greatest mythology of our time and then entrusted it to the Walt Disney Company." George was in his seat. He got a long, rapturous standing ovation. Willow was sitting in the row behind him and took a wonderful picture of him, surrounded by a few thousand people, all on their feet. I was happy to look at it later and see how pleased and grateful George was at the outpouring of admiration for him.

The movie opened and set a slew of box-office records, and we all breathed a sigh of relief. Our first *Star Wars* film was behind us and the *Star Wars* faithful appeared to have loved it. Shortly after the release, though, an interview George had done a few weeks earlier with Charlie Rose aired. George talked about his frustration that we hadn't followed his outlines and said that selling to Disney was like selling his children to "white slavers." It was an unfortunate and awkward way for him to describe the feeling of having sold something that he considered his children. I decided to stay quiet and let it pass. There was nothing to be gained from engaging in any public discourse or waging a defense. Mellody sent me an apologetic email, explaining how difficult this had all been for him. Then George called me. "I was out of line," he said. "I shouldn't have said it like that. I was trying to explain how hard it is to let this thing go."

I told him I understood. Four and a half years earlier, I'd sat with George at breakfast and tried to convey that I knew how difficult this would be for him, but that when he was ready, he could trust me. All of the negotiations—over the money, and then over the question of his ongoing involvement with *Star Wars*—were exercises in balancing my respect for what George had done, and how deeply personal I knew this was for him, with my responsibility to the company. I could empathize with George, but I couldn't give him what he wanted. At every step of the way it was necessary to be clear about where I stood, while being sensitive toward how emotional the entire process was for him.

Looking back on the acquisitions of Pixar, Marvel, and Lucasfilm, the thread that runs through all of them (other than that, taken together, they transformed Disney) is that each deal depended on building trust with a single controlling entity. There were complicated issues to negotiate in all of the deals, and our respective teams spent long days and weeks reaching agreement on them. But the personal component of each of these deals was going to make or break them, and authenticity was crucial. Steve had to believe my promise that we would respect the essence of Pixar. Ike needed to know that the Marvel team would be valued and given the chance to thrive in their new company. And George had to trust that his legacy, his "baby," would be in good hands at Disney.

CHAPTER 12

IF YOU DON'T INNOVATE, YOU DIE

AFTER THE DUST settled on the last of our "big three" acquisitions, we began to focus even more on the dramatic changes we were experiencing in our media businesses and the profound disruption we were feeling. The future of those businesses had begun to seriously worry us, and we concluded it was time for us to start delivering our content in new and modern ways, and to do so without intermediaries, on our own technology platform.

The questions for us were: Could we find the technology we needed to accomplish that and be at the forefront of change rather than simply being undone by it? Did we have the stomach to start cannibalizing our own still-profitable businesses in order to begin building a new model? Could we disrupt ourselves, and would Wall Street tolerate the losses that we would inevitably incur as we tried to truly modernize and transform the company?

We had to do it, I was sure of that. It was the old lesson all over again about the need to constantly innovate. So the next question was: Do we build a tech platform or do we buy one? Kevin Mayer warned me that building one would take five years and would be a massive investment. Buying one would give us the ability to pivot immediately, and the speed at which everything was changing made clear that patience was not an option. When we looked at acquisitions, Google, Apple, Amazon, and Facebook were obviously off the table, given their size, and as far as we knew, none of them was looking to buy us. (Although I did believe that if Steve were still alive, we would have combined our companies, or at least discussed the possibility very seriously.)

What was left was Snapchat, Spotify, and Twitter. They were all digestible in terms of size, but who was potentially for sale, and who delivered the qualities we needed to reach our consumers most effectively and rapidly? We landed on Twitter. We were less interested in them as a social media company than as a new distribution platform with global reach, which we could use to deliver movies, television, sports, and news.

In the summer of 2016, we expressed interest to Twitter. They were intrigued, but felt they had an obligation to test the market, and so we reluctantly entered into an auction to buy them. By early fall, we'd virtually closed a deal. Twitter's board supported the sale, and on a Friday afternoon in October, our board gave their approval to finalize a deal. Then, that weekend, I decided not to go through with it. If earlier acquisitions, especially Pixar, were about trusting my instinct that it was the right thing for the company, the acquisition of Twitter was the opposite of that. Something inside me didn't *feel* right. Echoing in my head was something Tom Murphy had said to me years earlier: "If something doesn't feel right *to* you, then it's probably not right *for* you." I could see clearly how the platform could work to serve our new purposes, but there were brand-related issues that gnawed at me.

Twitter was a potentially powerful platform for us, but I couldn't get past the challenges that would come with it. The challenges and controversies were almost too much to list, but they included how to manage hate speech, and making fraught decisions regarding freedom of speech, what to do about fake accounts algorithmically spewing out political "messaging" to influence elections, and the general rage and lack of civility that was sometimes evident on the platform. Those would become our problems. They were so unlike any we'd encountered, and I felt they would be corrosive to the Disney brand. On the Sunday after the board had just given me the go-ahead to pursue the acquisition of Twitter, I sent a note to all of the members telling them I had "cold feet," and explaining my reasoning for withdrawing. Then I called Jack Dorsey, Twitter's CEO, who was also a member of the Disney board. Jack was stunned, but very polite. I wished Jack luck, and I hung up feeling relieved.

AROUND THE SAME TIME that we entered into the Twitter negotiations, we also invested in a company called BAMTech, which was primarily owned by Major League Baseball and had perfected a streaming technology that allowed fans to subscribe to an online service and watch all of their favorite teams' games live. (They'd also been hired, after HBO failed to build its own streaming service, to come in and, under intense time pressure, build HBO Now in time for the release of season five of *Game of Thrones*.)

In August 2016, we agreed to pay about $1 billion for a 33 percent stake in the company, with an option to buy a controlling interest in 2020. The initial plan was to address the threats to ESPN's business by creating a subscription service that would exist alongside the programming on ESPN's networks, but as tech companies invested more deeply in their entertainment subscription services, the urgency for us to create direct-to-consumer bundles not just for sports but for television and movies intensified.

Ten months later, in June 2017, we held our annual board retreat at Walt Disney World in Orlando. The yearly retreat is an extended board meeting, in which we present our five-year plan, including financial projections, and discuss specific strategic issues and challenges. We decided to spend the entire 2017 session talking about disruption, and I instructed each of our business leaders to present to the board the level of disruption they were seeing and what impact they predicted it would have on the health of their business.

I knew the board would demand solutions, and, as a general rule, I don't like to lay out problems without offering a plan for addressing them. (This is something I exhort my team to do, too—it's okay to come to me with problems, but also offer possible solutions.) So after detailing the changes we were both experiencing and projecting, we then presented to the board a bold, aggressive, comprehensive solution: We would accelerate our option to buy a controlling stake in BAMTech, and then use that platform to launch Disney and an ESPN direct-to-consumer, "over the top" video streaming services.

The board not only supported the plan, but urged me to move as quickly as possible, saying "speed was of the essence." (This is also an endorsement for populating boards with people who are not only wise and confident in their opinions, but also have direct and relevant experience of current market dynamics. In our case, Mark Parker from Nike and Mary Barra from General Motors are two perfect examples. Both have witnessed profound disruption to their businesses, and both are keenly aware of the perils of not adapting quickly to change.) I met with my team immediately after the board retreat and gave them the feedback I received, instructing Kevin to move quickly to purchase control of BAMTech and telling everyone else to prepare for a significant strategic shift into the streaming business.

On our August 2017 earnings call—exactly two years after a fateful call in which we'd watched our stock get clobbered as I spoke frankly about disruption—we announced that we were accelerating our agreement to buy full control of BAMTech, and we shared our plans to launch two streaming services: one for ESPN in 2018, and one for Disney in 2019. This time, our stock soared.

Investors understood our strategy and recognized both the need for change and the opportunity that existed.

THAT ANNOUNCEMENT MARKED the beginning of the reinvention of the Walt Disney Company. We would continue supporting our television channels in the traditional space, for as long as they continued to generate decent returns, and we would continue to present our films on big screens in movie theaters all over the world, but we were now fully committed to also becoming a distributor of our own content, straight to consumers, without intermediaries. In essence, we were now hastening the disruption of our own businesses, and the short-term losses were going to be significant. (As one example, pulling all of our TV shows and movies—including Pixar and Marvel and Star Wars—from Netflix's platform and consolidating them all under our own subscription service would mean sacrificing hundreds of millions of dollars in licensing fees.)

At some point over the years, I referred to a concept I called "management by press release"—meaning that if I say something with great conviction to the outside world, it tends to resonate powerfully inside our company. The investment community's reaction in 2015 was overwhelmingly negative, but speaking candidly about the reality punctured our denial and motivated people within Disney to conclude, *He's serious about this, so we better be, too.* The 2017 call had a similarly bracing effect. The team knew how serious I was about doing this, but hearing it communicated broadly, particularly to investors, and witnessing the reaction to it, fueled everyone with the energy and the commitment to move forward.

Before we'd made the announcement, I'd assumed we would transition to the new model in baby steps, slowly building the apps and determining what content would live on them. Now, because the response was so positive, the entire strategy took on a greater sense of urgency. There were now expectations that we had to live up to. That meant added pressure, but it also gave me a powerful communications tool within the company, where there would naturally be some resistance to changing so much, so fast.

The decision to disrupt businesses that are fundamentally working but whose future is in question—intentionally taking on short-term losses in the hope of generating long-term growth—requires no small amount of courage. Routines and priorities get disrupted, jobs change, responsibility is reallocated. People can easily become unsettled as their traditional way of doing business begins to erode and a new model emerges. It's a lot to manage, from a personnel perspective, and the need to be *present* for your people—which is a vital leadership quality under any circumstances—is heightened even more. It's easy for leaders to send a signal that their schedules are too full, their time too valuable, to be dealing with individual problems and concerns. But being present for your people—and making sure they know that you're available to them—is so important for the morale and effectiveness of a company. With a company the size of Disney, this can mean traveling around the world and holding regular town hall–style meetings with our various business units, communicating my thinking and responding to concerns, but it also means responding in a timely way and being thoughtful about any issues brought to me by my direct reports—returning phone calls and replying to emails, making the time to talk through specific problems, being sensitive to the pressures people are feeling. All of this became an even more significant part of the job as we embarked on this new, uncertain path.

We immediately began working on two fronts in the wake of our August announcement. On the tech side, the team at BAM-Tech, along with a group that was already in place at Disney, started building the interfaces for our new services, ESPN+ and Disney+. For the next several months, Kevin and I met in New York and Los Angeles with the team at BAMTech to test various iterations of the app: analyzing the size and color and placement of the tiles; honing the experience of moving through the app to make it more instinctive and easier to use; determining how the algorithms and data collection would function, as well as how our content and brands would be presented.

At the same time, back in L.A., we were putting a team together to develop and produce the content that would be available on Disney+. We had a vast library of films and TV shows (though we had to buy back some rights that we'd licensed to third parties over the years), but the big question was: What original content would we make for these new services? I met with the heads of our movie studios and television operations to determine what projects in our pipeline would be released in theaters or placed on our TV channels and what would go on the app. What new projects would we create expressly for the service, including original Star Wars and Marvel and Pixar stories, that would feel as ambitious as anything we make? I brought together the senior people from all of our studios and told them, "I don't want to create a new studio to make products for Disney+. I want you to do it."

These are all executives who have been trained for years to grow their own businesses and are compensated based on their profitability. Suddenly I was saying to them, essentially, "I want you to pay less attention to the business at which you've been very successful, and start paying more attention to this other thing. And by the way, you have to work on this new thing along with these other very competitive people from other teams, whose interests don't necessarily line up with yours. And one more thing, it won't make money for a while."

In order to get them all on board, I not only had to reinforce why these changes were necessary, but I also had to create an entirely new incentive structure to reward them for their work. I couldn't penalize them for the purposeful erosion and disruption of their businesses, and yet there were no early bottom-line metrics to assess "success" in the new business. We were asking them to work *more,* considerably more, and, if we were using traditional compensation methods, earn *less.* That would not work.

I went to our board's compensation committee and explained the dilemma. When you innovate, everything needs to change, not just the way you make or deliver a product. Many of the practices and structures within the company need to adapt, too, including, in this case, how the board rewards our executives. I proposed a radical idea—essentially, that I would determine compensation, based on how much they contributed to this new strategy, even though, without easily measured financial results, this was going to be far more subjective than our typical compensation practices. I proposed stock grants that would vest or mature based on my own assessment of whether executives were stepping up to make this new initiative successful. The committee was skeptical at first; we'd never done anything like that. "I know why companies fail to innovate," I said to them at one point. "It's tradition. Tradition generates so much friction, every step of the way." I talked about the investment community, which so often punishes established companies for reducing profits under any circumstances, which often leads businesses to play it safe and keep doing what they've been doing, rather than spend capital in order to generate long-term growth or adapt to change. "There's even you," I said, "a board that doesn't know how to grant stock because there's only one way we've ever done it." At every stage, we were swimming upstream. "It's your choice," I said. "Do you want to fall prey to the 'innovator's dilemma' or do you want to fight it?"

They likely would have come around even without the rousing speech (I've had a great relationship with our board, and they've been supportive of nearly everything I've wanted to do), but while I was finishing my diatribe, one member of the committee said, "I move on it," and another seconded immediately, resulting in approval of my plan. I went back to our executives and explained how the new stock plan would work. I would decide at the end of each year how much stock would vest, and that it was going to be based not on revenue but on how well they were able to work together. "I don't want any politics," I said. "This is too important. It's for the good of the company, and it's good for you. I need you to step up."

LESS THAN TWO weeks after the August earnings call and our BAMTech announcement, I got a call from Rupert Murdoch asking me to come by his house late one afternoon for a glass of wine. Rupert lives in Bel Air, in a beautiful 1940s home that overlooks his winery, Moraga Vineyards. He and I come from very different worlds; we're of different generations; we have different political views, but we've long respected each other's business instincts, and I've always been impressed with how he built his media and entertainment empire from scratch.

Since 2005, when I became CEO, Rupert and I would occasionally get together for a meal or a drink. We were both partners in Hulu, so sometimes we'd have specific business to discuss. More often we'd just chat about the changing media landscape and catch up with each other.

When he invited me to come to his house, though, I suspected Rupert was probing whether I was considering a 2020 run for the White House. There was already a fair amount of "chatter" about my interest in politics and the possibility of my exploring a run for the presidency. Some members of the Trump administration, including Kellyanne Conway and Anthony Scaramucci, had raised the question with people within our company, so I suspected Rupert wanted to find out for himself if this was true.

I have always been interested in politics and policy, and I often thought about serving the country after I left Disney. Many people had planted ideas in my head over the years about what office I might run for, including the presidency, which intrigued me but also had an absurd ring to it. Before the 2016 election, I was convinced America was ready to elect someone from outside the political system, that there was rampant dissatisfaction with traditional politics, including our political parties, and, like our businesses, government and politics were being profoundly disrupted. (Donald Trump's victory was proof, at least in part, that my premonition was correct.)

At the time I met with Rupert, I had in fact been exploring a run for the presidency, even though I knew it was a terrific long shot. I'd spoken with a couple dozen influential people within the Democratic Party—a few former members of the Obama administration, some members of Congress, pollsters, and fundraisers and staffers from previous presidential campaigns. I also started studying like crazy, reading papers and articles about everything from healthcare to taxation, from immigration law to international trade policy to environmental issues to Middle Eastern history and federal interest rates. I also read some of the greatest speeches ever delivered, including Ronald Reagan's speech on the fortieth anniversary of D-Day; Robert Kennedy's impromptu speech in Indianapolis when Martin Luther King, Jr., was killed; Franklin Roosevelt's and John F. Kennedy's inauguration speeches; Obama's speech after the massacre at the A.M.E. church in Charleston, South Carolina; and numerous Churchill addresses. I even reread the Constitution and the Bill of Rights. (I don't know if this was a sign that I should or shouldn't run, but I was waking in the middle of the night with nightmares about being on a debate stage and feeling unprepared.) I was also trying not to be presumptuous. The simple fact that I ran a large multinational company did not necessarily qualify me to be president of the United States, nor did it create a clear or easy path to winning—so I was far from committed to doing it. (In actuality, I was skeptical of the Democratic Party's willingness and ability to support a successful business person.)

When I walked into Rupert's home, we sat down and an aide poured us wine, then the first thing he said was "Are you running for president?"

Well, I thought, *I was right about that,* but I had no desire to be candid with Rupert about my thinking, figuring it would end up on Fox News. So I said, "No, I'm not. A lot of people have talked with me about it, and I have given it some consideration, but it's a crazy idea and it's very unlikely I would ever give it a try. Plus," I said, "my wife hates the thought of it." That was true. At one point Willow had joked, "You can run for any office you want, but not with this wife." She knew me well enough to know the challenge would appeal to me, but she was terribly worried about what it would mean for our family and our lives. (Sometime later she said that she'd married me "for better or worse, so if you feel you have to do it, I'll stand by you, but with tremendous reluctance.")

I wondered what Rupert and I would talk about for the rest of our time together, but he proceeded to spend most of the next hour talking about the threats to our respective businesses: the incursion of big tech companies, the speed at which things were changing, how much scale mattered. He was clearly worried about the future of 21st Century Fox. "We don't have scale," he said several times. "The only company that has scale is you."

As I said goodbye to him that evening, I couldn't help but think he was signaling an interest in doing the unthinkable. I called Alan Braverman on my drive home and said, "I just met with Rupert. I think he might be interested in selling."

I asked Alan to start making a list of all of the Fox assets that, from a regulatory perspective, we could or couldn't buy, and I called Kevin Mayer to tell him about the meeting and get his initial reaction. I asked Kevin to assemble a list, too, and to start thinking about the feasibility of acquiring all or some of Fox's assets.

The next day I followed up with a phone call to Rupert. "If I am reading you right, if I said we are interested in acquiring your company, or most of it, would you be open to it?"

"Yes," he said. "Are you seriously interested in buying?" I told him I was intrigued, but to give me some time to think about it. Then he said, "I would not do anything unless you agree to remain at the company beyond your current retirement date," which at that point was June 2019. I told Rupert I didn't think our board would ever consider an acquisition of this magnitude unless I agreed to extend my term, and we ended our call with an agreement to talk again in a few weeks. I suddenly had the feeling that my life was about to change, and a run for the presidency wasn't going to be the catalyst.

OVER THE NEXT couple of weeks Alan and Kevin and I began to wrap our minds around whether a Fox acquisition was possible and what it might mean for us. Alan ruled out several Fox assets right away. Rules dictate that you can't own two over-the-air broadcast networks in the United States (it's a little dated and silly in today's world, but it's the rule), so the Fox television network was off the table. We compete with their two primary sports networks, so owning them would result in too much market share in the business, so we wouldn't be buying them.

Then there was Fox News. This was one of Rupert's prize possessions, so I never expected him to offer it up. Plus, I didn't see us buying it. If we ran it as it is, we would be the scourge of the left; and if we dared try to move it to the center, we would be the scourge of the right. It didn't matter what I thought about Fox News, though, since there was no way Rupert was ever going to put it on the table.

There were some other smaller assets, but those were the big ones that were off-limits. That left us with a broad portfolio of assets: the movie studio, including Fox Searchlight Pictures; their stake in Hulu, which would give us a majority stake in that platform; the FX Networks; the regional Fox Sports Networks (which we would later have to divest); a controlling stake in National Geographic; a sprawling and varied set of international operations, particularly in India; and a 39 percent stake in Sky, Europe's largest and most successful satellite platform.

Kevin was tasked with doing a financial and strategic analysis of these assets. In very basic terms, that means putting together a team to do a painstaking examination of all of the businesses, not only looking at how they were performing at the moment but projecting what they would do in the future, and how they would perform in the disruptive world we were now witnessing. We also brought in our newly named CFO, Christine McCarthy, who had not been involved in our previous acquisitions but was eager to pitch in on this one—and it was going to challenge her to the extreme.

Once we got a sense of the present and future worth of their businesses, the next question was: What are these two companies worth together? How could we mine more value by combining them? Clearly there would be efficiencies by running them together. For instance, we would now have two movie studios, but under one umbrella, they could be run more efficiently. Then there's leverage in the marketplace. What improved access to markets would we achieve because of suddenly owning more local assets? They had a big business in India, for instance, where we had only nascent operations, and they'd already placed big bets on direct-to-consumer businesses there. They also had a great television studio and had invested heavily in creative talent, and we lagged far behind them. As with our other acquisitions, we assessed their talent. Would bringing in their people lead to more success for our businesses? The answer was a resounding yes.

The upshot was that we estimated that the combined company would be worth billions more than the two separately. (That number grew even larger when the corporate tax laws changed.) Kevin gave me a fairly comprehensive look at the whole thing, then said, "There are some great assets there, Bob."

"I know there are a ton of assets," I said. "But what's the narrative?"

"It's yours!" Kevin said. We hadn't even begun to negotiate, but the gears in Kevin's mind were already turning. "It's your narrative! High-quality content. Technology. Global reach." It got even

CHAPTER 13

NO PRICE ON INTEGRITY

RUPERT'S DECISION TO sell was a direct response to the same forces that led us to create an entirely new strategy for our company. As he pondered the future of his company in such a disrupted world, he concluded the smartest thing to do was to sell and give his shareholders and his family a chance to convert its 21st Century Fox stock into Disney stock, believing we were better positioned to withstand the change and, combined, we'd be even stronger.

It's hard to overstate how sweeping the disruption is in our industry, but his decision—to break up a company he'd built from almost nothing—was as good a marker as any of its inevitability. Just as Rupert and I were entering the beginning phase of what would become an almost two-year journey to close a massive deal that would alter the media landscape, a transformative social change was also under way, one more profound than the mega-technology changes we were experiencing. Numerous serious allegations about thoroughly unacceptable behavior, specifically in our industry, became the catalyst for long overdue action—about sexually predatory behavior, and about equal opportunity and equal pay for women in Hollywood and elsewhere. Specific and horrific allegations against Harvey Weinstein opened the floodgates and emboldened many others to come forward with their own claims of abuse. Nearly every company in the entertainment industry had to contend with and adjudicate complaints within their organizations.

At Disney, we always believed it was vital to create and maintain an environment in which people felt safe. But it was clear now that we needed to do even more to make sure that anyone who'd been abused—or anyone who'd witnessed abuse—could come forward knowing their claims would be heard, taken seriously, acted upon, and they would be protected from retribution. We felt an urgent need to assess whether our standards and our values were being adhered to, and so I charged our human resources team with doing a thorough analysis, which included opening a dialogue and putting in place processes at all levels of the company that would allow for candor and would reinforce our promise to protect anyone who came forward.

In the fall of 2017, we heard complaints about John Lasseter from women and men at Pixar, about what they described as unwanted physical contact. Everyone knew John as a hugger, and while many dismissed this behavior as innocuous, it quickly became evident the feeling was not unanimous. I'd spoken with John about this some years back, but these new allegations were more serious, and it was clear to me that he had to be confronted.

Alan Horn and I met with John in November of that year, and together we agreed that the best course was for him to take a six-month leave to reflect on his behavior and give us time to assess the situation. John issued a statement to his teams before he left. "Collectively, you mean the world to me," he wrote, "and I deeply apologize if I have let you down. I especially want to apologize to anyone who has ever been on the receiving end of an unwanted hug or any other gesture they felt crossed the line in any way, shape, or form. No matter how benign my intent, everyone has the right to set their own boundaries and have them respected."

In John's absence, we put a leadership structure in place at Pixar and Disney Animation and we conducted dozens of interviews with people at both studios to determine what was best for the organization.

THE NEXT SIX MONTHS—working on our direct-to-consumer strategy, contending with high-profile personnel issues, and analyzing and negotiating a Fox deal—were as challenging as any stretch of my career. I grew increasingly convinced that what Fox had in terms of content, global reach, talent, and technology would be transformative for us. If we could acquire them and integrate them quickly and smoothly while executing our direct-to-consumer vision—a daunting series of *ifs*—Disney would be facing the future in a stronger position than it had ever been in.

As our discussions proceeded, Rupert had three things in mind. The first was that, of the possible companies that might be interested in buying Fox, Disney provided the most likely path to regulatory approval. The second was the value of Disney stock. He could continue to have a controlling interest in Fox as it struggled among much bigger fish, or he could have a piece of a much more robust combined company. The third was his confidence that we could integrate the two companies smoothly and set the newly combined company on a dynamic path.

Among Rupert's many challenges as we negotiated throughout the fall of 2017 was managing the decision with his sons, Lachlan and James. They'd watched their father build the company since they were kids, hoping and assuming that someday it would be theirs. Now he was selling it to someone else. It wasn't an easy situation for any of them, and my stance from the outset was to let Rupert manage his family dynamics and stay focused on the business aspects of our discussions.

Throughout that fall, Kevin Mayer and I met several times with Rupert and his CFO, John Nallen. We'd determined that we were willing to make an all-stock offer of $28 a share—or $52.4 billion—for the acquisition. In the months after our initial conversation with Rupert, word had leaked that he was contemplating a sale, which invited others to start considering an acquisition. Comcast emerged as our competitor, making an all-stock bid that was considerably higher than ours. We were confident that even though Comcast's initial bid was higher, the Fox board would still favor us, in part because of the regulatory challenges Comcast was likely to face (they already owned NBC-Universal, as well as one of the largest distribution businesses in the country, and they were likely to face intense regulatory scrutiny).

At the end of Thanksgiving weekend, Kevin and I met Rupert and John once more at the winery in Bel Air. The four of us went for a long walk through rows of grapevines. Near the end of the walk, Rupert informed us that he wouldn't go below $29 a share, which translated to about $5 billion more than we wanted to spend. I suspected that he thought I was worried about Comcast's offer and would feel the need to go higher. As much as I wanted to make the deal, though, I was willing to walk away from it. I was enamored of many parts of their company, and had begun imagining in detail what they could do for our new business, but there were huge executional risks involved. Making it all work was going to require an enormous amount of time and energy. Even if we could execute a deal and get regulatory approval and successfully merge the two companies, there were still plenty of unknowns in the marketplace that concerned me. I was also torn about remaining at the company for what would be three more years. Would this be good for me or for Disney? I wasn't completely sure, but I didn't have much time to think about it. By the end of the meeting, I felt it was vital that we get all of the possible value out of the deal, so I told Rupert as we were leaving, "Twenty-eight is as high as we can go."

I don't know if Rupert was surprised that I was holding my

ground, but Kevin worried we would lose the deal by not going up. I felt confident we would prevail, though—that the risks of going with Comcast were too big for them—and when I came into the office on Monday morning, I told Kevin to call Nallen and tell him we needed an answer by the close of business. At the end of the day, Rupert called and accepted our bid, and invited me back to his winery—Lachlan was also there, and I wondered how it must all be settling with him—to toast the deal. We spent the next two weeks ironing out fine points, and then I flew to London for the premiere of *Star Wars: The Last Jedi* on December 12. While there, I went to Rupert's office to take a picture of us shaking hands on his balcony, which would be released along with an announcement of the deal on the 14th.

I flew back to L.A. on the thirteenth, arriving late in the afternoon, and went straight into a prep meeting for the announcement the next morning. I was scheduled to go on *Good Morning America* at 7:00 A.M. EST, which meant being at the studio on the Disney lot at 3:00 A.M. PST, to get made up and be ready to go live at 4:00 A.M. In the middle of our prep meeting, Jayne Parker, our head of Human Resources, came in and asked me if John Skipper, the president of ESPN, had been in touch with me.

"No," I said. "What's up?"

The look on Jayne's face said it was a problem, and I asked immediately if it was something that needed to be dealt with right away or whether it could wait until after we made the announcement the next day. "It's bad," Jayne said. "But it can wait."

December 14 ranks as another of the most *compartmentalized* days of my career. Looking back at the notes in my calendar, here's what turns up: GMA announcement at 4:00 A.M. Conference call with investors at 5:00 A.M. CNBC Live at 6:00 A.M. Bloomberg at 6:20 A.M. Webcast with investors at 7:00 A.M. From 8:00 A.M. till noon were calls with Senators Chuck Schumer and Mitch McConnell, then Representative Nancy Pelosi and several other members of Congress, in anticipation of the regulatory process that was about to unfold. Finally, that afternoon, Jayne came into my office to have the conversation that we'd punted on the day before. She told me that John Skipper had admitted to a drug problem, which had led to other serious complications in his life and could potentially jeopardize the company. I scheduled a call with John the next day, then went home and, because I'd scheduled it long before I ever could have known that all of these things would converge at the same time, Skyped with a group of students at Ithaca College, my alma mater, about the future of the entertainment and media industries.

The next morning, John and I talked. He admitted that he had terrible personal issues, and I told him that, based on what Jayne had described and what he'd confirmed, we needed him to resign the following Monday. I regarded John highly; he is smart and worldly and was a talented, loyal executive. This was a clear example, though, of how a company's integrity depends on the integrity of its people, and while I had great personal affection and concern for him, he'd made choices that violated Disney policy. It was a painful decision to let him go, but the right one—even if it meant that, as we entered what was the most taxing stretch for the company and for me since I'd become CEO, we were now without leaders in two of our most important businesses: ESPN and Animation.

THE AGREEMENT WITH Rupert set the complicated process of seeking regulatory approval in motion. This involves a series of filings with the Securities and Exchange Commission laying out the details of the deal, the financial aspects for both companies, as well as a "ticking clock" that transparently narrates how the deal transpired (including, in our case, a description of the initial meeting with Rupert and all of our subsequent conversations). Once the SEC approves the filing, each company then mails a proxy ballot to its shareholders, which includes all of the details in the filing and a recommendation from each company's board that its shareholders approve the deal. It also stipulates a voting period, which ends with a shareholder meeting at which all of the votes are counted. This whole process can take up to six months, and during this period, other entities can make competing bids.

As complex as our deal was, we assumed we had a clean path to regulatory approval (which, again, was part of why Fox's board had approved our bid over Comcast's in the first place) and Fox's shareholders would ratify it at their meeting that was scheduled for June 2018. There was only one possible hitch. As all of this moved forward, a district court judge in New York was contemplating a lawsuit brought by the Department of Justice against AT&T, to block its acquisition of Time Warner. Comcast was watching this carefully. If the judge ruled in favor of the Justice Department and the deal was blocked, Comcast would conclude that they, too, would face a similar hurdle, and their hopes for making another bid for Fox would be dead. If AT&T won, however, they could be emboldened to come back with a higher offer, assuming that Fox's board and shareholders would no longer be dissuaded by the regulatory obstacles.

All we could do was go forward under the assumption that we would be acquiring Fox, and begin preparing for that reality. Shortly after we agreed to the deal with Rupert, I began focusing on the question of exactly how we would merge these two huge companies. We couldn't just add them to what already existed; we had to integrate them carefully in order to preserve and create value. So I asked myself: What would, could, or should the new company look like? If I were to erase history and build something totally new today, with all of these assets, how would it be structured? I came back from our Christmas holiday and dragged a whiteboard into the conference room next to my office and began to play around. (It was the first time I'd stood before a whiteboard since I was with Steve Jobs in 2005!)

The first thing I did was separate "content" from "technology."

We would have three content groups: movies (Walt Disney Animation, Disney Studios, Pixar, Marvel, Lucasfilm, Twentieth
Century Fox, Fox 2000, Fox Searchlight), television (ABC, ABC
News, our television stations, Disney channels, Freeform, FX, National Geographic), and sports (ESPN). All of that went on the left
side of the whiteboard. On the other side went tech: apps, user interfaces, customer acquisition and retention, data management,
sales, distribution, and so on. The idea was simply to let the content
people focus on creativity and let the tech people focus on how to
distribute things and, for the most part, generate revenue in the
most successful ways. Then, in the middle of the board I wrote
"physical entertainment and goods," an umbrella for various large
and sprawling businesses: consumer products, Disney stores, all of
our global merchandise and licensing agreements, cruises, resorts,
and our six theme-park businesses.

I stepped back and looked at the board and thought, *There it is.
That's what a modern media company should look like.* I felt energized
just by looking at it, and spent the next few days refining the structure on my own. At the end of that week, I invited my team in to
look at it—Kevin Mayer, Jayne Parker, Alan Braverman, Christine
McCarthy, and Nancy Lee, my chief of staff. "I'm going to bounce
something different off you," I said, and then I showed them the
whiteboard. "This is what the new company would look like."

"You just did this?" Kevin asked.

"Yes. What do you think?"

He nodded. Yes, it made sense. The task now was to put the right
names in the right places. The moment that we announced the deal,
there was understandable anxiety throughout both companies about
who would run what, who would report to whom, whose roles would
expand or contract and how. Throughout the winter and spring, I
traveled all over meeting with Fox executives—in L.A. and New
York, London, India, and Latin America—getting to know them
and their businesses, fielding their questions and alleviating their
worries, and gauging them against their Disney counterparts. Once

the shareholders voted—assuming the AT&T ruling didn't break Comcast's way—I would have to make a lot of difficult personnel choices very quickly, and I needed to be prepared to start restructuring immediately.

IN LATE MAY, as we were closing in on the judge's decision and, soon after that, the Fox shareholder vote, I arrived at my office a little before 7:00 A.M. and opened an email from Ben Sherwood, the president of ABC. It included the text of a tweet that Roseanne Barr had posted that morning, in which she said that Valerie Jarrett, the former Obama administration adviser, was the product of "the Muslim Brotherhood and Planet of the Apes." Ben's message read: "We have a serious problem here. . . . This is completely abhorrent and unacceptable."

I immediately wrote back: "We sure do. I'm in the office. I'm not sure the show survives this."

A year earlier, in May 2017, we'd announced that we were bringing *Roseanne* back to ABC prime time. I'd been enthusiastic about the idea, in part because of how much I'd grown to like Roseanne when we worked together in the late '80s and early '90s when I was running ABC Entertainment, and in part because the idea of the show—that it would reflect a range of political reactions to the controversial subjects of the day—appealed to me.

I hadn't been aware of the controversial tweets that Roseanne had posted in the past, before we considered bringing the show back on the air, but once it was on, she took up tweeting again and said some thoughtless, occasionally offensive things on a variety of subjects. If she kept it up, it would be a problem. In April, a few weeks before the Valerie Jarrett tweet, I had lunch with her. It couldn't have been nicer. Roseanne showed up with cookies that she'd baked for me, and she spent part of our conversation recalling that I was one of the few people in her corner way back when and said that she'd always trusted me.

Near the end of the lunch I said to her, "You've got to stay off Twitter." The show was getting incredible ratings, and I felt personally happy to see her thriving again. "You've got a great thing going here," I said. "Don't blow it."

"Yes, Bob," she said, in her funny, drawn-out, nasal voice. She promised me that she wouldn't go on Twitter again, and I left the lunch feeling reassured that she understood that the success she was enjoying then was rare and could easily go away.

What I'd forgotten, or minimized in my mind, was how unpredictable and volatile Roseanne has always been. We were close in the early days of my tenure as president of ABC Entertainment. I inherited the show, which was in its first season when I arrived, and I thought she was wonderfully talented, but I also got a close-up look at how mercurial and volatile she could be. There were times when she was so depressed she couldn't get out of bed, and Ted Harbert and I would sometimes go to her home and talk with her until she got going. Maybe it was something to do with my father and his depression that made me sympathetic to her, but I felt the need to look out for her, and she appreciated that.

After reading Ben's email, I connected with Zenia, Alan, Ben, and Channing Dungey, then the head of ABC Entertainment, and asked them what they thought our choices were. They were considering a variety of responses, which ranged from a suspension and loss of pay to a severe warning and public rebuke. None of them seemed enough, and while they didn't mention firing her, I knew it was in the backs of their minds. "We don't have a choice here," I finally said. "We have to do what's right. Not what's politically correct, and not what's commercially correct. Just what's right. If any of our employees tweeted what she tweeted, they'd be immediately terminated." I told them to feel free to push back or tell me I was crazy, but no one did.

Zenia drafted a statement that Channing would eventually issue. I called Valerie Jarrett and apologized and told her we'd just decided to cancel the show and would be making an announcement in fifteen minutes. She thanked me and then called back later to say she was scheduled to be on MSNBC that evening, on a panel about racism, related to the news of Starbucks closing their stores that day for sensitivity training. "Can I mention that you called me?" she asked. I told her she could.

I then sent an email to the Disney board: "This morning we all woke up to a tweet by Roseanne Barr, in which she referred to Valerie Jarrett as a product of the Muslim Brotherhood and Planet of the Apes. We found this comment, no matter what its context was, to be intolerable and deplorable, and we made the decision to cancel Roseanne's show. I don't mean to stand on a high horse, but as a company, we have always tried to do what we felt was right, no matter what the politics or the commerce. In other words, demanding quality and integrity from all of our people and of all of our products is paramount, and there is no room for second chances, or for tolerance when it comes to an overt transgression that discredits the company in any way. Roseanne's tweet violated that tenet and our only choice was to do what was morally right. A statement will be released momentarily."

It was an easy decision, really. I never asked what the financial repercussions would be, and didn't care. In moments like that, you have to look past whatever the commercial losses are and be guided, again, by the simple rule that there's nothing more important than the quality and integrity of your people and your product. Everything depends on upholding that principle.

I received a fair amount of praise and some damnation throughout that day and the rest of the week. I took heart that the praise came from many quarters: heads of studios; politicians; some people in the sports world, including Robert Kraft, the owner of the New England Patriots. Valerie Jarrett wrote me immediately to say how much she appreciated our response. President Obama sent his appreciation, too. I was attacked on Twitter by President Trump, who asked where my apology was for him and said something about the "horrible" statements we'd made about him while report-

CHAPTER 14

CORE VALUES

O N JUNE 12, 2018, a district court judge in lower Manhattan ruled in favor of AT&T buying Time Warner. The next day, Brian Roberts announced Comcast's new offer: an all-cash bid of $35 per share ($64 billion) to our $28 per share. Not only was the number significantly higher, but the all-cash offer would be attractive to many shareholders who would rather have cash than stock. Suddenly we were in danger of losing the deal that we'd been dreaming about and working so hard on for the past six months.

The Fox board had scheduled a meeting, to take place a week later in London, during which they would vote on the Comcast offer. We could bid again, and we needed to decide quickly what our number would be. We could raise our bid but still come in slightly under theirs, and hope that their board would continue to believe that the path to regulatory approval, despite the AT&T decision, was still easier with us. We could match Comcast's offer and hope that they wouldn't scuttle our deal for an equivalent offer, even if many investors would prefer cash over stock. Or we could go higher and hope that Comcast didn't have much room left to go up.

Various executives and bankers were involved in the discussion. All of them were advising me to go in low, or at the most match Comcast's offer, and bet on the regulatory issues still weighing in our favor. I decided I wanted a knockout bid, and the board gave me approval to raise our number and do just that. Meanwhile, Alan Braverman had been in ongoing discussions with the Justice Department, trying to clear a way to regulatory approval, should we prevail in the bidding war for Fox.

Two days before the Fox board was set to vote on the Comcast offer, I flew to London with Alan, Kevin, Christine, and Nancy Lee. I made sure that only a few people on our team knew what our bid would be, and cautioned everyone that confidentiality was critical. We did not want Comcast to have any inkling of our plan to bid higher. We reserved a room in a hotel in London that we never stay in, under different names. I don't know if it's true, but some people told us that Comcast sometimes tracks the movements of competitors' private jets, so rather than flying into London, we flew first to Belfast, where we then chartered a different plane for the short jump to London.

Right before we boarded the plane to London, I called Rupert and said, "I want to have a meeting with you tomorrow." Late the next afternoon, Kevin and I went to meet with Rupert and John Nallen at Rupert's office. The four of us sat around his sleek marble table, looking out on the balcony where he and I had posed for a picture back in December. I got right to the matter. "We'd like to make a $38 offer," I said. "Half cash, half stock." I told him that this was as far as we could go.

As for the $38 price, I suspected that Comcast could possibly go higher than what they'd already bid, and that if we went to $35, they'd go to $36. If we went to $36, they'd go to $37, at each stage convincing themselves that it's only a little more, until eventually we'd go up to $40 per share. Whereas if we started at $38, they'd have to think hard about going up at least $3 per share. (Since they were offering all cash, it would mean borrowing even more money and significantly raising their debt.)

Comcast assumed the Fox board was voting on their offer the next morning. Instead, Rupert brought our new offer to his board, and they approved it. When their meeting ended, they informed Comcast they were accepting our new bid, which we announced jointly and immediately. We needed to explain this new move to investors, but we didn't have a conference room set up in London, because we didn't want anyone to know we were there. So we brought a speakerphone into my hotel room and held the investor conference call from there. It was a surreal scene, the small group of us gathered in a hotel room as Christine and I spoke with investors, while on the television set in the background CNBC was covering the news we had just made.

Shortly after we made our final bid, I exhorted Alan Braverman to see if he could reach an agreement with the Department of Justice regarding our acquisition. He knew our concentration in television sports and owning the Fox regional sports networks would be a big problem. We decided we would be better off agreeing to divest them in order to do a fast deal with Justice, which is what happened. This would give us a huge advantage over Comcast, who could still have a complicated and lengthy U.S. regulatory process, on top of their need to beat our $38 offer. In a matter of two weeks, we got a guarantee from the DoJ that, if we agreed to sell off the sports networks, they would not sue to block our deal. That guarantee proved to be crucial.

After the Fox board's vote, a new proxy, along with the board's unanimous recommendation to vote for the deal, was sent to their shareholders. The vote would take place in late July, which still gave Comcast plenty of time to come back with a higher bid. It was a nerve-racking several weeks. Every time I opened my computer or looked at email or turned on CNBC, I expected to see that Comcast had outbid us. In late July, I went to Italy with Kevin for three days of meetings, and from there back to London.

We were in a car in London when I received a call from David Faber, the host of CNBC's *Squawk on the Street*. I answered the phone, and David said, "Do you have a comment on this statement?"

"What statement?"

"Comcast's statement."

My anxiety immediately spiked. "I don't know what it is," I said.

David told me that the news had just broken: "Brian Roberts announced that they're out."

I was so expecting him to say that they'd topped our offer that my instantaneous reaction was "Holy crap!" I paused for a moment, then dictated a more formal statement to him. "You can tell your audience you told me," I said. Which he did—and he also told them I'd said, "Holy crap."

BEFORE WE COULD actually close the deal, we still needed to contend with the global regulatory process, outside of the United States securing approval in most of the places we'd now be doing business—Russia and China and Ukraine and the EU, India and South Korea and Brazil and Mexico among them. We got approval one region at a time, over the course of months, until finally, in March 2019, nineteen months after my first conversations with Rupert, we officially closed the deal and began to move forward as one company.

It all happened just in time. The next month, on April 11, we hosted an elaborate, highly produced, painstakingly rehearsed event on the Disney lot, to present the details of our new direct-to-consumer businesses to investors. It would have been a very different meeting if we hadn't closed the Fox deal in time. As it was, though, hundreds of investors and members of the media filled rows of bleachers in one of our soundstages, facing a giant stage and backdrop.

We'd promised Wall Street that when we were ready, we would share some information on our new streaming services. That led to an internal debate over just how detailed that information should be. I wanted to show them everything. We'd been candid about the challenges facing us in the past—in that fateful earnings call in 2015, when I spoke about the disruption we were all seeing—and I wanted to be just as candid now about what we'd done to face that disruption, to embrace it and become disrupters ourselves. I wanted to show them the content we'd created and the technology we'd developed to deliver it. It was also crucial to demonstrate how Fox fit perfectly into this new strategy and dramatically fueled it. Transparency about how much this would cost, the short-term damage it would do to our bottom line, and what we projected the long-term gains would be was also critical.

I took the stage and talked only for about a minute and a half, following a beautifully produced film we'd made to showcase the history of these two newly merged companies, Disney and 21st Century Fox. It was our way of saying, *We're moving in a new direction, but creativity is at the heart of what we do.* For years and years, these two companies have made extraordinary, indelible entertainment, and now, combined, we would do that more emphatically than ever.

This gathering was a bookend to my first interview with the Disney board back in 2004. It was all about the future, and our future depended on three things: making high-quality branded content, investing in technology, and growing globally. I couldn't have anticipated back then how everything we would do would emerge from that template, and I could have never predicted a day like this one, in which those three pillars would be so overtly on display as we demonstrated the company's plans for the future.

One after another, the heads of many of our businesses came onstage and introduced the original and curated content that would be available on our new streaming service. Disney. Pixar. Marvel. Star Wars. National Geographic. We would be releasing three new, original Marvel shows and two new series from Lucasfilm, including the first ever *Star Wars* live-action series, *The Mandalorian*. There would be a Pixar series, new Disney television shows, and original, live-action films, including *Lady and the Tramp*. All in all, more than twenty-five new series and ten original films or specials were slated to come out in the first year of the service alone, and all of them had been made with the same level of ambition and attention to quality as any films or television shows our studios produced. Virtually the entire Disney library, every animated film ever made since *Snow White and the Seven Dwarfs* in 1937, would also be available, including several Marvel titles, among them *Captain Marvel* and *Avengers: Endgame*. The addition of Fox meant that we would also be offering all six hundred or so episodes of *The Simpsons*.

Later in the presentation, Uday Shankar, the new president of our operations in Asia, took the stage to talk about Hotstar, India's largest streaming service. We'd made the decision to pivot toward a direct-to-consumer strategy, and now, as a result of the Fox acquisition, we owned the largest direct-to-consumer businesses in one of the most vital and thriving markets in the world. There was global growth.

When Kevin Mayer came onstage to demonstrate how the app would work—on a smart TV, on a tablet, on a phone—it was impossible not to recall Steve standing in my office in 2005, holding out the prototype of the new video iPod. We'd embraced change then, much to the chagrin of the rest of our industry, and now we were doing it again. We were addressing some of the same questions we asked ourselves almost fifteen years earlier: Are high-quality branded products likely to become even more valuable in a changed marketplace? How do we deliver our products to consumers in more relevant, more inventive ways? What new habits of consumption are being formed, and how do we adapt to them? How do we deploy technology as a powerful new tool for growth instead of falling victim to its disruption and destruction?

The cost of building the app and creating the content, combined with the losses incurred by undercutting our own traditional businesses, meant we'd reduce our profits by a few billion dollars a year over the first few years. It would take some time before success would be measured in profits. First, it would be measured in subscribers. We wanted the service to be accessible to as many people as possible around the world, and we had settled on a price that we estimated would bring in somewhere between sixty and ninety million subscribers in the first five years. When Kevin announced we would be selling it for $6.99 a month, there was an audible gasp in the room.

The response from Wall Street went far beyond anything we anticipated. In 2015, our stock dropped like a stone when I talked about disruption. Now it was soaring. The day after our investors conference it jumped 11 percent, to a record high. By the end of the month, it was up nearly 30 percent. That stretch, through the spring of 2019, was as good as any in my tenure as CEO. We released *Avengers: Endgame,* which would eventually go on to become the highest-grossing movie of all time. That was followed by the opening of our new Star Wars land, Galaxy's Edge, at Disneyland; and that was followed by an agreement to purchase Comcast's remaining stake in Hulu, which will serve as our subscription streaming service for the content that will not be on Disney+, a move that investors again rewarded. If the past had taught me anything, it was that with a company this size, with such a big footprint in the world and so many employees, something unpredictable will always happen; bad news becomes an inevitability. But for now it felt good, really good, like the fifteen years of hard work had paid off.

BEFORE WE ENTERED into the Fox negotiations, June 2019 was supposed to have been my retirement date from the Walt Disney Company. (I'd had some previous plans to retire that didn't quite happen as expected, but now I was determined to walk away, forty-five years after I started at ABC.) Not only was I not retiring, however, I was working harder and felt more responsibility than I ever had in my fourteen years in the job. That's not to say I wasn't fully engaged with or fulfilled by the work, just that it wasn't what I imagined my life would look like at age sixty-eight. The intensity of the work didn't fully inoculate me against a kind of wistfulness creeping in, though. The future that we were planning and working so feverishly on would happen without me. My new retirement date is December 2021, but I can see it out of the corner of my eye. It surfaces at unexpected times. It's not enough to distract me, but it is enough to remind me that this ride is coming to an end. As a joke a few years back, dear friends of mine gave me a license plate holder, which I immediately attached to my car, that says, "Is there life after Disney?" The answer is yes, of course, but that question feels more existential than it used to.

I'm comforted by something I've come to believe more and more in recent years—that it's not always good for one person to have too much power for too long. Even when a CEO is working productively and effectively, it's important for a company to have change at the top. I don't know if other CEOs agree with this, but I've noticed that you can accumulate so much power in a job that it becomes harder to keep a check on how you wield it. Little things can start to shift. Your confidence can easily tip over into overconfidence and become a liability. You can start to feel that you've heard every idea, and so you become impatient and dismissive of others' opinions. It's not intentional, it just comes with the territory. You have to make a conscious effort to listen, to pay attention to the multitude of opinions. I've raised the issue with the executives I work most closely with as a kind of safeguard. "If you notice me being too dismissive or impatient, you need to tell me." They've had to on occasion, but I hope not too often.

It would be easy in a book like this to act as if all the success Disney experienced during my tenure is the result of the perfectly executed vision that I had from the beginning, that I knew, for instance, that focusing on three specific core strategies rather than others would lead us to where we are now. But you can only put that story together in retrospect. In truth, I needed to come up with a plan for the future in order to lead the company. I believed that quality would matter most. I believed we needed to embrace technology and disruption rather than fear it. I believed that expanding into new markets would be vital. I had no real idea, though, especially then, where this journey would take me.

Determining principles of leadership is impossible to do without experience, but I had great mentors. Michael, for sure, and Tom and Dan before him, and Roone before them. Each was a master in his own way, and I'd absorbed everything I could from them. Beyond that, I trusted my instincts, and I encouraged the people around me to trust theirs. Only much later did those instincts start to shape themselves into particular qualities of leadership that I could articulate.

I recently reread the email I sent to all the employees of Disney on my first day as CEO. I talked about the three pillars of our strategy going forward, but I also shared some memories of my childhood, watching *The Wonderful World of Disney* and *The Mickey Mouse Club*, and about imagining as a kid what it would be like to someday visit Disneyland. I recalled my early days at ABC, too, how nervous I felt starting there in the summer of 1974. "I never dreamed I would one day lead the company responsible for so many of my greatest childhood memories," I wrote, "or that my professional journey would eventually bring me here."

There's a way in which I still can't quite believe it. It's a strange thing, to think on the one hand that the narrative of your life makes complete sense. Day connects to day, job to job, life choice to life choice. The story line is coherent and unbroken. There are so many moments along the way where things could have gone differently, though, and if not for a lucky break, or the right mentor, or some instinct that said to do *this* rather than *that*, I would not be telling this story. I can't emphasize enough how much success is also dependent on luck, and I've been extraordinarily lucky along the way. Looking back, there's something dreamlike about it all.

How could that kid, sitting in his living room in Brooklyn watching Annette Funicello and the Mickey Mouse Club, or going with his grandparents to his first movie, *Cinderella,* or lying in his bed a few years later replaying scenes of *Davy Crockett* in his head, find himself all those years later becoming the steward of Walt Disney's legacy?

Maybe this is the case for many of us: No matter who we become or what we accomplish, we still feel that we're essentially the kid we were at some simpler time long ago. Somehow that's the trick of leadership, too, I think, to hold on to that awareness of yourself even as the world tells you how powerful and important you are. The moment you start to believe it all too much, the moment you look yourself in the mirror and see a title emblazoned on your forehead, you've lost your way. That may be the hardest but also the most necessary lesson to keep in mind, that wherever you are along the path, you're the same person you've always been.

LESSONS TO LEAD BY

A T THE END of this book on leadership, it struck me that it might be useful to collect all of these variations on the theme in one place. Some are concrete and prescriptive; some a bit more philosophical. When I read through these bits and pieces of collected wisdom, they are a kind of map to the last forty-five years: *This is what I was taught every day by this person, and this is what I learned from that one. Here is the thing that I didn't understand then but do now, that could only come with experience.* My hope is that these ideas, and the stories I've told throughout this book to give them some context, might feel relatable to you, too. They are the lessons that shaped my professional life, and I hope they are useful for yours.

- To tell great stories, you need great talent.

- Now more than ever: innovate or die. There can be no innovation if you operate out of fear of the new.

- I talk a lot about "the relentless pursuit of perfection." In practice, this can mean a lot of things, and it's hard to define. It's a mindset, more than a specific set of rules. It's not about perfectionism at all costs. It's about creating an environment in which people refuse to accept mediocrity. It's about pushing back against the urge to say that "good enough" is good enough.

- Take responsibility when you screw up. In work, in life, you'll be more respected and trusted by the people around you if you own up to your mistakes. It's impossible to avoid them; but it is possible to acknowledge them, learn from them, and set an example that it's okay to get things wrong sometimes.

- Be decent to people. Treat everyone with fairness and empathy. This doesn't mean that you lower your expectations or convey the message that mistakes don't matter. It means that you create an environment where people know you'll hear them out, that you're emotionally consistent and fair-minded, and that they'll be given second chances for honest mistakes.

- Excellence and fairness don't have to be mutually exclusive. Strive for perfection but always be aware of the pitfalls of caring only about the product and never the people.

- True integrity—a sense of knowing who you are and being guided by your own clear sense of right and wrong—is a kind of secret leadership weapon. If you trust your own instincts and treat people with respect, the company will come to represent the values you live by.

- Value ability more than experience, and put people in roles that require more of them than they know they have in them.

- Ask the questions you need to ask, admit without apology what you don't understand, and do the work to learn what you need to learn as quickly as you can.

- Managing creativity is an art, not a science. When giving notes, be mindful of how much of themselves the person you're speaking to has poured into the project and how much is at stake for them.

- Don't start negatively, and don't start small. People will often focus on little details as a way of masking a lack of any clear, coherent, big thoughts. If you start petty, you seem petty.

- Of all the lessons I learned in my first year running prime time at ABC, the acceptance that creativity isn't a science was the most profound. I became comfortable with failure—not with lack of effort, but with the fact that if you want innovation, you need to grant permission to fail.

- Don't be in the business of playing it safe. Be in the business of creating possibilities for greatness.

- Don't let ambition get ahead of opportunity. By fixating on a future job or project, you become impatient with where you are. You don't tend enough to the responsibilities you *do* have, and so ambition can become counterproductive. It's important to know how to find the balance—do the job you have well; be patient; look for opportunities to pitch in and expand and grow; and make yourself one of the people, through attitude and energy and focus, whom your bosses feel they have to turn to when an opportunity arises.

- My former boss Dan Burke once handed me a note that said: "Avoid getting into the business of manufacturing trombone oil. You may become the greatest trombone-oil manufacturer in the world, but in the end, the world only consumes a few quarts of trombone oil a year!" He was telling me not to invest in small projects that would sap my and the company's resources and not give much back. I still have that note in my desk, and I use it when talking to our executives about what to pursue and where to put their energy.

- When the people at the top of a company have a dysfunctional relationship, there's no way that the rest of the company can be functional. It's like having two parents who fight all the time. The kids know, and they start to reflect the animosity back onto the parents and at each other.

- As a leader, if you don't do the work, the people around you are going to know, and you'll lose their respect fast. You have to be attentive. You often have to sit through meetings that, if given the choice, you might choose not to sit through. You have to listen to other people's problems and help find solutions. It's all part of the job.

- We all want to believe we're indispensable. You have to be self-aware enough that you don't cling to the notion that *you* are the only person who can do this job. At its essence, good leadership isn't about being indispensable; it's about helping others be prepared to step into your shoes—giving them access to your own decision-making, identifying the skills they need to develop and helping them improve, and sometimes being honest with them about why they're not ready for the next step up.

- A company's reputation is the sum total of the actions of its people and the quality of its products. You have to demand integrity from your people and your products at all times.

- Michael Eisner used to say, "micromanaging is underrated." I agree with him—to a point. Sweating the details can show how much you care. "Great" is often a collection of very small things, after all. The downside of micromanagement is that it can be stultifying, and it can reinforce the feeling that you don't trust the people who work for you.

- Too often, we lead from a place of *fear* rather than courage, stubbornly trying to build a bulwark to protect old models that can't possibly survive the sea change that is under way. It's hard to look at your current models, sometimes even ones that are profitable in the moment, and make a decision to undermine them in order to face the change that's coming.

- If you walk up and down the halls constantly telling people "the sky is falling," a sense of doom and gloom will, over time, permeate the company. You can't communicate pessimism to the people around you. It's ruinous to morale. No one wants to follow a pessimist.

- Pessimism leads to paranoia, which leads to defensiveness, which leads to risk aversion.

- Optimism emerges from faith in yourself and in the people who work for you. It's not about saying things are good when they're not, and it's not about conveying some blind faith that "things will work out." It's about believing in your and others' abilities.

- People sometimes shy away from big swings because they build a case against trying something before they even step up to the plate. Long shots aren't usually as long as they seem. With enough thoughtfulness and commitment, the boldest ideas can be executed.

- You have to convey your priorities clearly and repeatedly. If you don't articulate your priorities clearly, then the people around you don't know what their own should be. Time and energy and capital get wasted.

- You can do a lot for the morale of the people around you (and therefore the people around them) just by taking the guesswork out of their day-to-day life. A lot of work is complex and requires intense amounts of focus and energy, but this kind of messaging is fairly simple: *This is where we want to be. This is how we're going to get there.*

- Technological advancements will eventually make older business models obsolete. You can either bemoan that and try with all your might to protect the status quo, or you can work hard to understand and embrace it with more enthusiasm and creativity than your competitors.

- It should be about the future, not the past.

- It's easy to be optimistic when everyone is telling you you're great. It's much harder, and much more necessary, when your sense of yourself is on the line.

- Treating others with respect is an undervalued currency when it comes to negotiating. A little respect goes a long way, and the absence of it can be very costly.

- You have to do the homework. You have to be prepared. You certainly can't make a major acquisition, for example, without building the necessary models to help you determine whether a deal is the right one. But you also have to recognize that there is never 100 percent certainty. No matter how much data you've been given, it's still, ultimately, a risk, and the decision to take that risk or not comes down to one person's instinct.

- If something doesn't feel right *to* you, it won't be right *for* you.

- A lot of companies acquire others without much sensitivity toward what they're really buying. They think they're getting physical assets or manufacturing assets or intellectual property (in some industries, that's more true than others). But usually what they're really acquiring is *people*. In a creative business, that's where the value lies.

- As a leader, you are the embodiment of that company. What that means is this: Your values—your sense of integrity and decency and honesty, the way you comport yourself in the world—are a stand-in for the values of the company. You can be the head of a seven-person organization or a quarter-million-person organization, and the same truth holds: what people think of *you* is what they'll think of your company.

- There have been many times over the years when I've had to deliver difficult news to accomplished people, some of whom were friends, and some of whom had been unable to flourish in positions that I had put them in. I try to be as direct about the problem as possible, explaining what wasn't working and why I didn't think it was going to change. There's a kind of euphemistic corporate language that is often deployed in those situations, and that has always struck me as offensive. If you respect the person, then you owe them a clear explanation for the decision you're making. There's no way for the conversation not to be painful, but at least it can be honest.

- When hiring, try to surround yourself with people who are *good* in addition to being good at what they do. Genuine decency—an instinct for fairness and openness and mutual respect—is a rarer commodity in business than it should be, and you should look for it in the people you hire and nurture it in the people who work for you.

- In any negotiation, be clear about where you stand from the beginning. There's no short-term gain that's worth the long-term erosion of trust that occurs when you go back on the expectation you created early on.

- Projecting your anxiety onto your team is counterproductive. It's subtle, but there's a difference between communicating that you share their stress—that you're in it *with* them—and communicating that you need them to deliver in order to alleviate your stress.

- Most deals are personal. This is even more true if you're negotiating with someone over something he or she has created. You have to know what you want out of any deal, but to get there you also need be aware of what's at stake for the other person.

- If you're in the business of making something, be in the business of making something great.

- The decision to disrupt a business model that is working for you requires no small amount of courage. It means intentionally taking on short-term losses in the hope that a long-term risk will pay off. Routines and priorities get disrupted. Traditional ways of doing business get slowly marginalized and eroded—and start to lose money—as a new model takes over. That's a big ask, in terms of a company's culture and mindset. When you do it, you're saying to people who for their entire careers have been compensated based on the success of their traditional business: "Don't worry about that too much anymore. Worry about this instead." But *this* isn't profitable yet, and won't be for a while. Deal with this kind of uncertainty by going back to basics: Lay out your strategic priorities clearly. Remain optimistic in the face of the unknown. And be accessible and fair-minded to people whose work lives are being thrown into disarray.

- It's not good to have power for too long. You don't realize the way your voice seems to boom louder than every other voice in the room. You get used to people withholding their opinions until they hear what you have to say. People are afraid to bring ideas to you, afraid to dissent, afraid to engage. This can happen even to the most well-intentioned leaders. You have to work consciously and actively to fend off its corrosive effects.

- You have to approach your work and life with a sense of genuine humility. The success I've enjoyed has been due in part to my own efforts, but it's also been due to so much beyond me, the efforts and support and examples of so many people, and to twists of fate beyond my control.

- Hold on to your awareness of yourself, even as the world tells you how important and powerful you are. The moment you start to believe it all too much, the moment you look at your-self in the mirror and see a title emblazoned on your fore-head, you've lost your way.

ACKNOWLEDGMENTS

THERE'S AN OLD ADAGE that says success has many fathers and failure is an orphan. In my case, success has many fathers *and* mothers. Everything we've accomplished at Disney these last fifteen years has been the result of the collaborative efforts of countless people: our senior executive team, tens of thousands of Disney employees ("cast members," as we call them), and thousands more on the creative side of our business—directors, writers, actors, and legions of other talented people who have devoted so much time and effort to telling the stories I have referred to so often in this book.

I could go on for pages mentioning the names of individuals I owe thanks to, but will limit this list to the handful of people mentioned below, without whose efforts I and Disney wouldn't have been nearly as successful:

Stephanie Voltz, for sharing this ride with me from start to finish, for doing so much more than just keeping the trains running on time, and for years of endless smiles and tremendous support.

Alan Braverman and Zenia Mucha have also been with me

from the beginning, and both have been invaluable to me and to the company.

Kevin Mayer is a master strategist and dealmaker. A CEO couldn't ask for a better strategic partner.

Jayne Parker has been our head of human resources for a decade. You can't run a company well without a star in the HR role, and Jayne has been that and more.

I've also had the benefit of three excellent CFOs: Tom Staggs, Jay Rasulo, and Christine McCarthy. Their wisdom, perspective, and strategic and financial acumen made so much of what we have done possible.

Bob Chapek has also done a tremendous job running our consumer products and theme park businesses, and was invaluable in the run-up to the opening of Shanghai Disneyland.

George Bodenheimer and Jimmy Pitaro have guided ESPN honorably and ably.

Alan Horn is the best hire I've ever made. His leadership at our film studio has enabled us to shine commercially and artistically.

John Lasseter and Ed Catmull and their great team of directors and animators kept Pixar vibrant and creatively strong, and revitalized Walt Disney Animation.

Bob Weis and more than a thousand Imagineers designed and built Shanghai Disneyland. It is a triumph of vision, passion, creativity, patience, and extraordinary hard work and sacrifice.

In the almost fifteen years I've been in this job, I've had some great "chiefs of stuff," as I called them (until I officially changed the title to chief of staff): Leslie Stern, Kate McLean, Agnes Chu, Nancy Lee, and Nichole Smith have been invaluable to me. And thank you, too, to Heather Kiriakou for all of the help over the years.

I also owe a great debt of gratitude to the many members of the Walt Disney Company Board of Directors, notably George Mitchell, John Pepper, Orin Smith, and Susan Arnold. Thank you supporting our vision and for all of your advice and encou ment. Successful companies share one thing in common—a strong partnership between management and their boards, and ours has been critical to the success of the Walt Disney Company.

In the forty-five years I have been at this company, I've had many bosses. Some are mentioned in this book, but I want to thank all of them for guiding and believing in me:

Harvey Kalfin
Deet Jonker
Pat Shearer
Bob Apter
Irwin Weiner
Charlie Lavery
John Martin
Jim Spence
Roone Arledge
Steve Solomon
Dennis Swanson
John Sias
Dan Burke
Tom Murphy
Michael Eisner

And a final thanks for my book team:

Joel Lovell, with deep gratitude for your collaboration and your friendship. It has been great sharing these lessons, memories, and experiences with you.

Esther Newberg, for your guidance and for talking me into this book. You said it was going to be easy and you sure

e leadership, advice, and encouragement are

ROBERT IGER is chairman and CEO of the Walt Disney Company. He previously served as president and CEO, beginning in October 2005, and was president and COO from 2000 to 2005. Iger began his career at ABC in 1974, and as chairman of the ABC Group he oversaw the broadcast television network and station group and cable television properties, and guided the merger between Capital Cities/ABC and the Walt Disney Company. Iger officially joined the Disney senior management team in 1996 as chairman of the Disney-owned ABC Group, and in 1999 was given the additional responsibility of president, Walt Disney International. In that role, Iger expanded Disney's presence outside of the United States, establishing the blueprint for the company's international growth today.